Great Is the Mystery

Encountering the Formational Power of Liturgy

Joe Paprocki and D. Todd Williamson

LTP

LITURGY
TRAINING
PUBLICATIONS

Nihil Obstat
Very Reverend Daniel A. Smilanic, JCD
Vicar for Canonical Services
Archdiocese of Chicago
October 15, 2012

Imprimatur
Reverend Monsignor John F. Canary, STL, DMIN
Vicar General
Archdiocese of Chicago
October 15, 2012

The *Nihil Obstat* and *Imprimatur* are declarations that the material is free from doctrinal or moral error, and thus is granted permission to publish in accordance with c. 827. No legal responsibility is assumed by the grant of this permission. No implication is contained herein that those who have granted the *Nihil Obstat* and *Imprimatur* agree with the content, opinions, or statements expressed.

Authors: Joe Paprocki and D. Todd Williamson

GREAT IS THE MYSTERY: ENCOUNTERING THE FORMATIONAL POWER OF LITURGY © 2013 Archdiocese of Chicago: Liturgy Training Publications, 3949 South Racine Avenue, Chicago IL 60609; 1-800-933-1800; fax 1-800-933-7094; e-mail orders@ltp.org. All rights reserved. See our website at www.LTP.org.

Illustrations by Anna Manhart © 2012 LTP

Printed in the United States of America.

Library of Congress control Number: 2012953740

17 16 15 14 13   1 2 3 4 5

ISBN 978-1-61671-110-8

GIM

Without any doubt, the mystery of our religion is great:
He was revealed in flesh,
vindicated in spirit,
seen by angels,
proclaimed among Gentiles,
believed in throughout the world,
taken up in glory.

—1 Timothy 3:16

DEDICATION

To our dear friend and colleague

Miguel Arias,

who lived the great mystery of life to the fullest,
did it with profound faith,
invited others to do the same,
and now shares eternal life with God.

TABLE OF CONTENTS

How Do You Learn Mystery?

You don't. You enter into, encounter, and experience it. Just ask any man and woman about the birth of their first child. All the Lamaze classes in all the prenatal clinics in all the hospitals in the world couldn't truly prepare them for what they were going to encounter in the delivery room. Certainly the Lamaze classes, clinics, and hospital preparation helped the new parents remain open to the inevitable and anticipated experience of the great mystery of their child's birth. But undoubtedly, the actual encounter of the birth was much more than they expected.

How, then, do you teach or communicate mystery to another? Again, you don't. The most you can do is to proclaim your own experience (not easy to do with words alone!), invite others to enter into it, and then accompany them on the pathway that leads to and then through their own experience of mystery. Just ask any catechist who has worked with adults preparing for Baptism. All the teaching, explaining, and descriptions of what will happen in their Baptism could not possibly cover all that is actually experienced in their encounter with Christ in the living water, which first drags us to our death and then at the same time becomes the very womb from which our new life is born. To express our encounter through word and gesture, invite others to enter into it, and then be there to walk with them through the encounter is sometimes all that we can do. And that is the key!

Encountering the Paschal Mystery

Our encounters with Jesus are like this, for they are indeed an entry into mystery. To become a follower of Jesus is to enter into mystery, be touched and transformed by it, and proclaim that mystery of faith to others. Unfortunately, all too often, we tend to reduce "the faith" to a set of cognitive statements to be learned intellectually. The teaching of the faith, then, simply becomes the transmission of knowledge without the experience of mystery. This would be like a father attending Lamaze classes but skipping the birth of his child because he feels he's "gotten it all." For this reason, from the earliest days of the Church, followers of Jesus have been very careful to devote themselves to "the apostles' teaching and . . . to the breaking of bread,"[1] or as we would say in today's Church language, catechesis and liturgy.

The Church has always understood that experiencing the Paschal Mystery of Jesus must involve more than simply words. It must also involve ritual and gestures that immerse would-be followers of Jesus into an experience of mystery. Just read any of the great Jerusalem Catechesis sermons of Cyril. In a wonderfully poetic style, he gently speaks to those of his community who have been reborn in the waters of holy Baptism about the very symbols and actions they had just experienced. With them, he "breaks open" and explores the experiences of descending into the font, being lavishly anointed with sweet-smelling chrism, feeding for the first time on the bread of life, and drinking from the cup of salvation. Accompanying them through their experience, he asks them, "Do you now understand?" And with him, his newest brothers and sisters are led to a deeper understanding of their faith, the Church of which they are now members, and the mysterious God who called them to the encounter in the first place. To invite, be present to, and then walk with another through their encounter with mystery is how the Church best proclaims the Gospel of Jesus! The *Catechism of the Catholic Church* tells us that such "liturgical catechesis aims to initiate people into the mystery of Christ."[2]

"That is why, in the Church's most ancient tradition, the process of Christian formation always had an experiential character. While not neglecting a systematic understanding of the content of the faith, it centered on a vital and convincing encounter with Christ, as proclaimed by authentic witnesses. It is first and foremost the witness who introduces others to the mysteries. Naturally, this initial encounter gains depth through catechesis and finds its source and summit in the celebration of the Eucharist."

(Sacramentum Caritatis, 64)

Learning the Dance

To mature in faith means to recognize the awesome power of mystery and the need for this intimate relationship between word and gesture. Catechesis and liturgy are not inventions of the Catholic Church. Throughout history, many cultures have understood this dynamic and have initiated and formed their members by inviting them to experience mystery. Many Native American cultures knew the awesome power of the encounter with mystery. The Academy Award–winning movie *Dances with Wolves* is an excellent illustration of this.[3] In this movie, Lt. John Dunbar (played by Kevin Costner), is a somewhat depressed and directionless soldier in the U.S. Army in the years immediately following the Civil War. After suffering severe injury and attempting to end his own life, Dunbar is assigned to an abandoned fort in the yet-unsettled American frontier, where he finds himself completely alone except for the Lakota Sioux tribe who live on the land nearby. The movie chronicles the relationship that slowly builds between Dunbar and the Sioux. As the story unfolds, Dunbar is transformed by the Sioux through his experiences of taking part in their lives, learning their culture, and, most importantly, participating in the sacred rituals that give meaning to their lives.

At a rather significant and poignant point in the film, Dunbar is invited to accompany the Sioux on the sacred buffalo hunt. With bison literally darkening the Dakota landscape, the Sioux embark on their sacred hunt, killing only enough to support the village. Following the hunt, the Sioux participate in a ritual celebration in order to give thanks to the Great Spirit who gave the bison, as well as to the bison themselves, who gave their lives in order to provide for the village. The Sioux invite Dunbar to take part in not only the sacred hunt, but also the sacred and ancient ritual celebration. In a great festive spirit, the whole village celebrates while everyone eats his or her fill, feasting on the meat of the kill. In the middle of the village, there burns a great bonfire, around which the Sioux dance throughout the night. With drums and music reaching the feverish pitch that truly makes a celebration out of a ritual, they dance around the fire, some covered in the skin of the bison, some carrying spears, some dancing with ceremonial staffs. Those not dancing are off to the side, telling and retelling the stories of the hunt just finished.

Shortly after this scene, Dunbar takes his leave of the Sioux, returning to his post. As the camera follows him walking away alone, he repeatedly looks back over his shoulder at the people who are having a most strange and transforming effect on him. He is, after all, not one of them. He is one who has been let inside for a brief time. Yet, in that brief time, something has happened to him—he is different now. How do we know this? In a dramatic scene, in the darkness of the lonely night, in the middle of the field surrounding the fort, Dunbar builds a tremendous bonfire, imitating the fire around which the Sioux danced. There, alone in the night, around that fire that he has built himself, Dunbar is dancing like a Sioux, imitating what he saw, practicing what he has become. As he dances and leaps around the fire, the film allows us to hear what is echoing within his heart and soul: the drums and the music that brought life into the Sioux ritual and into his being. He was practicing the dance that would make him a member of the Sioux people, with whom he longed to be. Caught up in the newness of life and change of identity, John Dunbar does the only thing he can think of doing: *he practices the dance*. John Dunbar didn't set out to "study" the Sioux people. Nor did the Sioux set out to "teach" John Dunbar what it meant to "be" a Sioux. And yet, both of them came face to face with the gradual, deepening encounter with mystery that changed each of them forever.

Jesus Teaches his Apostles to Dance

Jesus understood full well that his encounter with the will of the Father was too mysterious to be summed up in words alone. Thus, after three years of public ministry, after three years of teaching and apprenticing his disciples, Jesus summed up his message with one encounter which, at least for one early Christian community (the Johannine community), became the hallmark of all discipleship. On the night before he died, while sharing a meal with his disciples, he wrapped a towel around himself and, as the story says, "he . . . began to wash the disciples' feet."[4] He didn't lecture them on what it meant to be his disciple. He didn't deliver a treatise on the "Seven Habits of Effective Discipleship." He didn't give them a list of dos and don'ts to memorize and spit back to him. Instead, he invited them to an encounter with mystery. When he had washed their feet and put on his outer garments again he went back to the table. "Do you know," he asked, "what I have done for you?"[5]

Jesus invited his disciples to a deeper relationship by engaging them in gesture and then followed up the mysterious experience with more teaching to articulate and clarify. Jesus catechized liturgically. He taught his disciples a "dance" ("I have set you an example") and then instructed them to follow his steps ("that you also should do as I have done to you").[6] As followers of Jesus, we are commanded to teach as he did by engaging people in mystery and then breaking it open for reflection so that we can better understand what it means to follow him in our daily lives. This type of formation that engages people in liturgy and catechesis is what the Church used from its earliest days and has been retrieving ever since the reinstitution of the Rite of Christian Initiation of Adults in 1972. Most recently, the *General Directory for Catechesis* stated unequivocally that the catechumenate should serve as the model for all catechesis.[7]

What Are We Doing?

Catholic formation, done properly and respecting the intimacy between catechesis and liturgy, allows people the opportunities to "dance the dance" they learned and are learning from those who have gone before them, marked with the sign of faith. It is a dance that has brought them into newness of life. Their partner for this dance of new life is the community of the faithful—the Church. The music to which they dance, the music that plays in their hearts and souls, is the music of the Gospel of Jesus Christ. And the pattern of their dance is the living out of their newfound life, in imitation of the Master, which always—*always*—involves the building up of the kingdom of God!

"Catechesis is nothing other than the process of transmitting the Gospel, as the Christian community has received it, understands it, celebrates it and communicates it in many ways."

(General Directory for Catechesis, 105)

In our catechetical and liturgical formation, we need to stop and ask ourselves what it is that we are doing. If we are simply passing on the content of our faith, all we need to do is make sure that every baptized Catholic has access to the proper textbooks and documents along with some explanation for how to interpret or understand them. If, on the other hand, we are inviting people to enter into mystery, we must go well beyond words. We are not only about the task of providing accurate information, but of inviting people to enter into mystery, helping them to experience it, reflect upon it within a tradition, and integrate it into daily living. We are truly teaching people how to dance and then providing opportunities for them to practice the dance that has brought them to newness of life.

Liturgy Is the Place

If we are truly a Church proclaiming mystery, devoted to the "apostles' teaching and . . . the breaking of bread,"[8] then we need to catechize liturgically. Simply put, we cannot invite people to enter into the mystery of Christ unless we invite them to experience the mystery of the Eucharist as we celebrate it in sacred liturgy. In fact, the *Catechism of the Catholic Church* reminds us that "the liturgy is . . . the privileged place for catechizing the People of God."[9] This book is an invitation to that privileged place, the liturgy, where we encounter the great mystery of Christ that must be at the heart of our catechesis. This book is about mystery. It's about the great mystery that is God and our encounters with God and God's saving love for us. Specifically, it's about those encounters we have when we, God's people, gather to call upon the divine name; when we gather to express, through ritual, what we believe to be true of God, of ourselves, and the relationships we have to God and to one another. It is about those times when we gather to celebrate the rites that call us to conversion, transform us, and create us anew. It's about what we believe happens when we come to the table of the Lord, retell the stories of God's presence and action among us, and, in the name of the risen Christ, share the sacred meal that brings us to everlasting life.

This book is about walking with another through these holy encounters with mystery. Following the model set by the beloved bishop of Jerusalem, this book is about recalling some of those encounters, breaking them open and asking ourselves, "Do we understand?" There is great wisdom in Cyril's method of walking with the neophytes of his community, of using the very celebrations that had brought them to life as a touchstone for their continued conversion and deepening understanding of what it means to be a member of the Body of Christ.

This book is about the inseparable experience of mystery and its subsequent shaping of our worldview, our sense of identity, and our understanding of life and faith. As with John Dunbar and the Lakota Sioux, this book speaks of the melding of understanding and worship that takes place when we enter more deeply into the expressions of faith and belief that mark our rituals and rites. Today, we speak of this as *liturgical catechesis*—that is, the forming and shaping of our faith, beliefs, and understanding as a result of our preparation for, and celebration of, the liturgy, especially the Sunday Eucharistic liturgy. The Sioux understood this inseparable character of learning and ritualizing, of being formed through celebration, of teaching by living.

This book is about the ineffable reality of God the Father and his presence and action in our lives through the working of the Holy Spirit, in the person of Jesus Christ. It's about the continual conversion we are called to as a result of experiencing and celebrating that ineffable reality. It's about the meaning and insight that can come when we seek to put words to those experiences, when we seek to walk with another through those experiences, and to share with another the effect those experiences have on us. It's about liturgy and catechesis, formation and transformation, celebration and proclamation, conversion and discipleship.

This book is an invitation to would-be followers of Jesus to enter into the Paschal Mystery of the Lord within the context of the Eucharistic liturgy and emerge as proclaimers of the mystery of faith! This book is for catechists who long to engage their apprentices in the mystery of faith that has brought meaning to their own lives. It is for liturgists who long to teach the dance of faith and then break open the experience by asking, "Do you understand what God has just done to us through that experience?"

This book is for all those engaged in *mystagogia*, which, in its most ancient form, was that period following the celebration of initiation into the Body of Christ on Holy Saturday, characterized by an ever-deepening entrance into the Paschal Mystery through reflection upon the symbols, prayers, actions, and gestures that God uses to form us into a Eucharistic people. Today, we understand *mystagogia* in a broader sense, referring to the kind of catechesis and formation that is the result of careful attention to and reflection afterwards on the celebration of *any* liturgy. Benedict XVI spoke of this very dynamic in his first apostolic exhortation after being elected Pope, *Sacramentum Caritatis*. In this document, the Pope noted, "The Church's great liturgical tradition teaches us that fruitful participation in the liturgy requires that one be personally conformed to the mystery being celebrated, offering one's life to God in unity with the sacrifice of Christ for the salvation of the whole world. For this reason, the Synod of Bishops asked that the faithful be helped to make their interior dispositions correspond to their gestures and words. Otherwise, however carefully planned and executed our liturgies may be, they would risk falling into a certain ritualism. Hence the need to provide an education in eucharistic faith capable of enabling the faithful to live personally what they celebrate."[10]

What we often do not recognize is that all baptized Catholics are called to immerse themselves in *mystagogia*! Our understanding of *mystagogia* should not be limited to the formal period of fifty days after Easter celebrated by the community with the neophytes (the newly baptized). Instead, *mystagogia* should characterize all of our lives. We are a people who are called to enter deeper and deeper into mystery, celebrate it well, reflect upon it, learn from it, and proclaim it to others!

PART ONE

Proclaiming the Mystery of Sign, Symbol, and Ritual

CHAPTER 1

THE MYSTERY OF GOD

Encountering Mystery

When my mother-in-law, Sophie, was in hospice during the last days of her 94-year life, we gathered around her as a family, three or four at a time, to be present with her. Gradually, it seemed as though she was less engaged in conversation with us and more and more engaged in a private conversation with others whom we could not see. The hospice workers told us that she was most likely not speaking with us anymore, but with loved ones in the communion of saints. Two of Sophie's granddaughters thought it would be good to pray the Rosary aloud since Sophie had such a devotion to the Blessed Mother. The only problem was that they hadn't recited the Rosary in years. They found themselves stuck at a certain point, not knowing which mystery was next. Sophie interrupted her private conversation with the communion of saints and promptly indicated which mystery of the Rosary was next. Later, as Sophie drew her final breaths, the conversation had grown silent. Surrounded by her daughters, Sophie lifted her head, looked around the room, gave the biggest smile, and then closed her eyes for the last time. All of us knew, during those last moments of Sophie's life, that we had entered into an encounter with mystery. God's mysterious presence had become very real to us. We were in awe of the mystery of life, the mystery of death, the mystery of faith, and the mystery of God. This was not a mystery to be solved or understood, but a moment to be entered into and treasured.

~Joe

God is, above all else, a mystery. Unfortunately, most of us have an insufficient understanding of what the word *mystery* means. Most people would define *mystery* as "something that cannot be understood." There is a problem with this definition, however. Well-known author and speaker Rev. Richard Fragomeni often explains that, according to this definition, when we are invited to proclaim the mystery of faith at Mass, it is as if we are being invited to proclaim that which we do not and cannot understand. Obviously, our understanding of *mystery* leaves something to be desired. Not only do we approach mystery as something that we do not understand, we also tend to think of it as something that can be solved, like an Agatha Christie novel or an episode of *CSI: Crime Scene Investigation*.

God is not that kind of a mystery. God is not beyond our understanding, yet we can never fully understand God. As *The Cloud of Unknowing*, an anonymous work of Christian mysticism written in the latter half of the 14th century, reminds us, God is known, not so much by thought, as by love. Meister Eckhart wrote that, "The sublime and glorious reality that we call God, is to be sought first and foremost in the human heart."[11] God is beyond explanation. In fact, trying to explain God takes us in the opposite direction of where mystery is calling us. God is not a puzzle to be solved, although we can gather evidence leading to a fuller understanding of God's presence. In the biblical sense, a mystery is not something to be solved but rather something to surrender to. A mystery is something that is revealed to us and yet remains hidden. In this sense, a mystery is something that invites us. We encounter mystery and enter into relationship with that which we can never fully see, hear, or embrace.

What, then, does it mean for us to proclaim the mystery of faith? It means, first and foremost, that we must acknowledge God as mystery and reflect upon how we ourselves have surrendered to the mystery of God in our lives. It means that when we proclaim the mystery of faith, we are inviting others to surrender to a relationship with a God of mystery whom they can know and yet can never fully understand or embrace. It means that we cannot explain God to anyone, but can only describe how this God has transformed our lives and can transform the lives of others. It means that our task is not one of filling heads, but of opening hearts. It means that we are called to provide others with an opportunity to experience the living God, and not just learn about him.

I once facilitated a bilingual workshop in which I asked the participants to brainstorm what they would say if asked to explain the Catholic faith to a group of non-Catholics. When it was time to hear the results of the brainstorming, the English-speaking participants shared their extensive lists of doctrinal points, some of them even citing paragraph numbers of the *Catechism of the Catholic Church* in order to explain what we believe. It was quite impressive. We then listened as the translator told us what a young Hispanic woman was sharing from her group and we were astounded at the difference. She went on for several minutes sharing what her relationship with Jesus and the Church meant to her. There were no references to doctrinal points or paragraphs of the *Catechism*. She simply was sharing from the heart, not what she knew about God, but how she knew God and what it meant to her. It was a reminder to all of us that a life of faith must involve the heart and that proclaiming the mystery of faith must also flow from the heart.   **~Joe**

"God our Father, who by sending into the world / the Word of truth and the Spirit of sanctification, / made known to the human race your wondrous mystery."

(Collect of the Most Holy Trinity, *The Roman Missal*)

Beyond Logic

In the movie, *Star Trek V: The Final Frontier*,[12] the Starship *Enterprise* is commandeered by a maverick Vulcan (Spock's half brother, Sybok) who forces the crew to embark on a wild mission to the edge of the galaxy in hopes of encountering the supreme being. Upon reaching the planet where the supreme being allegedly resides, the crew beams down to literally meet their maker. Eventually, after thunder and lightning and earthquakes, a mysterious being appears, identifying himself as "God," just as they had hoped. While the rest of the landing crew trembles before the power of the supposed almighty, Captain Kirk boldly questions the mysterious figure's request to make use of the Starship Enterprise, asking, "Why does 'God' need a starship?" Kirk is the first to conclude that the strange alien they are communicating with cannot possibly be God since the mysterious transcendent God cannot possibly be contained in a vessel! In the end, the crew comes to realize that the mystery of God they are seeking cannot be comprehended and analyzed using their typical rational approach. Encountering mystery requires more than Mr. Spock's logic!

The truth is we do not discover God. God discovers us! Throughout history, mankind has attempted to discover God only to conclude, as Thomas Aquinas did, that "Man's utmost knowledge of God is to know that we do not know him."[13] For all of our human experience, knowledge, and wisdom, God remains a mystery. To encounter mystery means to encounter something that was previously hidden, is now revealed, and yet somehow remains hidden. In a nutshell, that describes our experience of God: God is indeed hidden from our eyes, revealed to us in a myriad of ways, and yet, is somehow still hidden from us. When we encounter the mystery of God, we are like Moses who cannot find words to express his encounter with the burning bush but instead takes his sandals off to indicate that he is somehow in the presence of sacred mystery.

Beyond Words

A few years ago, my family and I enjoyed a vacation that included our first visit to the Grand Canyon. With the video camera rolling, we spent hours strolling through this magnificent visual display. Upon arriving at home, we watched the video of our time at the Grand Canyon. Interestingly enough, as the camera pans across the great expanse of the colorful canyon, the only dialogue that can be heard from the usually talkative Paprocki family is the occasional utterance of "Wow!" or "Oh" or "Mmm." In the presence of such glorious mystery, words were suddenly quite useless!
                                                                          ~Joe

When my grandmother "Mimi" died, just before her 95th birthday, my dad (her son) and my mom were with her in the nursing home. Throughout the afternoon they held her hands, spoke to her, told her how much we all loved her. As the inevitable moment approached, my dad asked my mom to get her rosary from the bedside table. They gave Mimi her rosary and both held her hands around it. At the moment of her passing, they were silent. No one spoke; not my dad, nor my mom, nor Mimi. She died in the midst of human silence—yet, no doubt, the angels were singing her home at that moment.
                                                                          ~Todd

"God transcends all creatures. We must therefore continually purify our language of everything in it that is limited, image-bound or imperfect, if we are not to confuse our image of God—'the inexpressible, the incomprehensible, the invisible, the ungraspable'— with our human representations.[14] Our human words always fall short of the mystery of God."

(*Catechism of the Catholic Church*, 42)

Many of our encounters with God throughout our lives produce a similar loss for words. At those times when we encounter the great mystery of life, we are usually left speechless. When we encounter the mystery of birth or death, when we grapple with the meaning of some suffering that has entered our life, when we are held in the loving embrace of a family reconciliation, when we struggle with the loss of a relationship, when economic struggles threaten to negate our accomplishments, when we are overwhelmed by the awesomeness of nature, when we burst forth in joy over some success or achievement, when we feel the mysterious touch of the hand of God—all of these experiences invite us to enter into life more deeply and emerge with newfound knowledge of a mysterious God who has lifted the veil or curtain for a momentary glance at a presence that remains hidden.

In his book *I and Thou*, Martin Buber tells us that when we encounter mystery, the experience is "clouded yet it discloses itself . . . it does not use speech but begets it."[15] Our encounters with God leave us at a loss for words, and yet we attempt to put into words our understanding of these encounters. When we say that God is mystery, we are saying, in the words of Aquinas, that "we cannot grasp what He is but only what He is not and how other beings stand in relation to Him."[16]

It is for this reason that we necessarily rely upon more than words when we attempt to express our understanding of God. Even the words we use to describe God are filled with images, metaphors, similes, and analogies. When we express our understanding of what it means to encounter the mysterious God, we rely on sign, symbol, and ritual. By the same token, when God reveals himself to us, God uses images and symbols.

Author and liturgist Patrick Collins tells us that "God's truth is disclosed to us more fully through forms of imagination than through logic and concepts, words and notions."[17] Every contact with God is essentially mysterious since God is mystery. Our liturgy and catechesis, by necessity, must therefore also be experiences of mystery. If we try to reduce the mystery of God to words and concepts, we might as well be handing out pamphlets about the Grand Canyon without inviting people to ever visit it in person!

Make no mistake about it, God is mystery. Like people standing in awe over the majesty of the Grand Canyon, like those who stand with another at the moment of death, we stand before God, unable to grasp the vast expanse of his awesome and mysterious presence and unable to find the words to express our understanding of the experience. Yet, at the same time, we are called upon to proclaim this mystery of faith to others. Like Moses, we cannot proceed until we have acknowledged that we are standing on sacred ground in the presence of something and someone we do not and cannot fully comprehend. Only when we have acknowledged that we are in the presence of mystery, can we even begin to contemplate proclaiming the power of that mystery to others.

We Prepare to Celebrate These Sacred Mysteries

Ultimately, the place where we enter into and proclaim these mysteries most fully and profoundly is the liturgy. In fact, the Second Vatican Council's *Constitution on the Sacred Liturgy* tells us that "Liturgy . . . is the outstanding means whereby the faithful may express in their lives and manifest to others the mystery of Christ."[18] It is for this same reason that when we gather to celebrate liturgy, we hear the priest say in the Penitential Act, "Let us acknowledge our sins, / and so prepare ourselves to celebrate the sacred mysteries."[19] Despite the use of words, gestures, and rituals in our liturgy, God's sovereignty and transcendence are never in doubt.[20] Our celebration of the liturgy does not solve the mystery by making God appear upon command. Rather, our celebration of the liturgy immerses us even deeper in the mystery of God's presence and transcendence. The use of incense at Mass is designed to remind us of just this point: we are entering into the presence of mystery—following the Light of Christ but shrouded in the cloud of unknowing.

The very structure of our liturgical prayer, rooted in the Jewish *Berakah*, reveals that, when all is said and done, the only thing we can definitively say about God is that God has done wonderful things for us. The *Berakah* follows a set formula: praise of God, the invoking of God's name/divine titles, a litany of acknowledgment of God's wondrous deeds, and finally a petition. God may very well be mysterious and hidden, yet we are witnesses to his wonderfully saving actions and deeds. We may not be able to define God, but we can certainly proclaim his greatness!

> "I will call to mind the deeds of the LORD;
> I will remember your wonders of old.
> I will meditate on all your work,
> and muse on your mighty deeds."
>
> (Psalm 77:11–12)

Through our liturgical prayer, we acknowledge that we have been blessed and forever changed by our surrender into relationship with the God of mystery through the Paschal Mystery of Jesus Christ. This relationship, while mysterious, is intimate. In our prayer, we acknowledge our relationship with God, a relationship defined by names: Creator, Liberator, Father, Abba—names that, in turn, describe God's saving actions and express our trust. In our Eucharistic prayers, we give thanks to God for the countless ways in which God blesses us, redeems us, and sustains us through his saving actions, not the least of which is the sending of his only Son, Jesus Christ. Through the mystery of the Incarnation, the transcendent God becomes intimate with us and yet remains unsolved. It is to the mystery of Jesus that we now turn our attention as we seek ways to more powerfully proclaim the mystery of faith!

"In revealing his mysterious name, YHWH ('I AM HE WHO IS,' 'I AM WHO AM' or 'I AM WHO I AM'), God says who he is and by what name he is to be called. This divine name is mysterious just as God is mystery. It is at once a name revealed and something like the refusal of a name, and hence it better expresses God as what he is—infinitely above everything that we can understand or say: he is the 'hidden God,' his name is ineffable, and he is the God who makes himself close to men.[21]"

(Catechism of the Catholic Church, 206)

REFLECTION

» Do a "mystery inventory" of your parish community's liturgical celebrations. How is God's transcendence celebrated in your community's liturgical celebrations?

» Read Exodus chapter 32 about the golden calf. Reflect upon how the Israelites (and we) seem to be unable to cope with a God who is remote, invisible, and mysterious and instead try to bring him down into their own world. Reflect upon how the conversion process is not one of drawing God into our world but rather "going up" into God's.

» Take some time to ponder the mystery of God in the presence of God's beautiful creation. Take some time to go to a spot where the beauty of nature allows you to enter into God's mystery and just dwell in the presence of mystery.

» When was a time when you were totally at a loss for words? When was a time you communicated something meaningful and profound without using words (such as when you offered an embrace as a gesture of comfort, healing, or reconciliation)? How does the Catholic faith provide you with an opportunity to enter more deeply into mystery?

» What does it mean to you to say that God is mystery? Think back over the more profound experiences in your life. How would you describe the reality of mystery in such experiences?

» Read 1 Kings 19. How can encounters with the mysterious God be compared to "a sound of sheer silence"?[22] Have you encountered the mysterious God in more dramatic fashion, such as in the earthquake or thunder described in Elijah's encounter?

CHAPTER 2

THE MYSTERY OF JESUS

The Mystery of Relationship

God is indeed mystery. If the heart of the mystery of God is to be found in being in relationship with God, then the one who exemplifies this relationship best is none other than God's Incarnation: Jesus of Nazareth. As author Dick Westley describes it, "Christianity . . . is an account of the divinization of the human race by means of redemptive intimacy between the Lord God and humankind as incarnated in Jesus."[23] Jesus, in turn, reveals the depth of intimacy that exists between himself and the Father.

• Jesus was the one who called God "Abba," the one who always did the will of the Father, the one who said, "Whoever has seen me has seen the Father."[24]

• Jesus was the one who prayed, "I know that you always hear me."[25]

• He was the one who, as Paul says, emptied himself of everything to the Father, so that the Father would, in turn, glorify him.[26]

The core of Jesus's relationship with the Father is described in John's account of the Gospel—"Father, the world does not know you, but I know you."[27] Jesus *knew* God, and God *knew* Jesus. To understand the dynamics of this relationship, we have to understand what it means, in Scripture, "to know" someone else. To "know" in the Hebrew, scriptural sense is not a cognitive act, or an exercise of the mind where one studies what one wishes to know. Nor is it a casual sense of knowing, as one might be aware of something or someone else. To know in the biblical sense is much more than an activity of the mind. It is, in fact, first and foremost, an activity of the heart. To know in the biblical sense is to have intimate experience of the one who is known. It is to be connected at a profound level with that other person.

"And this is eternal life, that they may know you, the only true God, and Jesus Christ whom you have sent."

(John 17:3)

To know in the biblical sense is the way that Adam and Eve knew God, as they walked together with God in the garden during the "time of the evening breeze."[28] It is the way that Moses knew God, as they spoke in the desert about the complaining Israelites. There, God had had enough and was ready to abandon the relationship he had established with Moses's people. But Moses pleaded to God: "How shall it be known that I have found favor in your sight, I and your people, unless you go with us?" God relents and says to Moses, "I will do the very thing that you have asked; for you have found favor in my sight, and *I know you by name.*"[29]

To know in the biblical sense is to know in the way that:

- the author of the Song of Songs knows the beloved: "My beloved is all radiant and ruddy / distinguished among ten thousand";[30]

- Elijah knew the Lord in a gentle breeze that caressed his brow and touched his heart;[31]

- the psalmist experiences being known by God when the psalmist writes, "my frame was not hidden from you, / when I was being made in secret . . .";[32]

- Paul speaks of knowing when, after his beautiful hymn to love, he writes, "Now I know only in part; then [when the perfect comes] I will know fully, even as I have been fully known."[33]

Intimacy, Favor, and Beloved

This biblical sense of knowing indicates a very deep level of intimacy. Dick Westley tells us, "The truth is that intimacy is both a human and a Gospel imperative; we can be neither human nor Christian without it. It is intimacy, or if you prefer, 'incarnation,' which redeems us. Jesus is our Savior/Redeemer because he is the complete embodiment of the absolute intimacy of God and all of humanity."[34] The intimacy that is part of this relational knowing is an intimacy that was at the heart of Jesus's relationship with the Father. This intimacy was first publicly revealed on the banks of the Jordan River as Jesus was baptized by John. Mark records in his account of the Gospel that, as Jesus came up from the waters, the sky was torn apart and the Spirit descended on Jesus in the form of a dove. A voice from the heavens expresses God's favor of Jesus, "You are my Son, the Beloved; with you I am well pleased."[35]

In Scripture, to be favored denotes a particular level of relationship.

- The righteous who practice kindness and fidelity find favor with God.[36]
- Recall that Moses had "found favor" with God.
- The Acts of the Apostles states that David had God's favor.[37]
- The angel Gabriel greets Mary of Nazareth by calling her "favored one."[38]

To be favored is to know God's presence and action in our midst. To be favored is to recognize God's initiative toward us and to respond to that divine initiative wholeheartedly. As with Moses, David, and Mary, the favored one is the one who responds to God with trust and with faith. The level of relationship that is created by this invitation and response is what leads to the holy intimacy that countless men and woman of faith have shared with God. It is this level of depth and profundity that makes one "beloved."

In our own Baptism each one of us was raised out of the waters and declared to be "the beloved." In our own Baptism we believe that God's favor rests on us and we are adopted as sons and daughters in the image of Christ. Recreated into the image of the beloved, we can thus share in the intimacy that exists between the Father and Jesus. Through Christ, in whose image we have been reborn, we are in the Father and the Father is in us. This reciprocal intimacy between God, in Christ, and us is most obvious and most clearly expressed when we gather to praise God in liturgy.

The Power of Liturgy

I once took part in a commissioning rite for pastoral ministers in a large urban parish of New York City. This parish was known all over mid-Manhattan as a community of outreach. The list of services and ministries was vast and ranged from day care for low-income families, to a soup kitchen that served over 800 meals a week, to an AIDS ministry that served in home hospices. As part of this commissioning rite, all those who had been prepared and trained for the community's life of service were called forward and were sent to various stations in the church. At these stations were a chair, a large bowl, numerous pitchers of water, and a small supply of bath towels. Those being commissioned then proceeded to wash the feet of any member of the assembly who wanted to take part, as a way of symbolizing the Christ-like service that they had undertaken.

I knew one of the people who were being commissioned that day. Her name was Jackie and she had just entered her second year of living with cancer. The illness had interrupted her training several times, and at this point it threatened her plans for full-time ministry in the parish. Yet, she felt called to serve, and the determination she had developed carried her through to this point.

At a particular point in the service, when I felt moved to do so, I made my way to where Jackie was washing the feet of another parishioner. As I approached to wait my turn, I watched as Jackie poured the water over the other woman's feet in the large white bowl. She put the pitcher down and began to slowly rub the woman's feet, gently washing them with the water in the bowl. When she finished, Jackie lifted the woman's feet and wrapped them with one of the towels. I watched as all of Jackie's attention was focused on this woman. I was struck by how tenderly she handled and dried the woman's feet, not just patting them with the towel in a quick manner, but rather deliberately drying them, taking her time, careful to get all the water from between the toes. Then, as a final act of service to this woman, I watched as Jackie bent down and kissed both the woman's feet. When the woman got up to leave the chair, she was visibly touched by this rite and was quietly crying. As I sat in the chair, before Jackie, I began to be so moved.

Familiar with all that Jackie had gone through because of the cancer, and aware of the overwhelming sense of call to ministry which she felt, I placed my feet in the bowl and let Jackie wash them for me. I watched again as Jackie poured her whole self into that act of service for me. There was nothing perfunctory, nothing insincere about it. She was giving of herself to serve me. And I opened myself to her and received what she had to give. At that moment, we were intimately connected in the act of giving ourselves to each other. In this act of faith we were united to one another through Christ, who is at once and all times servant of God and Son of God.

~Todd

Liturgy has the power to connect people to one another, and then to connect us to the Father through Christ. This power is at work every time the Church gathers. In every instance of liturgy, the Church unites her praise and thanksgiving to the praise and thanksgiving offered to the Father by Christ. At the final doxology of the Eucharist, we recognize this. It is there that we acknowledge that all that has come before this point has been prayed, has been offered, "through him, and with him, and in him," and that, "in the unity of the Holy Spirit, / all honor and glory" is to the Father, for ever and ever.[39]

"May the oblation of this day's feast / be pleasing to you, O Lord, we pray, / that through this most holy exchange / we may be found in the likeness of Christ, / in whom our nature is united to you. / Who lives and reigns for ever and ever."

(Prayer over the Offerings, Christmas Mass during the Night, *The Roman Missal*)

Through Him

The glory and honor that Christ gave to the Father was indeed the ultimate prayer. That prayer of Jesus—with utter and complete trust in the act of giving his life to God—was rooted in Jesus's experience of intimacy with the one he called "Abba." The Beloved, the Favored One, lived his life out of that complete trust, and because of that, Jesus's whole life was a prayer to God. As Paul reminds us in the Philippian hymn, Jesus's life was a constant pouring of himself out to God. His life was total gift to the loving Father. In every instance, in every situation, Jesus gave himself over to God in trust. Through his self-emptying, which finally led to the cross, Jesus gave to the Father the ultimate form of praise. And through that praise, God's glory shone in the Resurrection.[40]

For us Catholics, the Eucharist is the ultimate form of praise. For in the Eucharistic liturgy, we too, in utter and complete trust, empty ourselves to God and offer the gift of our own lives. With the bread and the wine, all that we are, and all that we have, is given over to God. It is only through Christ—who first gave so completely of himself to God—that we are even able to offer such a gift. And in this offering, united with that of Christ, the glory of God who raised Christ on high is once again revealed.

"Let the same mind be in you that was in Christ Jesus, who, though he was in the form of God, did not regard equality with God as something to be exploited, / but emptied himself, taking the form of a slave, being born in human likeness. / And being found in human form, he humbled himself and became obedient to the point of death—even death on a cross. / Therefore God also highly exalted him and gave him the name that is above every name."

(Philippians 2:5b–9)

With Him

On the night before he died, Jesus did the only thing that the beloved could do. For all that he had, for all that he was, for all that he had experienced, he blessed God. Gathered with his friends and all those who recognized in him and in his life the love and presence of God, and aware of all that was happening around him, Jesus shared a meal with them. What did he do on that night before he died, knowing what his life had led him to? He took bread and he blessed God. In spite of what was taking place around him, what did Jesus do on the night before the cross? He took a cup of wine, and he blessed God. In trust and with faith in God's favor, even then, Jesus never stopped praising the ever-faithful one. With confidence in the loving care of the one whom he knew, Jesus never ceased giving thanks to the Father.

In our liturgies, in every act of public worship, we are called to unite our praise and thanksgiving to that of the beloved. In the same trust and with the same confidence, we raise all that is in our lives at any given moment—all our concerns, all our struggles, all our hopes, and all our joys—and in praise and thanksgiving we *bless* God. With Christ, we trust in the Father's favor for us, and believe that no matter what our lives hold, we too are beloved by God, who *knows us by name.*

"The Church, therefore, earnestly desires that Christ's faithful, when present at this mystery of faith, should not be there as strangers or silent spectators; on the contrary, through a good understanding of the rites and prayers they should take part in the sacred service conscious of what they are doing, with devotion and full involvement. They should be instructed by God's word and be nourished at the table of the Lord's body; they should give thanks to God; by offering the immaculate Victim, not only through the hands of the priest, but also with him, they should learn to offer themselves as well; through Christ the Mediator,[41] they should be formed day by day into an ever more perfect unity with God and with each other, so that finally God may be all in all."

(*Constitution on the Sacred Liturgy*, 48)

In Him

Paul writes, in his letter to the church of Ephesus, that it is in Christ Jesus that we have full access to God. Through Christ, he says, we are part of God's household, united in one body.[42] It is as one body, then, that we offer our praise and thanks to God. United to one another in Christ, we come before the Father as the Church. In Christ, we are God's holy people, favored and beloved. As the Church, we raise our voices in prayer. With faith and trust we raise our lives to God. In utter dependence on the one whose love first formed us, we offer all that we are. United with Christ, we too are able to empty ourselves into the hands of the one whose glory shines in the Resurrection.

In offering our praise, in our total thanksgiving, we are transformed, recreated, made anew, and shaped ever more into the image of Christ: crucified, dead, and risen. And in this, united with Christ through the Holy Spirit, all honor and glory is indeed the Father's, for ever and ever.

"Rightly, then, the liturgy is considered as an exercise of the priestly office of Jesus Christ. In the liturgy . . . the whole public worship is performed by the Mystical Body of Jesus Christ, that is, by the Head and his members. From this it follows that every liturgical celebration, because it is an action of Christ the Priest and of his Body which is the Church, is a sacred action surpassing all others; no other action of the Church can equal its effectiveness by the same title and to the same degree."

(*Constitution on the Sacred Liturgy*, 7)

Trust and Faith

Jesus, indeed, has shown us what it means to be in relationship with the Father. Jesus has taught us that we too may call upon God as "Abba." Through his intimate relationship with the Father, Jesus has taught us what it means to trust, and this trust is the very essence of our faith. Each of us is called to enter into relationship with our Lord Jesus Christ—a relationship of profound trust, a relationship of faith. Through him, with him, and in him, we live, move, and have our being. Ultimately, we place our faith, not only in a set of dogmas or cognitive principles, but also in a relationship that promises to lead us to new life!

"'The definitive aim of catechesis is to put people not only in touch, but also in communion and intimacy, with Jesus Christ.'[43] All evangelizing activity . . . proposes . . . 'to know better this Jesus . . . : to know his "mystery.""'[44]

(General Directory for Catechesis, 80)

REFLECTION

» Spend time considering the many ways in which all Catholic liturgical prayer is offered "through, with, and in" Christ. Look at the liturgies that make up the worship life of your parish and identify instances in which the community's prayer is united with Christ's.

» "Gratitude Journals" have become popular in recent years. Create a "Journal of Praise and Thanksgiving" and record the people, events, and situations for which you give praise and thanks to God.

» Read the various Scripture stories of God's relationships with people that are cited in this chapter. Read the stories in their entirety. Consider whether or not you see yourself in these stories. Think of similar ways God may be establishing such a relationship with you.

» Consider the many aspects of your life. Identify where you feel the most connected to or united with Christ (at work, in your struggles, in your joys). Develop ways to help yourself be more aware of your relationship to God in Christ.

» What does it mean to you to pray to God "through, with, and in" Christ Jesus? How do you understand such ritual phrases as, "We ask this through Christ our Lord," or "Grant this in the name of Jesus your Son," or "We ask this through Jesus Christ, our Lord, who lives and reigns with you in the unity of the Holy Spirit, one God forever and ever"?

» Think about the many ways in which you are coming to "know" God in your experience of daily living. Through whom or through what circumstances is Jesus showing you the presence, action, and love of God in your life?

» How do you experience yourself as a beloved son or daughter of God? What does it mean for you and for your life to be God's favored?

CHAPTER 3

THE MYSTERY OF FAITH

Faith: Taking Someone at Their Word

We're all familiar with the phrase, "I'll take your word for it." At one time or another in our lives, we have needed to trust the word of someone else. Perhaps it was a friend assuring us that our blind date would not have to play beast to our beauty. Or maybe it was a colleague recommending someone to us for a job. Or, even more seriously, perhaps a doctor telling us that without surgery chances of survival would be diminished. Without knowing all of the facts, we may have responded, "I'll take your word for it."

When we take someone at their word, we are venturing into the realm of faith. When we take someone at their word, we acknowledge that we don't know everything that there is to know, yet we trust that the one giving us their word is worthy of being relied upon. If we are hesitant, no doubt they will assure us, "Trust me. Have I ever let you down before?" To take another at their word is to place our faith in them. To place our faith in someone is to commit ourselves to them and allow them, in some small (or not so small) way, to influence our lives. To place our faith in someone is to embrace them and stand by them. Faith is, first and foremost, not a religious concept, but rather a human response: someone presents their word (or actions) and we respond by either embracing them or distancing ourselves from them.

"Faith is the assurance of things hoped for, the conviction of things not seen."

(Hebrews 11:1)

A story attributed to an anonymous author illustrates this. Once upon a time, there was a young boy who woke up to the smell of smoke in his house. Since there was no way out of his room because of flames and thick smoke in the hallway, he ran to the window and started screaming for help. Down below, his father stood, having been forced out by the deadly fire, seeking a way to get his son out alive. The father yells, "Jump! I'll catch you!" to which the son yells back in fear, "But I can't see you!" The father quickly replies, "I know, but I *can* see you . . . take my word for it. *Jump!*"

Faith, as understood in religious terms, is no different. While faith is not blind, it involves a certain amount of un-seeing and a high degree of trust in someone who can see. Faith is not simply the acknowledgment of a supreme being or the intellectual assent to a set of ideas or beliefs about God. Faith is taking God at God's word. Faith is trusting that God's promise will be backed up. Faith is committing ourselves to God and allowing God to influence our lives (in no small way). Faith is embracing God and standing by God.

How can we place our faith in God? Because God has given us his own Word! The Gospel according to John describes the Incarnation as the Word made flesh. God literally gave us his Word by sending us his only Son, Jesus Christ. We can take God at his Word or we can distance ourselves. To have faith in God is to embrace the relationship that has been extended to us through Jesus Christ. To proclaim the mystery of faith, then, means to proclaim the relationship with the Father, through Jesus, that we embrace, commit ourselves to, and surrender to. To have faith in God is to acknowledge that we do not know everything that there is to know, but we trust the word of the one who assures us that we need not be afraid.

"In the beginning was the Word, and the Word was with God, and the Word was God. . . . And the Word became flesh and lived among us."

(John 1:1, 14a)

Getting in the Last Word

The late Sofia Cavalletti wrote, "From the beginning of the world, up to today, the history of salvation has been gradually constructed through a continuous dialogue between God and humankind. It is a dialogue in which God always has the first word but in which he also awaits the response of all people and of each person."[45] Since God has already given us his word, this means that faith is always a response. God has already initiated the relationship and the dialogue as a gift to us, and now it is up to us to respond. We literally get the last word in this conversation because God's word always comes first! God always initiates! The extent to which we respond or embrace this relationship freely given is the extent to which we can say we have faith. It is for this very reason that we feel compelled to proclaim faith: we announce God's initiative and invite others to listen to God's word (evangelization), we seek a deeper understanding of God's initiative in our lives (catechesis), and we offer praise and thanksgiving for God's initiative and pray for it to continue (liturgy). The liturgy is the place where all three of these come together in one moment of encounter with mystery.

"Do not let your hearts be troubled. Believe in God, believe also in me."

(John 14:1)

Try it On!

If we refer to faith as a gift, then it would serve us well to pause and reflect upon what it is we do with gifts. Sometimes, we put them back in the box and return them. Other times we acknowledge how nice they are and hide them on a shelf. If we truly want to embrace a gift (as a way of embracing the giver of the gift), however, we own it, we wear it, we display it, we try it on, we do whatever it takes to show that our response is one of gratitude and that it is our greatest desire to pursue this relationship further. The gift of faith that God invites us to enter into through relationship with Jesus is a gift that we can either return, ignore, take for granted, or embrace in thanksgiving and desire for pursuing the relationship further. If we truly want to show someone that we embrace the new shirt, tie, scarf, or jewelry that they gave us as a gift, we will "put it on" and wear it so that when others notice, we will proudly tell them from whom we received it and make our association with that person known. We do the same with faith in Jesus. St. Paul tells us that we are to "put on" Christ as though wearing a new garment. We respond in faith by wrapping ourselves in Jesus's cloak, wearing his mantle of love for all to see, proudly announcing our association with the one who has bestowed the gift of grace upon us.

O ne of the most popular moments on TV each year is the arrival of actors and actresses on the red carpet at the Academy Awards. I have to admit that I often join my wife on the couch in front of the TV to look for the best and worst dressed in Hollywood. If you're familiar with this ritual, you know that each celebrity is greeted by the interviewer, told how stunning he or she looks, and then is asked, "So, who are you wearing tonight?" The celebrity then proceeds to tell us about his or her outfit and the designer of the outfit and accessories. Perhaps this is what St. Paul was envisioning when he taught us to "put on Christ"—that others will ask us to describe who we have "put on" and we will respond by talking about the Person who has designed our life: Jesus!   **~Joe**

It is this understanding of faith as an expression of one's embracing of and association with Jesus that prompted James to insist that faith must be accompanied by good works, because to embrace Jesus is to embrace neighbor—and that may call us to some kind of action. Faith brings us into relationship not only with God but with one another. Faith is not an intellectual assent to a set of ideas or beliefs about God but commitment to (embrace of) the character of God and a willingness to let God shape our lives. We desire to embrace the One whom we do not and cannot fully embrace and, in doing so, place our trust in the One whom we cannot fully see yet has been revealed to us. Whenever we accept a gift, we trust that the one who offers it has our best intentions and interests in mind and that the relationship will sustain us.

"Let us then lay aside the works of darkness and put on the armor of light; let us live honorably as in the day, not in reveling and drunkenness, not in debauchery and licentiousness, not in quarreling and jealousy. Instead, put on the Lord Jesus Christ, and make no provision for the flesh."

(Romans 13:12b–14)

In God We Trust

Faith is very powerful but it is not because of any power that we have. Faith is powerful because the One whom we embrace, namely God, is powerful. Even the smallest amount of faith can "move mountains" because when we have faith, we have faith in the one who can (and does) move mountains. To have faith is not to develop supernatural powers like Luke Skywalker tapping into the power of "the force" to battle Darth Vader. To be a person of great faith means to be someone who surrenders to the higher power of God, thus allowing God's will to be revealed. When we live in a manner that reflects the motto on United States currency, "In God we trust," we surrender our will to the will of the one with whom we have entered into relationship and we attempt to sustain that relationship by praying over and over again, "thy will be done!"

This surrender to the will of the Father is the heart and soul of Jesus's Paschal Mystery. When we celebrate Eucharist and the priest says, "The mystery of faith," our response summarizes the Paschal Mystery: "Save us, Savior of the world, / for by your Cross and Resurrection / you have set us free."[46] Ultimately, when we proclaim the mystery of faith, we are announcing that we embrace a relationship with Jesus that calls us to surrender to the will of the Father, leading us to salvation—that is, a transformation from death to new life.

"The mature fruit of mystagogy is an awareness that one's life is being progressively transformed by the holy mysteries being celebrated. The aim of all Christian education, moreover, is to train the believer in an adult faith that can make him a 'new creation,' capable of bearing witness in his surroundings to the Christian hope that inspires him. . . . Each Christian community is called to be a place where people can be taught about the mysteries celebrated in faith."

(*Sacramentum Caritatis*, 64)

Ronald Rolheiser tells us that the Paschal Mystery, "is the central mystery within Christianity . . . a process of transformation, within which we are given both new life and new spirit."[47] Rolheiser asserts that the Paschal Mystery is so central to our faith because it deals with the ultimate mysteries of suffering, death, and transformation. When we gather to celebrate Eucharist, we are about much more than creating a feel-good experience or simply a sense of belonging to community. Rather, we are coming face to face with the ultimate meaning of our lives and proclaiming that the only way to find our way is to embrace the suffering, Death, and Resurrection of Jesus Christ!

"[T]hrough the Paschal Mystery / we have been buried with Christ in Baptism, / so that we may walk with him in newness of life."

(Renewal of Baptismal Promises, Sunday of the Resurrection, *The Roman Missal*)

We Remember . . .

As we grow older, we tend to have trouble remembering things! Whether important or insignificant, it is human nature to forget in the face of distractions and neglect. Unfortunately, the same holds true for our faith life. In fact, for most of us, the greatest danger that threatens to weaken our faith is not outright rejection of our faith but the forgetting that comes about through distraction and neglect. This "spiritual amnesia" that plagues all too many of us is the tendency to simply forget all of the wonderful things that God has done for us. The reason we recite the Creed week in and week out at our liturgies is to ward off spiritual amnesia. It is no coincidence that the word amnesia and the word *anamnesis* both come from the same root word in Greek, meaning to recall or remember. *Anamnesis*, of course, refers to the part of the Eucharistic prayer following the institution narrative in which the presider calls upon the assembly to recall the deeds of the Father, accomplished through Christ, namely, the Paschal Mystery. We recall how Jesus suffered, died, and rose again, because if we don't, we run the risk of forgetting.

It is for this same reason that God gave us the First Commandment, which most of us recall as "I am the Lord your God, you shall have no other gods before me." If you take a look at the actual Scripture verse, however, you'll notice that the entire sentence is "I am the LORD your God, *who brought you out of the land of Egypt, out of the house of slavery;* you shall have no other gods before me."[48] God, like a good parent, reminds us in that First Commandment of God's previous glorious deeds. In essence, God is saying: Remember what I have done! God does not need the First Commandment because God craves our attention. We need the First Commandment because, without it, we tend to forget our true source of salvation.

"Therefore, O Lord, / as we now celebrate the memorial of our redemption, / we remember Christ's Death."

(Eucharistic Prayer IV, *The Roman Missal*)

Liturgy and catechesis team up together to ensure that no one ever forgets the great deeds of the Father that culminate in the Death and Resurrection of his Son, Jesus Christ. Liturgy and catechesis team up together to proclaim the mystery of our faith, namely that Christ has died, is risen, and will come again. Liturgy and catechesis teach us to remember Jesus's Paschal Mystery so that we may be transformed through our own sufferings and deaths, which are intimately bound to Jesus's.

"Catechetics forms part of that 'memory' of the Church which vividly maintains the presence of the Lord among us.[49] Use of memory, therefore, forms a constitutive aspect of the pedagogy of the faith since the beginning of Christianity."

(*The General Directory for Catechesis*, 154)

Forming Faith—Proclaiming Faith

How is faith formed? Where is faith formed?

Unfortunately, in many cases, liturgy and catechesis have undergone, not a divorce, but an amicable separation. We may acknowledge that the two still belong together, yet, all too often, we operate in such a manner that we tend to keep them in "separate rooms." At times, it seems as though liturgists and catechists are stuck inside some present-day "tower of Babel," unable to understand what the other is saying because we are speaking different languages.

"Catechesis is intrinsically linked with the whole of liturgical and sacramental activity, for it is in the sacraments, especially in the Eucharist, that Christ Jesus works in fullness for the transformation of human beings."

(*Catechesi tradendae, 23*)

Yet liturgy and catechesis, if understood properly, are two sides of the same coin. Catechesis without liturgy is like a parent explaining to their child *how* to celebrate their birthday without ever actually getting them a cake, lighting the candles, or singing the "Happy Birthday" song. Liturgy without catechesis, on the other hand, is like the same parent throwing lavish birthday parties for their child without ever sitting down with them to tell them about the day they were born, showing them pictures/videos of their birth or previous birthdays, or telling them stories about their family history. When both are done and the boundary lines between the two are erased, we find that liturgy takes on a catechetical flavor and catechesis takes on a liturgical flavor.

For this reason, the *General Directory for Catechesis* tells us that "'Catechesis is intrinsically bound to every liturgical and sacramental action.' [50] Frequently, however, the practice of catechetics testifies to a weak and fragmentary link with the liturgy: limited attention to liturgical symbols and rites, scant use of the liturgical fonts, catechetical courses with little or no connection with the liturgical year; the marginalization of liturgical celebrations in catechetical programs."[51] Not by coincidence, the *Catechism of the Catholic Church* tells us that liturgy is "the privileged place for catechizing the people of God."[52] The liturgy is "the central context for our formation because it is there that we hear and encounter the truths we assent to live."[53]

It is in and through liturgical action and expression that we are formed in faith and proclaim faith. In order to encounter mystery and enter into it, we must make use of a language of mystery, namely, the language of liturgy. This language goes beyond words to involve sign, symbol, and ritual—all vehicles for communicating God's mysterious presence and intention. Encountering God's presence always leads us to proclaim that presence to others. Pope Paul VI, in his Apostolic Exhortation *Evangelii Nuntiandi*, says that "it is unthinkable that a person should accept the Word and give himself to the kingdom without becoming a person who bears witness to it and proclaims it in his turn."[54] Let us turn to the liturgy to encounter the mystery of faith and discover the language needed to enter into it and proclaim it to others.

"The disciple of Christ must not only keep the faith and live on it, but also profess it, confidently bear witness to it, and spread it."

(*Catechism of the Catholic Church*, 1816)

REFLECTION

» During liturgy, pay attention to all of the times and ways in which God's deeds are proclaimed. Reflect upon how the liturgy catechizes.

» Reflect on the role that memorization plays or can play in your catechetical formation.

» Read the letter to the Hebrews, chapter 11, and meditate on the various examples of faith in our salvation history referred to there. Look up some of the examples in the Old Testament.

» In your daily living, how are you inviting others into deeper relationship with the Lord?

» What distractions get in the way of your ability to remember the deeds of the Lord?

» Think of someone you have entered into relationship with. What have you surrendered to this relationship? How do you allow this relationship to influence you? In what ways do you need to surrender to God as you deepen your faith relationship?

» When was a time that you needed to take someone at their word? Who do you consider to be a person of great faith?

CHAPTER 4

THE MYSTERY OF RITUAL

Encountering Ritual

Bill was seventy-eight years old. For over fifty of those years he and Elaine had lived together as husband and wife. Both of them were very well known in the parish. You saw them every Sunday, week after week, month after month. Faithfully they would come to Mass and each week I would get the update on their lives: what they had been up to, which of their children they'd spoken to, whether or not they had decided to go to Florida or Arizona for their vacation. Bill would tell the same joke he had told the last two weeks, and each time Elaine would smile and shake her head at him in mock disapproval. Each week they would sit in the same section of the church, and each week they would both kneel to say a prayer before Mass began. On the way out of the church after the liturgy, Bill would make sure to give one more quip, and then off they'd go for another week.

It hadn't always been this way. For the first twenty years or so, Bill didn't go into the church with Elaine. He'd wait in the car in the parking lot, reading the Sunday paper while Elaine went to Mass by herself. See, Bill wasn't baptized. At one point, a priest told Elaine that Bill didn't have to wait in the car if he didn't want to; he could come in to Mass with her if he wished. Ultimately they decided on that course and that's how it remained for the next thirty years. They would come to Mass together and at communion, Elaine would go up and Bill would wait in his seat for her to come back before he would kneel down with her in prayer. Then, after seventy-eight years, Bill decided that he wanted to be baptized, and that he wanted to go with Elaine to communion. He became part of the parish's RCIA process and each Sunday he would include, in the weekly report before Mass began, an update on his process of initiation.

When the Easter Vigil finally came that year, much had been made of Bill's intent to be baptized. Week after week the parish community had seen him among those who were dismissed after the homily, always walking a bit slower than his younger fellow catechumens. During Lent the community prayed with him and over him at the Rite of Sending to the Cathedral in preparation for the Rite of Election, and again they prayed over him at the Scrutinies. Sometimes during the homily, when the priest would direct a portion of his comments directly to the catechumens and candidates, he would always include a friendly, good-natured jab at Bill.

No words, no explanation could ever even come close to describing the experience of that Holy Saturday night. With his wife, Elaine, as his sponsor, Bill was called to the front of the church as the Litany of the Saints began. There, he sat in a chair while the other catechumens knelt, until they all began to make their way in procession to the baptismal font. After the water was blessed the catechumens were called, one by one, into the tomb of the font, only to be reborn moments later, in the image of the Risen Christ.

Whether by design or by coincidence, Bill was the last one to be called. As he stepped down into the font, his tall frail body covered by a gray robe, the pastor addressed him. "Bill, after all this time, profess your belief in the God who created you and who has called you to this water. I ask you: Do you believe in God the Father almighty, creator of heaven and earth?" To each of the baptismal questions, Bill's "I do" was loud and strong. Then, with no other words, the pastor helped Bill to kneel down into the water. Everyone in the church strained to get a glimpse of what was about to happen. However, even if one couldn't see from the far end of the church, there was no mistaking the sound: an abundant amount of water loudly poured over that 78-year-old body.

The water flowed over a head that contained years of thinking. It flowed over eyes that had spent years searching and questioning. It ran over arms that had embraced his wife at prayer for fifty years and hands that had been extended countless times in the sign of peace, yet had never reached out for the bread of life. It washed over legs that had carried this man for seventy-eight years on a journey that no one but God knew completely. And it splashed down into a pool that had become the womb from which a brand new life was to begin.

In that moment, in that ancient ritual of death and new life, nothing could be said to adequately express all the meaning, all the depth, and all the profundity of what was taking place. The most any of us could do, was to give over to the power of the ritual and let it express everything that was in our minds, our hearts, and our souls. Our opportunity came with the "Alleluia" that literally burst forth upon Bill's coming up out of the water of the font, and the applause that followed as he made his way out of the church with the rest of the newly baptized to change into their white garments—an applause that continued well after they had left and the rest of us had begun to make our way to the same font so that we could renew our own baptism which Bill now shared with us.   **~Todd**

How can we put words to all that we have been considering in the previous chapters? How can we talk about the great mystery that is God? How can we express our understanding of the intimate relationship with the Father to which we are called in Christ Jesus? How can we put words to the depth of faith and trust that we have experienced through that relationship? How can we do any of this? The answer is, through ritual.

Ritual is the uniquely human ability to express what can't be expressed in mere words. Ritual is the only adequate response to an experience or situation that touches us so deeply that it can overwhelm us. Ritual is the means by which we give voice, meaning, and understanding to that profound reality which is beyond all of it. Ritual is a key to communicating truths that are far greater than we are.

"Then Moses called all the elders of Israel and said to them, 'Go, select lambs for your families, and slaughter the passover lamb. . . . You shall observe this rite as a perpetual ordinance for you and your children. When you come to the land that the Lord will give you, as he has promised, you shall keep this observance. And when your children ask you, "What do you mean by this observance?" you shall say, "It is the passover sacrifice to the Lord, for he passed over the houses of the Israelites in Egypt, when he struck down the Egyptians but spared our houses."' And the people bowed down and worshiped. The Israelites went and did just as the Lord had commanded Moses and Aaron."

(Exodus 12:21, 24–28)

A most basic element of ritual is that it engages the imagination of those who participate in it. It is for this reason that many lament the decline of ritual in our times and in our society. Some believe that we have lost the ability to ritualize because we have lost our sense of imagination. Our culture is one of explicit excess. Nothing is left to the imagination anymore. The intensity of a scary movie used to be measured by the level of suspense and fear that it generated in the viewer. Today, a scary movie is measured by the amount of gore, how realistic it looks, and by how graphic it is. The sense is that the more explicit a film is, the scarier it is. Nothing is implied anymore. The advancement of live-action video games and the continued fascination with reality TV has left nothing to the imagination.

Perhaps that is why ritual can be so *countercultural* for us as Catholics. In the face of a video-oriented, technological society in which the semblance of reality is valued over all else, we rely on the power of ritual to express what we know to be real and true. In the face of a culture that wants to explain it all for us and provide us with "ultimate reality," we look to ritual to stir our imaginations and point us to what may be unseen, but what is nonetheless authentic.

"A mystagogical catechesis must also be concerned with *presenting the meaning of the signs* contained in the rites. This is particularly important in a highly technological age like our own, which risks losing the ability to appreciate signs and symbols. More than simply conveying information, a mystagogical catechesis should be capable of making the faithful more sensitive to the language of signs and gestures which, together with the word, make up the rite."

(*Sacramentum Caritatis*, 64)

The Language of Ritual

Ritual has its own language. Like all languages it has a specific structure, pattern, and vocabulary. It has its own nuances and rules of construction and grammar. Like all languages, we learn its structure, pattern, and vocabulary slowly, over a period of time—sometimes years. First we observe, hearing it and experiencing it—getting used to its sights, sounds, gestures, and movements. Little by little, we learn the ins and outs and we begin to recognize its structures and patterns. Then, taking our place with the others who have learned this beautiful language, we too begin to understand it and to speak it. We enter into it and we share in the meaning it expresses.

"Gestures, language, and actions are the *physical, visible,* and *public* expressions by which human beings understand and manifest their inner life. Since human beings on this earth are always made of flesh and blood, they not only will and think but also speak and sing, move and celebrate. These human actions as well as physical objects are also signs by which Christians express and deepen their relationship to God."[55]

(Built of Living Stones, 23)

The language of ritual is made up of many elements. It involves the use of signs, symbols, and gestures: water sprinkled on us, hands extended over us, and oil rubbed into our hands or on our foreheads. It uses special, designated objects to convey its meaning: books that are used for specific purposes at specific times, special cups and other vessels, and clothing that is immediately identifiable. Even time and the seasons enter into its structures and help in giving the ritual a voice with which to speak to us. Think of the large bonfire lighted in the dark of the first Saturday night after the first full moon after the Spring equinox (Holy Saturday night), or the celebration of All Saints and All Souls during the autumn of the northern hemisphere that signals the end of the harvest and speaks of the inevitability of death.

The language of ritual is a patterned structure. It is ordered and repetitive. This order and repetition is often misunderstood as *routine*. Yet, there is a profound difference between ritual and routine. Routines are done without thought. We know them well enough to do them with our eyes closed. They may serve certain purposes, as in our morning routines that help us wake up and get ready for the day, and our bedtime routines that similarly help us wind down from the day and prepare us for sleep. But, while these routines may have purpose, they don't have any great meaning beyond the purposes they serve.

Rituals, on the other hand, are rife with meanings. They express these meanings and our understandings in profound ways. The repetition of routines serves nothing except the routine. The repetition of rituals, however, serves to take us deeper and deeper into the truths they express. Each time we experience the ritual, we are drawn ever deeper into the meaning of the mystery that the ritual celebrates. For this reason, we need to be careful about glibly "changing" rituals in order to make them seem more contemporary.

Once, a group of catechists were discussing this repetitive nature of ritual. One of the participants shared a story about her mother's birthday party. This person recalled her mother commenting about how much she liked this certain pie that her daughter once made. So, for her birthday, she thought she would surprise her mother with this particular pie. The family gathered and participated in the familiar birthday ritual, but her mother seemed upset. Afterward, she asked her mother what was wrong and she replied, "Why did you make a pie? Birthdays call for cake! You don't mess with the cake!"

The same is true of our liturgical rituals: we wash feet, not hands, on Holy Thursday; we use unleavened bread and wine, not crackers and grape soda pop, for Eucharist; we confess sins verbally to an ordained priest, we don't write them on paper and then throw them into a bonfire. In short, we don't "mess with the cake!"

Ritual relies on a shared understanding among those who speak its language. All those taking part know what certain gestures mean, they have the same understanding of the symbols, and they share a sense of what the ritual expresses. Anyone who has ever had an experience of ritual where there wasn't a shared understanding of the symbols used, or the gestures made, or the objects employed, knows the difficulty of being able to enter into the experience.

"The rites should be marked by a noble simplicity; they should be short, clear, and unencumbered by useless repetitions; they should be within the people's powers of comprehension and as a rule not require much explanation."

(Constitution on the Sacred Liturgy, 34)

The language of ritual is multileveled and multidimensional. It communicates meaning to different people at different levels in different ways, all of which combine to express the truth and mystery that it proclaims. The meaning conveyed to one person may not be the same exact meaning that another person understands. And yet a truth has been proclaimed. What a particular ritual stirs in one person's imagination and memory may not be what is stirred in another person, and yet an experience of the same mystery is communicated to both people.

Ritual Creates and Sustains Relationships

The concept of ritual is not something that was created by liturgists in liturgical laboratories or by theologians in ivory towers. Rather, ritual is a very human experience and is something that is learned and practiced at a very young age as the following story illustrates. Every night, my friend Chris would read a book to his two-year-old daughter, Carole. The book, called *Blue Hat, Green Hat*, showed four animals on every page: each animal wearing a different color hat or shirt, the last one being a turkey who always wore things the wrong way: hat on his feet, pants on his head, and so forth.[56] Chris would point to each picture one at a time and describe the four animals wearing different color clothes: "blue hat, green hat, red hat, . . . OOPS!" At the sight of the turkey and the sound of Dad saying, "OOPS!" Carole would double over in laughter and roll on the floor. As soon as she would calm down, she would insist, "Again! Again!" and Dad would read it again. And again, Carole would giggle at the sound of "OOPS!" and the sight of the turkey.

Then, one morning, Chris got up early and saw that Carole was "reading" the book *Blue Hat, Green Hat* on her own in her bedroom. While Chris secretly watched, Carole, who of course could not read, pointed silently to each animal, the first, then the second, then the third. After pointing at the fourth picture, the turkey with pants on his head or a hat on his feet, she would say, "OOPS!" and double over in laughter and roll on the floor. As Chris spied on her, Carole would do it over and over again. It seemed that Carole didn't need to know how to read to make the "magic" happen. She just had to perform the ritual that she learned from her father.

This simple story of a family ritual reveals to us both the utter simplicity and the mysterious complexity of ritual. Ritual puts us in contact with something other than ourselves. It places us in relationship with something or someone else. More than that, ritual sustains relationships. The ritual of "Red hat, blue hat, green hat, . . . OOPS!" not only created a special dynamic in the relationship between Carole and her father, but it sustained that relationship for Carole in the absence of her father. The ritual not only allowed for the usual response of laughter but it also maintained the relationship and, in fact, helped Carole to experience her father's presence although he was physically absent.

This dynamic is a very common and fundamental element to most family rituals. Think of a major holiday the first time it was celebrated with a certain family member absent. Did the particular rituals that are part of the holiday serve, among other things, to make that person's presence felt again? Think of the more intimate relationships among friends. Are there not individual rituals that are part of those friendships? These rituals serve to deepen the relationship and to connect the friends at a profound level. It could be a special meal shared together, a specific place that has some significance to the people involved, or a certain annual event. Whatever it is, the experience of the ritual among the people who share it is often beyond explanation, beyond definition, yet it expresses a very real truth about the relationship and the friendship.

Sometimes a ritual defines the relationship itself. There is an American Russian Orthodox Cathedral to which I go every year on the celebration of Great Friday (the Orthodox Good Friday). The liturgy is sung Matins and it is a beautiful experience of chanting psalms, venerating an icon of Christ's burial shroud, and lighting and processing with candles outside and around the church. There is a woman in the parish who, over the years, has "figured me out." She knows I am not a regular parishioner, that I come to the cathedral only for this service each year, and she probably knows that I am not even Orthodox. But she also knows that I love to come each year and sing the liturgy with the bishop and the other members of the parish.

Each year she and I greet one another, make some comment about the past year, and even, on occasion, save candles for one another. One year I missed the Great Friday celebration because I was out of town. The next year I was once again able to go and arrived in plenty of time before the liturgy began. Now, bear in mind that it had been two years since I was last to this liturgy. When I entered the cathedral and this woman saw me, she made it a point to seek me out and to say, "It's so good to see you! I missed you last year." She then handed me the candle that was to be my light throughout the whole liturgy. We know each other only through our mutual participation in this annual ritual, and yet that was enough for her to note my absence the year before and it was enough to allow her to look for me and to make note of it the next year. Rituals create and sustain relationships. **~Todd**

Catholic Ritual

The rites and liturgies that make up our Catholic worship have every one of these dynamics of ritual. These rites and liturgies engage our religious imagination and allow us to express what we know and believe about God, about ourselves, about our Church, and about what God has called us to be. They allow us to express our faith on intimate levels. They allow us to speak a language using certain symbols, objects, gestures, and movements, the meaning of which is shared among all of us who participate. They call us into relationship with the Father, through Christ, and with one another. Our rituals sustain these relationships, strengthening them so that each time we celebrate them, we enter deeper and deeper into the mystery of these relationships.

> "O God, who by invisible power / accomplish a wondrous effect / through sacramental signs."
>
> (Blessing of Water from the Easter Vigil, *The Roman Missal*)

Each time we celebrate these rituals, they reveal something of the Father, of Christ, and of ourselves. It's as if our eyes are opened during ritual and we see something of the divine: some truth, some dynamic of our relationship with God, some aspect of our faith. In the liturgy of Reconciliation, for example, the ritual reveals the forgiveness and mercy of a God who knows we are broken, but who longs for nothing more than to make us whole. In the liturgy of marriage, the ritual reveals the love and total commitment with which God has entered into covenant with us who are beloved. In the liturgy of Anointing of the Sick, the ritual reveals the tender care and concern of God in regard to our struggles and our suffering. And in the Liturgy of the Eucharist, the ritual reveals the abundance with which God nourishes us and sustains us by his presence and action in our midst.

Most important, these rituals allow us to experience salvation. We have to remember one of the most important realities about our Catholic rites and rituals: through them, God acts on us. Our rites are *efficacious*. That is to say, they have an effect on us—an actual effect. We believe that, through our rites, God does something to us. Ideally, we are not the same after we participate in the rites and liturgies of our faith as we were before. God acts on us and does something to us in these rites. In the end, through our rites, God renews the covenant first made with each of us at our Baptism. With each celebration of these rituals we are drawn deeper and deeper into that covenant. All of the ritual elements—the prayers, symbols, gestures, objects used—reveal to us more and more the mystery of our salvation.

> "Christ, taking on human flesh, reveals the Father. . . . Christ is himself the sacrament of the Father. In his risen glory, he is no longer visible in this world. . . . And so washing and anointing, breaking bread and sharing the cup, raising arms in blessing and imposing hands are *visible* signs by which Christ manifests and accomplishes our sanctification and salvation in the Church."[57]
>
> (*Built of Living Stones*, 25)

REFLECTION

» Reflect on the difference between ritual and routine and observe how you celebrate liturgy.

» Look at the different and varied rituals of the Catholic Church. Identify the patterns that mark our worship. List the elements that speak the most to you now in your faith journey.

» Identify the rituals you follow in your own life. Identify any family rituals that you have, including those that are part of the holidays. Identify what rituals you share with some of your closest friends. Compare those rituals and ones that make up our Catholic liturgies. Reflect upon what they tell you about the rituals that we celebrate as a people of faith.

» How do you experience the power of ritual in your community's life of worship and in your specific liturgical ministry? What helps you or hinders you as you enter into the ritual?

» What strikes you the most about our Catholic rituals? How are they helping you to express your developing faith? How do you experience the power of ritual to help sustain your relationship with God and with the faith community?

» Spend time in reflection on a liturgy you have recently experienced. See if you can identify the ritual element that struck you most. Why do you think that element spoke to you so powerfully?

CHAPTER 5

THE MYSTERY OF SIGN AND SYMBOL

The "Dark Mark"

In J.K. Rowling's *Harry Potter and the Goblet of Fire*, an event occurs that reveals the power of sign and symbol.[58] Harry and his friends are camping out in a field with hundreds of other wizard families following a major sporting event they had attended. When a band of thugs appears, terrorizing the campground, Harry and his friends Ron and Hermione, along with dozens of other frightened children, run into the dark forest to hide. Suddenly, Harry hears a voice call out a mysterious spell followed by a flash of green glittering light that flies up into the sky to form an image of a skull. Harry does not understand the significance of this symbol, but the others around him, who are more aware of wizard culture, react with fear. His friend Hermione tells him that this is the Dark Mark—the sign of "You-Know-Who," which is the code name for Lord Voldemort, a wizard so evil that even speaking his name would frighten people. The Dark Mark that appeared in the sky was his official sign. Its presence communicated to the people that evil and danger were lurking in their presence.

One does not need to be a wizard to understand how signs and symbols work. In fact, it is no coincidence that signs and symbols play such an important role in children's literature. A great example is Dr. Seuss's *How the Grinch Stole Christmas!*, a tale of what happens when a curmudgeonly character called the Grinch attempts to "steal" Christmas by removing all of the signs and symbols of the holiday, only to realize that the event comes from within people.[59] Likewise, the classic book *The Wonderful Wizard of Oz* reveals how the Scarecrow's brains, the Tin Woodman's heart, and the Cowardly Lion's courage are "realized" when the wizard presents them with symbols: a head full of bran, pins, and needles for the Scarecrow; a silk heart stuffed with sawdust for the Tin Woodman; and a potion of "courage" for the Cowardly Lion.[60] In reality, all three had already possessed what they sought, but the symbols made these realities more tangible for them.

Children understand that signs and symbols communicate something that words alone cannot. Perhaps it is because children have a more limited vocabulary that they understand signs and symbols in a way that adults don't. It is easier for adults to rely on the power of words, thinking that somehow our vocabulary can capture the essence of our experience. Yet, there is so much in our experience that words alone cannot capture or express. Most certainly, in the area of our understanding of God, words alone cannot express the reality of the divine presence in our midst.

As children of God, we continue to rely upon signs and symbols to help us both encounter and express the mystery of God.

The Grinch Who Stole . . . God?

What would happen if Dr. Seuss's nasty old Grinch decided to steal the presence of God from Catholics? Imagine the Grinch creeping into all of the church buildings around the world and stealing the bread, wine, water, oils, candles, statues, incense, and so on, in hopes of eliminating God's presence from our midst. Tucked away in his mountain retreat with all of his liturgical booty, the Grinch would wake up on Sunday morning and bend his ear, hoping to hear the sound of Catholics wailing over the loss of their God. Rather than hearing any mourning taking place, however, the Grinch would (we hope) hear the glorious sounds of praise and thanksgiving coming from every Catholic church, despite the loss of our signs and symbols. The truth is, we Catholics know full well that God's presence is not confined, contained, or isolated in our liturgical signs and symbols but, rather, is communicated (made manifest) through them. Like the Whos in Dr. Seuss's Whoville, we rely on sign and symbol to encounter and express that which we know and believe is already within us and around us—in our case, the presence of our Risen Lord, Jesus Christ, the love of God the Father, and the fellowship of the Holy Spirit.

So, then, why do we bother with signs and symbols? Primarily because we acknowledge that our spoken language is inadequate to express the overwhelming reality of the divine presence. In our daily lives, we have many occasions upon which we rely on signs and symbols to express something beyond words. On Valentine's Day, we may say "I love you" to a very special someone; however, the expression of that love does not seem complete or sufficient without the presence of some symbolic gift such as chocolates, flowers, or a card accompanied by the "ritual" practice of going out for dinner. Without these outward expressions, the love between two people still exists, but, through sign and symbol, that love is made manifest and, in a mysterious way, is strengthened and formed in a way that would not be true if the signs, symbols, and ritual were ignored. Likewise, our birthday can come and go without the symbolic birthday cake, candles, cards, gifts, balloons and ritual song. Without the outward signs, it would still be our birthday. The presence of the traditional birthday symbols and the enactment of the ritual, however, make our birthday and the love that people have for us manifest. Some experiences are just too "big" or important to be limited to words. Encounters with God fit that description.

"In human life, signs and symbols occupy an important place. As a being at once body and spirit, man expresses and perceives spiritual realities through physical signs and symbols. As a social being, man needs signs and symbols to communicate with others, through language, gestures, and actions. The same holds true for his relationship with God. . . . The liturgy of the church presupposes, integrates and sanctifies elements from creation and human culture, conferring on them the dignity of signs of grace, of the new creation in Jesus Christ."

(*Catechism of the Catholic Church*, 1146, 1149)

God's Signs and Symbols

In Scripture, these encounters with God are continually communicated through signs and symbols. The burning bush, the pillar of cloud by day and the pillar of fire by night, the dark cloud that enveloped the mountaintop while God gave Moses the Ten Commandments, even Elijah's gentle, whispering breeze all convey the overwhelming presence of a God too great for words and too great for descriptions.

Not only is God's presence conveyed through signs and symbols, but so too is God's relationship with us. In the book of Genesis, God devises a sign that will communicate God's faithfulness to the promise God made to Noah: "This is the sign of the covenant that I make between me and you and every living creature that is with you, for all future generations: I have set my bow in the clouds, and it shall be a sign of the covenant between me and the earth. When I bring clouds over the earth and the bow is seen in the clouds, I will remember my covenant that is between me and you and every living creature of all flesh."[61] The prophet Ezekiel notes that the Sabbath is a sign between God and Israel that speaks of the holiness in which God had made his people.[62]

It is noteworthy that John's account of the Gospel speaks of Jesus's miracles as "signs." The changing of water into wine, the feeding of the multitudes, the healing of the official's son in Capernaum, the raising of Lazarus are all "signs" of God's presence, power, action, and love in Jesus. They speak of what was not immediately obvious, of what was "hidden," of what was to be known only through a deeper level of experiencing Christ. They *revealed* God, through Jesus, to those who witnessed these "signs." These signs and symbols that mark our encounters with God continue to reveal God to us in powerful and meaningful ways.

"And so, Father, by the power of your love, make this mixture of oil and perfume a sign and source of your blessing. Pour out the gifts of your Holy Spirit on our brothers and sisters who will be anointed with it. . . . Above all, Father, we pray that through this sign of your anointing you will grant increase to your church until it reaches the eternal glory where you, Father, will be all in all, together with Christ your Son, in the unity of the Holy Spirit, for ever and ever."

(Prayer of Consecration for Holy Chrism, *The Roman Pontifical*)

Sign . . . or Symbol?

In talking about signs and symbols, the question inevitably comes: What is the difference between the two? Smoke is indeed a sign of something, namely the presence of fire, as the old saying goes. At a celebration of Vespers, or Evening Prayer, however, when the Church sings Psalm 141, "Let my prayer arise like incense before you, O Lord," and the presider places a piece of resin on a coal, the rising smoke, rather than a sign of the presence of fire, acts as a symbol of our prayers rising up to God. Is the smoke a sign, or is it a symbol? Is it both? What's the difference?

All symbols are, quite literally, signs. That is, like a sign, they point to something beyond themselves. They communicate a determined meaning that is shared and understood by all. A red, octagon shape with white lettering means something very definite: it means *Stop*. The red, octagon shape with white lettering is so distinctive that even if the white lettering isn't in English, we know what it means. Because it has an agreed-upon meaning, the red, octagon shape with white lettering is a *conventional sign*. Smoke, on the other hand, is a *natural sign*, because its meaning (the presence of fire) is natural and is not determined by any agreement or convention.

All signs are not, however, symbols. The red, octagon shape with white lettering means nothing more than, *Stop*. It carries no other meaning or understanding with it. As a sign, smoke means nothing more than the presence of fire or the immediate danger of its presence. Symbols, on the other hand, not only point beyond themselves as a sign does, but their meaning is often varied and their understanding not limited to a single idea. As a symbol, smoke means much more than simply the presence of fire. If it is white smoke, and it is coming out of a particular chimney in the Vatican, it symbolizes the election of a new pope. If it is billowing out of a censer and envelops the casket of a loved one during a funeral liturgy, it symbolizes the royal and noble stature that the deceased person held as a baptized member of the Body of Christ.

Unlike signs, symbols have the unique ability to transmit more than one meaning at a time. It is this ability that gives symbols such richness and power. Like an onion, symbols are multilayered and the more you peel away at the layers, the more potent the symbol becomes. Unlike a sign, the meaning a symbol carries can never be summed up in a single explanation. Their meaning or their explanation is wondrously just a bit more than words are able to convey.

I have a friend who is a classmate of mine from college seminary. We have known one another for almost thirty years, and our friendship has been a wealth of emotional support and spiritual sustenance for me. At some point in our lives, Gari had developed a deep fondness for the symbol of wheat. For him it spoke in myriad ways about the Eucharist and its nurturing and sustaining power, about the Christian life and the Paschal Mystery, about the call to die in order to produce abundantly. Over the years, Gari has shared these varied and different meanings with me in countless, intimate moments. I am so aware of these meanings and they have touched me so profoundly that I cannot see a picture or image of wheat without thinking of Gari.

More than just thinking of him, the symbol of wheat has such a power that when I see an image of it, Gari is instantly and mysteriously present to me. It's not just that I think of him or about him. It's a sense of his presence to me, an awareness of him and of our friendship that is more than just memory. It is so powerful that when I see an image of wheat he is called to mind and heart and I am affected at a deep level. This is the power of symbol.   **~Todd**

After the Chicago Blackhawks won the Stanley Cup in 2010, ending a 49-year drought, I erected a "shrine" in my basement with all of the Blackhawks memorabilia I had acquired over the years: pucks, autographed sticks, photos, programs, and even bobbleheads. One item in my shrine often attracts attention: an empty cigar pack. This empty pack conjures up so many memories for me. I purchased the five-pack when the Hawks were one win away from going to the Stanley Cup Finals and I vowed to smoke one cigar for each of the five victories it would take to win the Cup. I did this as a tribute to my late Dad, a great hockey fan, who enjoyed a cigar on special occasions. Over the next few weeks of ups and downs, nervous stomachs, and white knuckles, I joyfully smoked the first four cigars in my backyard after each victory. On the day that the Hawks would clinch the Cup, I was in Seattle, over a thousand miles away from my backyard, giving a presentation. When the Hawks did indeed win the Stanley Cup, I stood outside my hotel in Seattle, proudly wearing a Blackhawks jersey and smoking the fifth and last cigar. As I posted pictures on Facebook of each cigar-smoking experience, family and friends promised that they would smoke a cigar with me when and if the Hawks won. Sure enough, in the weeks following the Stanley Cup victory, I spent many happy moments savoring more victory cigars with my wife, mom, son, daughter, brothers and sisters, cousins, and coworkers. That empty five-pack of cigars symbolizes the great fun we had in Chicago celebrating a long-awaited Stanley Cup championship. Thanks, Dad, for taking me to my first Blackhawks game when I was a kid!   **~Joe**

The Effect of Signs and Symbols

For us Catholics, our liturgical and faith symbols speak to us at significantly deep and profound levels, and do more than simply convey a single meaning. They convey understanding and power; they convey a richness and depth that stir our imaginations and touch our hearts; they convey the presence of something that is beyond us, something that is greater than we are. In a word, they convey the presence and, in fact, the action of the Father, in Christ, through the Spirit.

"Just as Christ invited those who heard him to share his personal union with the Father through material signs, so Christ leads the church through these same signs in the liturgy from the visible to the invisible.[63] As a result, effective liturgical signs have a teaching function and encourage full, conscious, and active participation, express and strengthen faith, and lead people to God. . . . It must likewise be kept in mind that the liturgy and its signs and symbols do not exercise merely a teaching function. They also touch and move a person to conversion of heart and not simply to enlightenment of mind."

(*Built of Living Stones*, 26)

What we do with these symbols—that is, the ritual gestures and liturgical movements that make use of these symbols—speaks just as much to us of God's presence and action. Oil that is rubbed into foreheads and hands; arms that are raised or hands that are laid in blessing; water that is poured deliberately—these all speak to us on a symbolic level. They convey the deepest of beliefs and the truest of realities: the reality that our God is one who longs to be with us and touch us, and, in so doing, to heal us, to comfort us, to strengthen us, to nourish us, and to save us.

Oil and fire, water and wine, bread and ashes, incense and extended hands—these are the symbols and the symbolic actions that we use to express our belief in God's presence among us. At the same time, they are the vehicles through which God *acts on us*, through which he does something to us. As such, they speak to us on levels that words never could. We Catholics are a very "earthy" people. We recognize that God uses natural, commonplace, ordinary objects, and natural, common, and ordinary gestures, to communicate to us his extraordinary presence and action.

"When God's people gather for prayer, the most intimate and all-embracing aspect of their life together occurs: the moment when they touch, taste, smell, hear, see, and share those hidden realities that would otherwise remain imperceptible. Together they adore the holiness of God and give expression to the unceasing life God has given them. God nourishes them as a community and makes them holy through the use of *ordinary* perceptible signs of water, oil, bread and wine, transformed by *extraordinary* grace."

(Built of Living Stones, 140)

I remember watching my sister bathe my nephew once, not long after he was born. She carefully and gently lifted him up out of the water and wrapped him in a big, fluffy towel. Tenderly, she patted him dry and worked to get the water from under his arms, from around his fingers, and from between his toes. I remember recalling, immediately, the number of times I'd seen members of the parish work just as carefully to dry the water from between the toes of the person whose foot they had just washed at the Holy Thursday liturgy of the Lord's Supper.

I watched as my sister lovingly brushed my nephew's tassel of hair from his forehead so that the water wouldn't drip into his eyes, and immediately thought of my pastor's gentle way of brushing wet hair out of the eyes of the woman whom he had just pulled from death's grip as she stood in the baptismal font that had just given birth to her new life in Christ. I watched as my sister took a palm full of baby oil and, with a parent's care and attention, rubbed it into my nephew's skin, and I couldn't help but think of the countless number of faithful who have similarly had oil rubbed, just as lovingly and just as carefully, onto their foreheads as they were confirmed as God's beloved son or daughter and were anointed with the oil of gladness in the image of their Lord and Savior.   **~Todd**

These signs, symbols, and ritual gestures all proclaim to us the mystery of faith that Christ is risen, alive, and active here, now, in *this* community, at *this* time, and during *this* celebration. They proclaim that this presence is balm for our wounded bodies, nourishment for our hungry spirits, strength for our journey, and salvation for our souls. Our only response—the only appropriate response—is to recognize God's overwhelming love and goodness and to proclaim with the rest of the Church, "blessed be God, for ever."

"To the central signs and word, the Church adds gestures and material elements such as incense, ashes, holy water, candles, and vestments to dispose us for the heavenly gifts of our crucified and Risen Lord and to deepen our reverence for the unceasing mercy and grace that come to us in the Church through the passion and death of Jesus, our Lord."

(Built of Living Stones, 25)

REFLECTION

» Reflect on all the symbols that are used in your parish's life of worship: water, oil, ashes, incense, bread and wine. How do they speak of God's presence and action in the lives of the faithful?

» Identify the signs and symbols that God is using now in your life to communicate God's encounters with you. (Note: They may not necessarily be liturgical or religious symbols—think of the many different areas of your life in considering this.)

» Spend some time reflecting on the symbols that are part of our Catholic faith. See if you can identify other areas of your life where these same objects and gestures are used (water or bread, for example). See how their liturgical use might influence your awareness of them in other areas of your life. Reflect on how your experience of them in other areas of your life might deepen your experience of these same symbols and gestures in liturgy.

» What Catholic symbols or gestures speak the loudest to you?

» Identify how Catholic symbols touch and speak to you on levels that are beyond words. How do they communicate to you the presence and action of God in your life at this point of your faith journey?

» Recall the stories from this chapter that deal with personal or familial signs and symbols. What are the signs and symbols from your own life that similarly communicate something that is just too "big" or too important for words? What is the experience or who is the person that these symbols represent? How do they speak to you?

PART TWO

Proclaiming the Mystery of the Church at Prayer

CHAPTER 6

THE MYSTERY OF THE ASSEMBLY

What is My Role?

Ever since we were children, most of us have struggled to figure out what our role is in various settings. How do we fit in with our friends? Where do we stand with our siblings or our parents? What is our role on our team? At work? We longed to be chosen when teams picked up sides so that we would know that we too have a role and are not just spectators.

What about when we go to Mass? What role do we play? At times, we think that the only people at Mass who have a role to play are the priest, lectors, servers, ushers, musicians, and extraordinary ministers of Holy Communion. What does that make the rest of us? Spectators? Unfortunately, for many of us, we approach the role of the assembly as just this: an audience passively watching while others perform their tasks, hoping that they will do so in a way that will engage us or even entertain us. Even the way we talk betrays what we think of our role. We speak of *"going to* Mass," *"attending* Mass," even *"watching* Mass."

How many of us talk about going to "participate" in Mass? How many of us would even think of speaking, as the *Constitution on the Sacred Liturgy* does, of "assist-ing" at Mass?[64]

"The celebrating assembly is the community of the baptized who, 'by regeneration and the anointing of the Holy Spirit, are consecrated to be a spiritual house and a holy priesthood, that . . . they may offer spiritual sacrifices.'[65] This 'common priesthood' is that of Christ the sole priest, in which all his members participate."[66]

(*Catechism of the Catholic Church*, 1141)

This can be especially true for those of us who are "cradle" Catholics. For many years, we have faithfully "attended" Mass as we were taught. The problem is, we some-times think of ourselves in this passive posture with no real role to play in the liturgy.

On one particular Palm Sunday, my wife and kids and I went to church to cel-ebrate our Lord's triumphal entry into Jerusalem. We sat in the back half of the church because I wasn't feeling particularly well and wanted to be close to an exit in case I needed to leave. Along came a gentleman who sat down next to us with his two-year-old daughter. For the next hour, the two of them proceeded to talk (out loud!) to each other—through the palm procession, through the proclamation of the Passion, the homily, the consecration, and so on. To make matters worse, a number of families around us were doing the same thing: talking amongst themselves, not paying attention or participating in the responses, and seemingly oblivious to the proceedings of the Mass.

My wife and kids and I looked at each other in frustration and amazement: it seemed that a number of people had absolutely no idea why they were there or what their role was. Upon departing, my wife commented to me that "it would be nice to go to church with people who really understood why they were there!" The problem is that so many of us do not understand our role as members of the assembly.

~Joe

When I was coordinating the Rite of Christian Initiation for Adults in a Chicago parish, we introduced the dismissal rite for the catechumens. The dismissal rite recognizes the role of those who are not yet baptized into the Catholic faith by inviting them to gather with the assembly for the Liturgy of the Word before dismissing them at the Liturgy of the Eucharist. The idea is that it is inappropriate and even inconsiderate to have someone who cannot yet partake in the Lord's meal remain and observe while others do so. (We would never invite someone over to our house and then tell them to watch while we eat dinner!)

Upon dismissal, the catechumens go to another space and reflect upon God's Word as they build their desire to come to the Lord's table at the Easter Vigil. Some weeks after Easter when all of our newly initiated were reflecting upon their journey through the RCIA, I asked them what they thought of the dismissal rite. After a moment or two, one of the women in the group responded: "The dismissal rite meant a great deal to me. When I started coming to church here by myself, I was so afraid. I didn't understand the Mass and I didn't know what I supposed to say or do or when to sit, kneel, or stand. I was embarrassed and thought people would notice me. When we began the dismissal rite and the priest would call the catechumens forward to dismiss us, I felt so proud because now I understood my role." She understood that everyone at Mass has a role, and she was coming to more fully understand her role in the assembly.

~Joe

The Responsibility of the Baptized

So just what is the role of the assembly? The process of initiation gives some excellent guidance in understanding the role of the assembly in our tradition's life of worship. For example, the Rite of Baptism for Children, when it is celebrated outside of Mass, ends at the altar for the Lord's Prayer. It does this for a reason: although the child cannot yet receive the Eucharist, as a member of the baptized, it will become the child's responsibility to gather around the Lord's table, with his or her faith community, praising and thanking God for all that God has done for us through his Son, Jesus Christ. The Rite of Baptism for Children ends at the altar as a sign that it is in order to gather around the table that this child is even baptized in the first place. While this is not the only reason why the child is baptized, this symbolic action is a very significant element of our baptismal understanding: it is a foretaste of what the child is called to do and who the child is called to be in his or her Baptism.

"Before the altar to prefigure the future sharing in the eucharist, the celebrant introduces and all recite the Lord's Prayer, in which God's children pray to their Father in heaven."

(Rite of Baptism for Children, 19)

For adults, too, in their process of full initiation, the culmination of months and sometimes years of preparation isn't found only in the waters of the font. The culmination of a person's death and new life in Christ Jesus is found around the altar. Baptism is what *allows* that person, in the first place, to gather with his or her brothers and sisters and to share the Lord's Meal. It is what allows a person to be part of the assembly.

When each one of us was baptized, we were initiated into the People of God—the Church. We became part of something that is bigger than each one of us. We took a place among God's holy people and we took upon ourselves the responsibilities that go along with that distinction. The word the Scriptures use to describe this body of God's people—*ekklesia*—gives us a sense of these responsibilities. Matthew's account of the Gospel is the only one to use this word, which in English is rendered "Church." This Greek word, *ekklesia* literally means, "the assembly." It denotes what this body of God's holy people, the baptized, did. They *assembled*. Baptism allowed them to take part in this *assembly*. And what did *assembling* allow them to do? Why did they *assemble*? We find the answer in another Greek word: *leitourgos*, which means, "the work of the people," or "the service of the people." This is the word from which our English word, *liturgy*, comes. Liturgy, then, was what the Church assembled for!

Liturgy is not the work of any one person or any one group of people. It is the work of all of us. Many people may have a misunderstanding of what we mean when we speak of the assembly. Many Catholics hear that term and immediately think of the *congregation*. They think of just the faithful laypeople, as opposed to the priest and liturgical ministers (those people who have "something to do" in the liturgy). In truth, an accurate understanding of the assembly is the whole gathered body, head (represented by the priest) and members (represented by every person who has gathered).

The Eucharist that we share every week is the prayer and the worship of every single member of the baptized. When we gather to retell our stories of faith; thank God for all that God has done and is doing for us; remember the life, Death, and Resurrection of Christ; share the meal of his Body and Blood; and then take that action out into the rest of the world, we are acting as the Church. We are doing the very thing for which we were baptized. Because we are members of worshiping communities, the Church, each one of us has a role to play and a part to take. Perhaps one is called to proclaim the Word. Perhaps another is called to help the community to share the Body and Blood of Christ. Perhaps one is called to help fill the prayer and worship with song. *All of us*, however, are called to be an active, participating part of the assembly. Whatever gifts we have, whatever talents, whatever our place in this family of ours, we are called to the hallmark of the Second Vatican Council's *Constitution on the Sacred Liturgy*: "full, conscious and active participation."[67]

"Whatever rites, according to their specific nature, make provision for communal celebration involving the presence and active participation of the faithful, it is to be stressed that this way of celebrating them is to be preferred, as far as possible, to a celebration that is individual and, so to speak, private."

(Constitution on the Sacred Liturgy, 27)

The Constitution's Charge

Those three descriptive words (full, conscious, active) carry with them the weight of *leitourgos*: "the work or service of the people." When they were first published, they sounded a very deliberate call in the work of reforming the Church's worship life. What did the *Constitution* and those in the Second Vatican Council who wrote it, envision as "full, conscious, and active"? What does that mean in our own lives of faith and worship? What does it mean for us, Sunday to Sunday, week to week, and season to season?

As noted earlier in these pages, we who are part of the North American culture in a technologically oriented society may have particular struggles with what we are discussing here. We're part of a society that is *used* to being entertained. We seem to always have the role of "spectator." We watch, we listen, and we sit for hours and stare. We are always being "talked at." We get our news that way, we relax that way, we take our minds off our cares and worries that way, and we are entertained that way. If we aren't careful, sometimes we think that we should also worship that way.

"The Church earnestly desires that all the faithful be led to that full, conscious, and active participation in liturgical celebrations called for by the very nature of the liturgy. Such participation by the Christian people as 'a chosen race, a royal priesthood, a holy nation, God's own people'[68] is their right and duty by reason of their baptism."

(Constitution on the Sacred Liturgy, 14)

Full Participation

Earlier, in Chapter 2, we noted the dynamic of liturgy that calls us to unite our own prayers of praise and thanksgiving to those of Jesus, and to offer them, along with the bread and wine, to God. This is partially what is meant by full participation. Here, "full" can refer to the disposition with which we come to celebrate the Eucharist. Ask yourself this question: When you are at Mass, are you fully there? Are you there in mind as well as body? Do you come with the understanding that this is the most important thing you will do all week?

To engage in full participation means that we participate in the Eucharist with all that we are and all that we bring on a particular Sunday morning. It means that we come aware of our mood: frustrated with the kids, aggravated by a spouse, anxious over the coming week, angry with an argument from earlier in the week, joyous over an accomplishment, sad because of an experienced loss. It means that we come aware of those areas of our lives that need the life-giving power of Jesus's presence and that of the Sacrament of the Eucharist. It means that we come with the desire to offer those areas to the Father, through Christ, and to have the Father give them back, transformed with the power of his Spirit, and that we do so with the faith that God will, indeed, accept them.

To participate fully means that we do so with the desire to experience the unity that the Eucharist brings about: unity with Christ Jesus and unity with all others who gather around the table of the Lord. To participate fully means that we do so with our whole person, with all that we are and with all that we have, fully attentive, fully aware, and fully deliberate in what is to take place in the Eucharist.

Conscious Participation

We all know people who pride themselves on being able to do many things at once. Multitasking is what it's called these days. They can talk to a client on the phone and print out a report for a coming meeting at the same time, and not miss a beat in either task. They can be sitting in front of you having what you think is a very deep and engaging conversation, and at the same time they're formulating a presentation for next week's staff meeting. Now, in a way, we may envy people like this. It would be great to do two things at once the way they do. We could be very productive if we were able to do two different tasks in the time it takes to do one.

What if we applied this "talent" to an experience of celebrating the Eucharist? Imagine how it might be described: "I went to Mass and during the readings I was able to rethink a proposal for work and have it ready for presentation on Monday. During the Preparation of the Gifts, I made a mental list of all the items I needed to secure in order to leave for vacation next weekend. During the Eucharistic Prayer, I jotted down a whole grocery list so that I could get in and out of the store quickly after Mass. During the Sign of Peace, I completed my list of everyone I needed to buy Christmas gifts for. . . ." With such a scenario, how participatory do you think one could actually be in what was taking place, in this case the celebration of the Eucharist? How genuinely could one be engaged in what was happening?

Now, in regard to the liturgical celebration of the Eucharist, "conscious participation" means much more than simply paying attention. Although that is part of it, what is called for in conscious participation is more than attention: what is called for is *presence*. Conscious participation calls us to be present to what is taking place in the celebration of the Eucharist. We are called to not only give over our attention, but to give over our whole selves to this celebration: to consciously and deliberately be a member of the assembly. It means being mindful—savoring the various elements of the Eucharistic liturgy.

Conscious participation, however, does not mean forced participation. It does not mean that I take part completely separated from my feelings, my mood, how I may be feeling at any particular celebration of the Eucharist. I may be feeling very distracted, for example, and for some particular reason it may be a struggle for me to pay attention or to be as present to the prayer as I would want to be. Does this mean I am not consciously participating? Not at all. In fact, if I am aware of these distractions and my preoccupation with them, and yet bring these too to the Eucharist to be offered to God, then my participation is, in fact, *very* conscious. In this case, my participation is very genuine: it's where I am at the moment, it's who I am as I come to this celebration, it's what I bring to Christ as he feeds me with his Body and Blood— it's genuinely me at the moment. That is what we mean by conscious participation.

Active Participation

"Let us pray." What do you do when you hear these words at Mass? Most of us watch for the altar server to bring the Roman Missal to the priest so that he can lead the prayer. It's interesting that in the *General Instruction of the Roman Missal*, the directives indicate that a short silence take place after this ritual invitation, so that all those gathered can actually do what they were just invited to do: to pray. How many of us take this invitation seriously?

"The Lord be with you." We know the response by heart, but what is actually meant by "And with your spirit"? Do we really mean it when we say it? In our liturgies, we have formal, established, and familiar ways of responding to greeting and invitations: "And with your spirit," "Amen," "We lift them up to the Lord," "Thanks be to God." When we say these responses, are we always aware of what we are saying? Do we really think about the responses we say, or do we just respond out of habit? Do we really mean "thanks be to God," after the Word of Life has just been proclaimed to us? When we say "and with your spirit," do we really mean that we want the Lord's Spirit to be with the presider who leads us through our common prayer, or do we just pay lip service to the formula and give the response halfheartedly, with no thought?

A priest friend of mine has a term he uses to describe a Eucharistic celebration where the people are less-than-actively participating. He calls them, "the-Lord-be-with-me-Masses," referring to the situation where very few would respond or take part in appropriate places.   **~Todd**

When we're invited to join in the gathering song, a song that is meant to unite us as one body and to help prepare us to enter into the celebration as a collected worshiping assembly, do we actually do so with that intention? When the Responsorial Psalm is intoned, do we respond full-heartedly and with enthusiasm, or do we let the cantor sing the psalm, because after all, that's his or her role in the Mass?

Active participation calls us to respond, both interiorly and exteriorly, to the liturgy's greetings, invitations, and songs as a way of fulfilling our role as the gathered worshiping assembly. Active participation means that we enter into the celebration with the understanding that our interior dispositions, our responses, and our participation are what we are called to as members of the assembly. Active participation means that we allow ourselves to be engaged by what is taking place and that we enter into the celebration, fully intending to take our place and to perform the roles that we have as baptized members of the community.

We all have a part to play at the celebration of the Eucharist. We each have a role, particular and distinct, according to our order (ordained or lay) and our area of ministry (lector, usher, extraordinary minister of Holy Communion, member of the congregation). Our responsibility, as a baptized member of this Body of Christ, is to carry out the parts of our role in the best way we possibly can. Whatever our role in the liturgy, we are called to carry it out in the fullest way possible. We are to be very conscious and deliberate about what we do and to be actively attentive to how we do it.

"For the celebration of the Eucharist is the action of the whole Church, and in it each one should carry out solely but totally that which pertains to him, in virtue of the place of each within the People of God. . . . For this people is the People of God, purchased by Christ's Blood, gathered together by the Lord, nourished by his word, the people called to present to God the prayers of the entire human family, a people that gives thanks in Christ for the mystery of salvation by offering his Sacrifice. . . . This people, though holy in its origin, nevertheless grows constantly in holiness by conscious, active, and fruitful participation in the mystery of the Eucharist"[69]

(*General Instruction of the Roman Missal,* 5)

REFLECTION

» Reflect on how you prepare to celebrate Sunday liturgy. Consider whether you spend time immediately before the liturgy in silent or communal prayer.

» Consider the many different roles you fill in your life right now (family roles, employment roles, relational roles). Identify what liturgical roles you fill in your community of faith. How do you understand your roles? Identify ways in which you can deepen your understanding of your roles.

» Is there another, different role that you have considered filling in the celebration of the liturgy in your parish? What different role have you considered? What are the responsibilities of that role as you understand them?

CHAPTER 7

THE MYSTERY OF REVERENCE

Reverence and "Fear of the Lord"

In C.S. Lewis's *The Lion, the Witch, and the Wardrobe*, a discussion between Lucy, a young girl from England who has entered the land of Narnia through a wardrobe, and Mr. and Mrs. Beaver, inhabitants of Narnia, sheds light on an understanding of the concept of reverence.[70] The true leader of Narnia, they explain, is a mysterious and powerful lion called Aslan. As Mr. and Mrs. Beaver attempt to explain the nature of Aslan to Lucy, she remains frightened, and asks whether it is safe to be around Aslan. Mr. and Mrs. Beaver respond by saying that of course he is safe—he is good, and he is the king.

The Beavers' characterization of Aslan captures what we mean when we talk about a spirit of reverence or fear of the Lord. Such an understanding of fear is not to be equated with trembling in fright like the Cowardly Lion before the great and powerful Oz! Rather, this kind of fear or reverence can be characterized as a blend of fear, awe, and the proper respect or honor owed to the Almighty. Proverbs 1:7 tells us that "fear of the LORD is the beginning of knowledge." If we are truly to know the mystery of God, we begin by approaching, not casually, but with proper reverence or fear of the Lord.

This is the spirit of the Second Commandment, which teaches us to have the proper respect for the name of God and everything God's name stands for. This Commandment addresses more than simply swearing; it instructs us to approach God in such a manner that we give God the honor and respect that is due to God.

"Respect for his name is an expression of the respect owed to the mystery of God himself and to the whole sacred reality it evokes."

(Catechism of the Catholic Church, 2144)

John Henry Cardinal Newman explained that feelings of fear and awe in the presence of God are, not only appropriate, but absolutely necessary: "In proportion as we believe that He is present, we have them (*feelings of fear and awe*); and not to have them, is not to realize, not to believe that He is present."

(John Henry Cardinal Newman, Parochial and Plain Sermons)

"Preaching and catechizing should be permeated with adoration and respect for the name of our Lord Jesus Christ."

(Catechism of the Catholic Church, 2145)

Oddly enough, it seems that in some of our liturgical and catechetical efforts to make God more present to people, we have tended to emphasize a more casual approach to God. Although we certainly want to proclaim a God who is approachable, that approach needs to be characterized by reverence. Today, all too often, we approach worship as casually as if we were going to the movies, rather than entering into an encounter with profound mystery.

Once, when I was attending Mass while going through a particularly difficult time in my life, I recall feeling very emotional and troubled. I was grappling with some deep, personal spiritual matters. As I made it to the front of the communion procession, the priest smiled at me and said, "Happy day!" I might as well have been entering Disney World! I was coming forward to mysteriously receive the living God into my heart at a time when I needed God desperately. While the "Happy day!" greeting was well-intentioned, it clearly did not measure up to the profound reverence that the moment called for. My wife, who was directly behind me in that procession, later commented, "It seems to me that some priests' approach to Mass is this: 'Don't worry! I'll make sure this doesn't feel like Mass.' It's as though some of them think they have to protect us from the mystery by making it casual and familiar." This comment can be extended to many of us who, as cantors, readers, musicians, ushers, extraordinary ministers of Holy Communion, or members of the assembly, have, from time to time, gone overboard in our efforts to make people feel more at home at Mass by making everything more casual at the expense of reverence.

~Joe

Hospitality, of course, plays an important part in our celebration of the Mass, and warm smiles, greetings, and words of friendship have their place, especially during the gathering. By the same token, reverence, or fear of the Lord, does not mean dour faces, strict silence, and rigid piety. Reverence simply means respecting the moment; nothing more and nothing less. Fear of the Lord and reverence, because they have not been properly understood, have gone out of vogue. Reverence, all too often, has been interpreted as haughty piety. Fear of the Lord has been interpreted as cowering before someone who is "unapproachable." If we are to properly enter into the mystery of faith, we need to restore a proper understanding of reverence and fear of the Lord.

Reverence at Mass

Shortly after my "happy day" experience at Mass, my wife and I decided to attend Mass at another parish that we visit occasionally. St. Ailbe Parish is a wonderfully vibrant African American parish on the south side of Chicago. A feeling of reverence is apparent from the moment one enters. Yes, there is a great deal of smiling, hugging, and talking as people gather. Yes, there is a great deal of handclapping accompanied by shouts of praise during the hymns. Yes, there is laughter at points during the homily when the pastor engages the congregation with imaginative yet pertinent stories. And yes, there is a great deal of reverence. What makes Mass at St. Ailbe reverent? The fact that people, from the priest and deacon to the choir, liturgical ministers, and all those gathered—the whole assembly have learned (and obviously teach to their young ones) how to respect the moment. When silence is called for, it is long and rich. When shouting is called for, it is loud and enthusiastic. Reverence is a matter of being keenly aware of the significance of the moment and responding accordingly.

~Joe

Reverence is not a "churchy" thing. It is a gift of the Holy Spirit that we are to use in all aspects of our lives. Our society's loss of reverence is not restricted to church. How often do we go to the movies and find people laughing at sad or tragic moments in the story? How often do we see the crowd at a sporting event cheer when a member of the opposing team goes down with an injury? How often have we attended commencement ceremonies only to have the dignity of the moment spoiled by people hooting and hollering for their favorite graduate? We are called to be keenly aware of the significance of each moment of our lives and respond accordingly and appropriately. We are called to show reverence and respect not only during those moments when we are in church, but also for other people, for the environment, and for life itself. The God we "fear" and revere is not relegated to the dimensions of our church building. If we truly believe that "through him, all things were made," then we must extend the same reverence owed to God in church to all things and all moments of our lives.

At Mass, reverence takes on different forms. At times, we show reverence by being quiet. At other times, we show reverence by singing loudly. Reverence calls us to be attentive to the Scripture readings and homily. Reverence also calls us to sit, stand, kneel, and process appropriately. Another form of expressing reverence is becoming lost in our society—namely, the act of bowing. Many oriental cultures have maintained the practice of bowing in the presence of another as a sign of reverence for them. In the Bible, bowing is the most common gesture of reverence toward another person considered to be a superior.[71] Bowing continues to have its place in the celebration of the Mass. The priest and liturgical ministers bow to the altar as they approach it during the opening and closing processions. As members of the assembly, we are invited to do the same. As we enter church and before we enter our pew, it is most appropriate that we bow to the altar (or genuflect if the tabernacle containing the Blessed Sacrament is also in the sanctuary). If incense is used at the preparation of the altar and the gifts, the minister bows to the people before he or she incenses them. The people are to *bow back* to the minister. Likewise, we are invited to bow as a sign of reverence when we come forward to receive Holy Communion. The key to reverence is being aware of the proper expression for the proper moment.

I live in a neighborhood of Chicago that is predominately Jewish. Because of this, I am often made keenly aware of the feast days and other events observed by our Jewish brothers and sisters. I recall one day during summer when a new synagogue in the neighborhood received its copy of the Torah. Although I did not know what the celebration was, you could hear the music from blocks away as the Torah was carried in procession to the new synagogue. At one point, I realized that the procession was going to pass right in front of my home. I was in the back yard working as the music and sounds of celebration got closer and closer. As it approached, I became aware of a sense of excitement growing inside me. I went out to the front yard to see what the celebration was all about. All up and down my street, people came out of their homes. I asked my neighbor, who is Jewish, what the occasion was, and she told me, "It's a new Torah from Israel, and it's being taken from the rabbi's house to the synagogue." I had to stay and watch.

As the procession drew near, it was being led by a group of musicians playing festive music. The musicians were followed by a group of men dancing in a circle and moving forward. This was followed by a large canopy that was surrounded with younger men carrying burning torches. Under the canopy was the tabernacle with the Torah inside. It was, literally, breathtaking to see such a display of reverence and celebration around the Word of the Lord.

As the canopy covering the Torah approached, I actually felt myself getting emotional. And as it passed directly in front of me, there in my front yard, I did the only thing I could think of doing—the only thing that seemed appropriate: I stopped speaking to my neighbor, drew a few steps back, and bowed as the Torah went by. What else could one possibly do in the presence of the Word?   **~Todd**

Reverence and Silence

My friend Larry and I were talking over lunch about the silent retreat he had just been on when he said something that I found quite curious. "It was nice to see some of the same people from previous retreats," Larry said. "We really had formed community." I asked him how you could form community when no one is speaking. He said, "You'd be surprised how much you can 'hear' about people when there's silence. People express themselves in very powerful ways when they are silent." Larry went on to explain how sharing a bond of silence with others was a unifying experience. "When the retreat was over and we could finally speak verbally to each other, it was as if we already knew one another. Sharing a week of silence with a group of people is a very intimate experience." In short, silence is a powerful form of communication.

~Joe

Silence is all too rare in our noise-filled society. We are constantly bombarded with sounds coming from our televisions, iPods, computers, car stereos, and from our own mouths. It is no wonder that we have difficulty understanding reverence when we never allow ourselves a moment of silence to even consider it!

Fr. Richard Fragomeni, author, speaker, and teacher, relates a story that illustrates how different our society's concept of silence is compared with that of other cultures. He describes how, at his office at Catholic Theological Union in Chicago, a student from Africa came to visit him saying, "Fr. Richard, I just thought I would spend some time with you." Fr. Fragomeni welcomed him in and the two sat facing one another for a period of silence that Fr. Fragomeni found uncomfortable and tried to remedy through small talk. After a few unsuccessful attempts, Fr. Richard just gave up and continued doing some paperwork, inviting the visitor to remain as long as he wished. After about ten minutes, the visiting seminarian simply stood up and said, "I enjoyed visiting with you!" and left. From a North American point of view, this visit was a disaster—the silence was unbearable and could only be interpreted as lack of connection. The gentleman from Africa, on the other hand, understood that sitting with someone in complete silence was an excellent way to bond with someone and get to know him or her.

Such an understanding of silence is lost in our society. The days of sitting together on the front porch after dinner without saying hardly a word are no longer a part of the lives of most 21st century Americans. Today, silence is usually an indication of a problem. If our computer is silent for a moment, we panic that it has frozen. Computer companies compete to create faster and faster Internet connections so that we never experience a lull or moment of silence. If our iPod goes silent, no doubt it is malfunctioning. If silence creeps into a conversation, we tend to squirm and get uncomfortable.

"Sacred silence also, as part of the celebration, is to be observed at the designated times."[72]

(*General Instruction of the Roman Missal*, 45)

Unfortunately, this notion of silence (or lack thereof) often creeps into our celebration of liturgy. From the moment we enter the church, we are often bombarded with a never-ending stream of sound. From the greeting of a minister of hospitality as we enter to the last line of the closing song as we leave, we may not experience more than three to five seconds of silence at any particular time. Some of our attempts to make liturgy more lively have resulted in a trampling of the role of silence. This loss of silence is accompanied by a loss of reverence: we are so busy talking that we are not allowing the depth and breadth of the mystery of God to surround us, enfold us, and engage us as only silence can do.

"Even fools who keep silent are considered wise; / when they close their lips, they are deemed intelligent."

(Proverbs 17:28)

Many TV news and sports broadcasters have learned what we in liturgy sometimes fail to understand: there are moments when we should stop talking. Occasionally, an event occurs in the news or in sports that is just so profound that any words would simply be superfluous. Walter Cronkite demonstrated this twice in his journalistic career when he simply could not find words to express what was happening. One such event was the 1963 announcement of the death of John F. Kennedy, when suddenly the words he was reading became so profound that he could do nothing other than pause in silence. The other event was the 1969 landing on the moon. For so long, Cronkite anticipated what he would say when a spaceship actually landed on the moon's surface. When the moment finally came, Cronkite found himself at a complete loss for words. Sometimes, like Elijah, who sensed the call of God not in an earthquake or fire but in a nearly silent whispering sound, our best response is to hide our face with our cloak and stand silently in awe of the presence of the divine.[73]

In our celebration of the liturgy, we encounter profound moments when we realize that the divine is in our midst. We experience these moments when we pause to consider our sinfulness, when we hear the invitation, "Let us pray," when we hear the Word of God proclaimed, when the Word of God is broken open for us in the homily, when bread and wine are consecrated as the Body and Blood of Jesus Christ, and when we receive the Lord's Body and Blood in Communion. All of these are profoundly reverent moments—moments whose reverence is often lost because we fail to pause in silence and dwell in the presence of mystery.

"To promote active participation, the people should be encouraged to take part . . . and at the proper times, all should observe a reverent silence."

(*Constitution on the Sacred Liturgy*, 30)

Catechesis Requires Silence

The word catechesis comes from the Greek, meaning "to echo." An echo occurs most successfully in a cavernous area, an area in which enough space is available for the sound to reverberate. In other words, in order for an echo to occur, some degree of silence is needed in order to allow the sound to bounce back and forth. In our catechesis, this same notion of silence is needed. Our catechesis, like our liturgy, is often far too noisy. If we are truly to allow the Word of God to echo within ourselves and in the hearts and minds of those whom we teach, it is necessary to recognize the profound nature of what we are teaching by simply responding in silence. Through catechesis, we have the opportunity to teach reverence by inviting those we teach to engage the Good News of Jesus in moments of silent reflection. The silence that we provide in our catechetical gatherings may indeed be the only significant periods of silence that our learners will experience for the entire week!

"But the LORD is in his holy temple; / let all the earth keep silence before him!"

(Habakkuk 2:20)

When I teach religious education classes, I regularly include an extended experience of prayer that includes a fair amount of silence. At first, my students (especially 8th graders!) are uncomfortable with it and react by being antsy. As the weeks go by and I persevere in teaching them how to be silent, they grow very comfortable with these silent moments that we call our "sacred space" and they begin to ask each week if it will be a part of class. Once after a particularly good chunk of silent prayer, I asked my 8th graders, "For how many of you was this the only silence you experienced today?" Every hand went up! At the end of the year, I asked the students to evaluate our experience together. To my surprise and delight, they voted our "sacred space" as their favorite component of our sessions!   **~Joe**

Catechesis Teaches Reverence

As we described earlier, reverence does not mean strict silence (although it calls us to be silent at the appropriate moments), dour expressions, or cowering in fear, but simply respecting the moment—being keenly aware of the significance of the moment and responding appropriately. One of the most important things that catechesis does is to teach reverence. Catechesis is not simply the memorization of doctrines, but the shaping of disciples of Christ. Disciples of Christ are called to reform their lives and believe in the Good News. This means that we are called to reform the way we see ourselves, others, and all of creation and to become keenly aware of the presence of

God in all people and in all things, resulting in a new way of responding to others and to life. Once we come to see with the eyes of Christ, we become keenly aware of the significance of each moment and each person and respond appropriately, with reverence. The Gospel teaches us to have reverence for tax collectors, lepers, prostitutes, Samaritans, and other outcasts. Catechesis is the process of facilitating this conversion. A catechized person is a reverent person! A catechized person recognizes that reverence is called for when worshiping the mystery of God in church as well as when encountering the mystery of God in the moments and people of our daily lives.

"In the Sermon on the Mount, the Lord recalls the commandment, 'You shall not kill,'[74] and adds to it the proscription of anger, hatred, and vengeance. Going further, Christ asks his disciples to turn the other cheek, to love their enemies."[75]

(*Catechism of the Catholic Church*, 2262)

REFLECTION

» Pay special attention to the role that silence plays in your parish community's celebration of the Eucharist. Reflect upon the moments that call for silence in the liturgy and the extent to which your community is observing those moments.

» Reflect upon the role of reverence in our society today. Take note for a day or two of the experiences in which you witness either a show of reverence or a lack thereof. Consider how the Gospel of Jesus sheds light on how we are to respond appropriately toward others if we truly recognize them as members of the Body of Christ. Read 1 Corinthians 12 and 13 with an eye toward reverence for others.

» In many cultures, bowing remains an appropriate form of showing reverence to others when greeting them. Try incorporating a slight bow into your greetings of others, especially strangers, without being overly dramatic or condescending. Remind yourself, each time you do this, that each person is made in the image of God and deserves reverence. How does the slight bow remind you to treat each person with reverence?

» Do you consider your worshiping community to be reverent? How do you present the concept of reverence to your community? What can be done to enhance reverence without making it sound like an imposition of overly pious rigidity?

» What does it mean when we say that a disciple of Jesus is one who is filled with reverence?

» How is reverence for God linked with reverence for others?

» What role does silence play in your life? Have you ever responded to a profound moment by keeping silent? What do you experience when you encounter silence? Are you comfortable with it, or does it make you uneasy? How can God be encountered in silence?

» How do you express/practice reverence at Mass? How do you understand the difference between being reverent and casual? How is reverence best expressed at the following moments during Mass: gathering, Penitential Rite, Liturgy of the Word, Eucharistic Prayer, Communion, and Dismissal?

CHAPTER 8

THE MYSTERY OF MOVEMENT

Wouldn't It Be Easier If . . . ?

Working with liturgy planning teams in the parish is always an enjoyable and interesting experience. Most liturgy teams are made up of dedicated, faithful, everyday parishioners who are devoted to the Eucharist and take great pride and joy in celebrating liturgy in a thoughtful and prayerful manner. At the same time, most folks involved in liturgy planning in the parish do not have advanced degrees in liturgy (thank goodness) but instead come at things from a very practical point of view. The result, it is hoped, is a healthy balance between liturgists who may be out of touch with the assembly and assembly representatives who may not have a full understanding of the liturgy. This makes for some interesting moments when some people's more practical sides clash with liturgical rubrics.

I recall working with a liturgy planning team as we were discussing the Gospel procession. We were discussing the location of the *Book of the Gospels* when one of the team members said, "Wouldn't it be easier if we put it right next to the ambo? That way, it won't take as long to get it from point A to point B." His suggestion was very practical. His goal was to get the book from point A to point B with as little effort as possible, making as little fuss about it as possible. His focus was on function. This provided us with a wonderful opportunity to discuss the purpose of processions as well as any other sacred movements during the liturgy that are less focused on function and more on expression. We talked about how the purpose of a Gospel procession was not to get from point A to point B, but to visually proclaim the reverence we have for the Word of God in our midst. We, in fact, end up going out of our way and walking in roundabout itineraries so that the Word of God may be exalted! **~Joe**

Once, during a sacraments course in a predominantly African American community, one of the participants commented on how a friend of his thought that we Catholics make too much "fuss" over everything. His friend thought that with all of our oils, incense, holy water, processions, and rituals, we Catholics simply make too much fuss over our faith. The participant went on to say that he responded to his friend by saying, "You're right that we Catholics make a fuss over our beliefs. I call it a holy fuss! We believe that God is so great and so glorious that we need to express that in as many ways as we can. Words alone won't do. We make a holy fuss over Almighty God's presence in our midst!" For the rest of our course, we used this term, *holy fuss*, to refer to our Catholic rituals, signs, and symbols.

This term can aptly be applied to the way we use movement in liturgy. When we think about how we move through processions at the entrance, Gospel, offertory, Communion, and dismissal, we are not trying to simply get from point A to point B, but are, in reality, making a holy fuss about how we encounter God in our comings and goings.

~Joe

What Could Possibly Take Three Hours?

In Chicago, we have many remarkable worshiping communities, each with its own flavor and style. One such parish is an African American parish on the south side of the city well known for liturgies that take between three and four hours. Most people think the celebrations take so long because the pastor just talks and talks and talks. But that's not it. While the pastor is a remarkable preacher and does preach longer than most Catholic priests, the real reason that Mass takes 3-4 hours at this parish is because every movement that is done during Mass is done with such thoughtfulness and detail that time is not even a consideration.

The opening procession moves gracefully, reverently, and joyfully at its own pace, accompanied by singing that does not stop after the third verse of the opening hymn. The opening procession alone may take 15-20 minutes, but nobody is watching the time. Each procession that follows, whether the Gospel procession, Offertory procession, Communion procession, or closing procession is an expression of praise and thanksgiving—and not simply a way of getting from point A to point B!

This is not to say that the only way to do liturgy properly is to imitate this African American parish in Chicago and take three to four hours for each Mass we celebrate! Each parish community must celebrate liturgy in a way that fits the culture and spirituality of the people who make up the assembly. It does say, however, that all of our *movements* during liturgy are moments of prayerful expression—giving thanks and praise to our God whose mysterious presence causes us to respond by making a *holy fuss!*

Getting From Here to There

We live in a highly mobile society. People are always on the move. It used to be that a family bought a house with a sense of permanency. But, studies have shown that a property being put on the market today will end up on the market again within five to eight years. Many of our friends have had more than two different jobs in the last ten years. We live in a society where things are constantly changing, where we are always "on the go." As a society, we don't like things that slow us down. This sense of movement, this sense of getting from here to there, is part of our cultural sensibilities. People speak of "moving on," of "moving up," of "getting there." Mistakes are spoken of as "steps backwards," and if by chance we've become bored or overcome by a sense of routine, we say, "I'm just not getting anywhere."

"The space within the church building for the faithful other than the priest celebrant and the ministers is sometimes called the *nave*. This space is critical in the overall plan because it accommodates a variety of ritual actions: processions during the Eucharist, the singing of the prayers, movement during baptismal rites, the sprinkling of the congregation with blessed water, the rites during the wedding and funeral liturgies, and personal devotion. This area is not comparable to the audience's space in a theater or public arena because in the liturgical assembly, there is no audience. Rather, the entire congregation acts."

(Built of Living Stones, 51)

This sense and imagery of movement is connected to something that is deep within us as human beings. At the heart of it all is the inescapable realization that *life is a journey*. We travel the road of life, going from place to place, walking with different traveling partners, always aware that we are moving forward. There is a purpose in this journey, a destination. Most of us would be hard pressed to name, specifically, what this destination is, but we are all aware of a sense of it, aware of an urging forward, mindful that although we may like where we are at any given moment, it just isn't "it"—it isn't our ultimate destination.

"For in this visible house that you have let us build / and where you never cease to show favor / to the family on pilgrimage to you in this place, / you wonderfully manifest and accomplish / the mystery of your communion with us."

(Preface to the Eucharistic Prayer, Common of the Dedication of a Church, *The Roman Missal*)

This sense of journeying, of traveling on the road, of moving forward is not only part of our understanding of the world and our life in it, it is also part of our understanding of faith. For centuries, mystics and spiritualists have visioned our growth and development in faith as a journey, as movement, as a pilgrimage or trek toward God. In the spirit of our ancestors, we are all on a *journey of faith*. Like Abraham, we have a sense of being called from our homeland and of being directed to journey out, to move. Like the Israelites who were led out of Egypt, we have a sense of being led through seas and deserts, of being led onward, beyond where we feel comfortable. And like those who were once exiled in a foreign land, we have a sense of a homeland, a place that has been promised to us and to which we have to travel. We know that it is there, waiting for us at the end of our journey.

Our Faith Journey in Three Dimensions

This sense of journeying, this sense of moving out in answer to a call, this sense of "going to the Promised Land" or of being on a pilgrimage is at the heart of every liturgical procession. In fact, when we really think about it, the whole of the Eucharistic liturgy can be seen, in one way, as one complete procession. In terms of journeying or of being on a pilgrimage, the whole Mass can be seen as an expression of what we believe is happening to us in our interior, or spiritual, journey. All of these different moments of movement in the Mass, when seen as a whole, are moments when our faith lives are "acted out," if you will, in three-dimensional expression.

"Churches are never 'simply gathering spaces but signify and make visible the church living in [a particular] place, the dwelling of God' among us, now 'reconciled and united in Christ.'[76] As such, the building itself becomes 'a sign of the pilgrim church on earth and reflects the church dwelling in heaven.'[77] Every church building is a gathering place for the assembly, a resting place, a place of encounter with God, as well as a point of departure on the church's unfinished journey toward the reign of God."

(Built of Living Stones, 17)

This weekly expression of our spiritual journey of faith begins even before we get to the church. Our procession to Mount Zion (an ancient image of the Church), our pilgrimage to the "Promised Land," begins to be acted out even before we leave our homes and make our way to the parish church. Moving from our homes to our cars, and then processing across town to the parking lot of the church begins our weekly pilgrimage. From there, we continue the journey to the entrance of the church, where we pass by water—the water of the font that reminds us of our Baptism; the water that refreshes us and renews us; the water for which every person who has ever been on a serious journey longs. From there, we continue the procession as we move to our places to listen to the Word proclaimed. It encourages us on our journey. It challenges us, comforts us, and nourishes us for this part of the pilgrimage.

From this spot of listening, we are called to move again. The procession of gifts is an expression of all that we bring to offer in this pilgrimage. As the gifts are brought forward we enact what we believe to be truly happening: our offerings are taken to the table, to be blessed, broken, and shared in the name of the risen Christ. Along with bread and wine, we include in the procession of gifts our own selves, our own lives as an offering to God the loving Father.

Then, we are once again called to move forward. The procession to the altar is the culminating movement of our gathering. It is the movement toward the gifts over which we have prayed and for which we have given thanks to God: the Bread of Life and the Cup of Salvation. The communion procession calls to mind the journey that is our own life. As we move toward the table, all as one group, as one body, so do we move toward the table of the heavenly banquet that awaits each of us at the end of our earthly lives.

"Blessed are those called to the supper of the Lamb."

(Invitation to Holy Communion, The Roman Missal)

The procession to the table is an enactment of the faith journey of every member with whom we travel. In the communion procession, we move toward Zion, toward the kingdom, toward the Promised Land for which we were baptized. The journey of our faith lives is symbolized in this journey to the table. From the table then, our journey continues. After we have all shared in the one Bread and one Cup, we are again asked to move. This time we move out into the coming week with our families and friends, in our jobs and our daily responsibilities, nourished by the Eucharist.

"Your solemn processions are seen, O God, / the processions of my God, my King, into the sanctuary— / the singers in front, the musicians last, / between them girls playing tambourines: / 'Bless God in the great congregation, / the Lord, O you who are of Israel's fountain!' / There is Benjamin, the least of them, in the lead, / the princes of Judah in a body, / the princes of Zebulun, the princes of Naphtali."

(Psalm 68:25–28)

The Journey of Discipleship

Each procession of the liturgy is an image of our own experience of discipleship. Moving along the road, we encounter Jesus the Christ. Indeed, processions are so much more than getting from here to there: they are images of a much greater journey that began in our Baptism and will not end until the time when we gather at the eternal banquet. Think of some of the more extraordinary processions that make up our liturgical lives. The procession of the Easter Vigil from the fire to the inside of the darkened church, led by the light of the paschal candle calls to mind the Israelites, journeying out of Egypt, following the pillar of fire. Think of the Palm Sunday procession, an image of the crowds that recognized Jesus as the Son of David and proclaimed him king. Think of the penitential procession at the start of Lent: an enactment of our journey to Jerusalem and to the cross, with the one whose death is our salvation. Think of the processions with the Blessed Sacrament on Holy Thursday, or on the Solemnity of the Most Holy Body and Blood of Christ (Corpus Christi), carrying that which is itself strength for our journey.

"For today by your gift we celebrate the festival of your city, / the heavenly Jerusalem, our mother, / where the great array of our brothers and sisters / already gives you eternal praise. / Towards her, we eagerly hasten, as pilgrims advancing by faith, / rejoicing in the glory bestowed upon those exalted members of the Church."

(Preface of the Eucharistic Prayer for the Solemnity of All Saints, The Roman Missal)

All of these examples are outward expressions of our interior faith. All of these are physical enactments of what we believe to be our own faith pilgrimages. All of these are examples of embodied prayer and ways of "praying with our feet." They are spiritual and holy fuss.

Sign Language

Once, during a training session, new members of a liturgy planning team were asked to imagine attending Mass and to imagine that they were deaf, focusing on the following question: if you were unable to hear at our liturgies, what parts of the Mass would still speak to you? The next meeting after completing this assignment was fascinating. The new liturgy planners had discovered that the celebration of the liturgy went well beyond words and involved a great deal of movement and gesture that spoke to them in very profound ways.

It was also discovered that, at times, the parish's celebration of the liturgy lacked reverence and thoughtfulness when it came to movement and gesture. The fact is, if we are going to praise God with all of our being, we need to do so in word, song, movement, and gesture, employing all of our senses: sound, sight, speech, smell, and touch. Unfortunately, American culture places little importance on how one moves. For the most part, Americans do not bow to one another, dance in their homes or neighborhoods, or even use their hands and arms when speaking! It is no wonder, then, that when we gather to celebrate Eucharist, we often lack an appreciation for the importance of movement. Liturgy presents us with a unique opportunity to explore a different language than the spoken word. It is a form of "sign language," it is the language of movement and gesture.

Once, I was asked to do a presentation on liturgy to a sixth grade religious education class, of which my daughter Amy was a participant. I began by asking the class if anyone knew sign language. Several children volunteered to show that they knew a word or phrase or two. I then proceeded to tell them that they all knew more sign language than they thought, especially if they went to Mass. At first, they looked at me like I had three heads. Next, I played a form of "charades" with them as I went through some of the various movements and gestures we use at Mass: bowing, genuflecting, making the sign of the cross, making a cross with our thumb on our forehead, lips, and chest, sharing a sign of peace, etc. They had to guess what part of the Mass we do each movement at and, more important, what the movement or gesture "meant." Not only did we have fun, but the young people came away from the lesson knowing that they did indeed know more sign language than they thought since we use a great deal of it at Mass to express ourselves reverently and prayerfully to our mysterious and glorious God!   **~Joe**

Embodied Prayer

What we have been discussing in this chapter is the idea of embodied prayer. We are human beings and, as such, we have physical bodies that we use to communicate. We greet with embraces and handshakes, we show affirmation by applauding and waving our arms, and we express anger with gesture and bodily postures. Praying with our bodies is part of our religious tradition. We kneel to show a spirit of penitence and adoration. We stand to show respect and openness to what God calls us to be. We prostrate ourselves in humility and in a spirit of service. We hold out our hands in a gesture of prayer in which we give over our very lives to God and in which we make ready to receive whatever it is that God's providence gives to us. We lay hands on another to express our belief in God's love and the outpouring of God's Spirit.

In short, as Catholics, we cannot pray without using our whole bodies! Our liturgical movements—our processions, our gestures, our postures—are all ways of expressing our prayer and our attitudes toward God and toward our brothers and sisters. They express our beliefs and our faith. They express our hopes as ones who have been redeemed by Christ and they express our desires for the coming of God's kingdom in its fullness. Does this mean that if we are not comfortable with such movements and gestures, or if we are not able because of limited ability to take part in such postures, that we are not faithful or are not prayerful? Certainly not! It is an invitation to those of us who may not be so demonstrative to enter fully, body and soul, into the praise and thanks, the prayer and supplication, the joy and celebration that we express in our prayer and in our liturgies.

"Whenever the cloud was taken up from the tabernacle, the Israelites would set out on each stage of their journey; but if the cloud was not taken up, then they did not set out until the day that it was taken up. For the cloud of the LORD was on the tabernacle by day, and fire was in the cloud by night, before the eyes of all the house of Israel at each stage of their journey."

(Exodus 40:36–38)

REFLECTION

» Next time you attend Mass at your parish, pay attention to the movement and gestures of the liturgy. Keep a journal of which parts of the Mass would still "speak" to you even if you couldn't hear.

» Think of everyday examples of gestures, and what they mean.

» Surf through various TV channels with the sound off and observe all of the ways in which people use movement and gesture especially in music videos, ballet, dance shows, sports, and just common conversations. Reflect on the extent to which you use (or don't use) movement and gesture in your everyday life. Reflect upon how this impacts your comfort (or lack thereof) with movement and gesture at Mass.

» How do you understand your own faith life as a journey? What elements of a journey are particularly pertinent to your faith life? What are the stages of this journey and how have you moved through each of them? How can your prayer life be compared to a pilgrimage?

» Reflect on the great biblical images of movement and journey: Abraham and Sarah, Moses and the Israelites, the exiles returning to Jerusalem, the disciples on the road to Emmaus. How do you see yourself in these fellow journeyers? What comparisons can be made between their journey and yours? How do you see your journey lived out each week at the Eucharistic celebration or in other liturgies in which you've taken part?

» What postures or gestures of liturgical prayer speak the most to you? With which are you the most comfortable? Which ones express best for you the praise and prayer you offer to God? With which gestures or postures are you the most uncomfortable? Why are they uncomfortable for you? Reflect on the many ways you pray with your body in liturgy.

CHAPTER 9

THE MYSTERY OF SONG

"Happy Birthday to You . . ."

What could possibly be so mysterious about song? Try this experiment. Say (do not sing) the following words out loud:

Happy birthday to you.

Happy birthday to you.

Happy birthday, dear ____.

Happy birthday to you.

Now don't you feel silly? Saying these words instead of singing them seems like utter nonsense. Now, for the mystery: think of how many times you have seen someone cry tears of joy because a group of people gathered to *sing* these silly words in their honor. For some mysterious reason, when these silly words are put to music and the song is lifted up by many voices, a part of us that cannot be reached in any other way is touched and the bonds of relationship are strengthened and reinforced.

Everyone knows that the words "happy birthday to you" are not meant to be spoken, but sung. It's part of the ritual. When we celebrate the anniversary of someone's birth, we gather to express our love for him or her, and we do so by spontaneously breaking into song. Anything less would not sufficiently express the feelings that we have for the person whose birthday we are celebrating. A well-prepared speech could never capture or express the depth of sentiment that a well-sung "Happy Birthday" can.

Take Me Out to the Ballgame

What would a baseball game be like if the crowd did not stand and break out into "Take Me Out to the Ballgame" during the seventh-inning stretch? Somehow, the singing of this song is a way of both expressing the joy and fun of being a part of our national pastime and, at the same time, uniting thousands of people not only with each other, but with all those who have gathered at baseball games over the decades to participate in this ritual. At Wrigley Field in Chicago, where the Chicago Cubs play, the late Hall of Fame announcer Harry Caray began a tradition of leading the crowd in this song. After Caray's death in 1997, the Cubs began a tradition of inviting "guest conductors" including politicians, actors, church leaders, pop stars, journalists, and other sports celebrities to lead the singing. Whether sung well or comically butchered, the traditional song unites those who are present at the park and those who are listening on the radio or watching on TV with one another, with the memory of Harry Caray, and with the thousands of people who have gathered over many decades to participate in this ritual of fun and frivolity.

Singing is human nature. Think for just a moment: what is it that could be called the "very first instrument?" The human voice, of course. It is the *primordial* instrument. Long before wind was forced through the holes of a wooden reed, or even before the rhythmic banging of some primitive drum, long before any wire-like material was strung tightly to reverberate with a defined pitch, the human voice was making music. As part of our human nature, something that has evolved and developed over time, we rely on singing to express what words alone cannot and to achieve unity where even the most persuasive speech is limited.

"A cry from deep within our being, music is a way for God to lead us to the realm of higher things.[78] As St. Augustine says, 'Singing is for the one who loves.'[79] Music is therefore a sign of God's love for us and of our love for him. In this sense, it is very personal. But unless music sounds, it is not music, and whenever it sounds, it is accessible to others. By its very nature song has both an individual and a communal dimension. Thus, it is no wonder that singing together in church expresses so well the sacramental presence of God to his people."

(Sing to the Lord, 2)

When Words Are Not Enough

Fiddler on the Roof. My Fair Lady. Phantom of the Opera. The Sound of Music. These are just some of the classic musicals that have entertained us over the years. There's something captivating about musicals that is missing from regular movies: it is the idea that at certain key moments in the story, characters break into song! The songs lift us up, touch us, engage us, and sometimes even make us sing along. Often these songs move the plot forward or help us understand a particular aspect of the scene that is being played out. They sometimes give us a greater sense of the overall story. Singing is a form of expression that unleashes power that spoken words alone cannot. Singing touches us at a level of our being that spoken words alone cannot. Singing is often the only appropriate and fitting expression for certain occasions.

I recall that at a reception to celebrate my brother Tom's installation as a pastor of a predominantly Polish Catholic parish on the north side of Chicago, a long line of people waited to greet him and present him with gifts and cards. Suddenly, the sound of talking in the reception hall was overtaken by the sound of fifteen or twenty people who had surrounded my brother and broken out into traditional Polish songs. My brother beamed (and blushed) as all eyes turned to watch this group of genuinely delighted people sing Polish song after Polish song. Those of us less versed in the Polish language could not understand the songs but were still touched by the sheer joy of the sounds of their voices lifted in song. Words alone could not communicate their feelings of joy over receiving a new pastor (and a Polish one at that!) or express the unity that they felt as a people. Only singing could accomplish that.

~Joe

How many of us have had experiences at prayer or liturgy where the music that was played or the song that was sung touched us at a profound level? How many have had the experience where the song that was sung touched us so deeply that something of the mystery of God was actually revealed to us? Music and singing have the power to lead us to such experiences.

One Lent, the parish was celebrating the last scrutiny with the elect who were preparing for Baptism and full initiation. In the celebration of this scrutiny, we hear the proclamation of John's account of the raising of Lazarus. An acclamation was used during it: the refrain from the very well known hymn, "I Am the Bread of Life," a song that is most often sung at funerals.

With the proclamation of this most profound Gospel story, in which the life-giving power of Christ is revealed to be greater than even death itself, I found myself recalling how moved I had been when singing "I Am the Bread of Life" at funerals. On this day, though, in the context of the scrutiny, in which we as a community were praying for and over those who would become our brothers and sisters in Christ, I became overwhelmingly aware of what our faith proclaims about death. It has no power in the face of Christ! Each time we sang the refrain throughout the scrutiny, I became more and more convinced of this aspect of my faith. All at once, this awareness was applied to the many people at whose funerals I could remember singing this song. This awareness was applied to my own family members who have died, marked with the sign of Christ, and it was applied to my sense of these elect who were celebrating the scrutiny. Not only was something of my faith revealed to me, but also something of God's love and power. By the end of the scrutiny, with that refrain and that Gospel proclamation, I had been so deeply moved and touched by God's grace—all through the singing of a piece of music that took me to a profound place of prayer.   **~Todd**

Music and Culture

Rich experiences of God through song may not occur in many settings unless a particular ethnic custom or a particular culture (for example, a Catholic culture in which a certain song is readily identifiable) supports them. The truth is that, in our American culture, the idea of singing together with others is no longer in vogue. True, we may sing Christmas carols during the holidays or join in the national anthem at a sporting event, but for the most part, we do not sing with one another. If we tried to get a busload of people on a commuter bus to sing along with us, we would no doubt be arrested—if we were able to get off the bus alive! What has happened to singing in American culture?

The fact is that singing has become less of a communal exercise and more of a form of entertainment. Aside from singing "Happy Birthday" and perhaps the national anthem, we don't tend to sing together often. Our most common experiences of live music are probably concerts, where an individual or group performs the music and the audience watches. Singing at liturgy is not like this. Music and singing at Mass are not performances centered around an individual or group while the audience passively watches. Rather, our singing at Mass is a way for us as the People of God to pray and to express our faith in a manner that the spoken word alone cannot capture. It is a way of engaging our entire being in response to God, whose saving deeds require appropriate expression. To respond to God in spoken word only would be like Julie Andrews reciting, "The hills are alive with the sound of music!" in response to the overwhelming beauty of God's creation.

Rejoice, let Mother Church also rejoice, / arrayed with the lightning of his glory, / let this holy building shake with joy, / filled with the mighty voices of the peoples."

(The Exsultet, *The Roman Missal*)

Love the Lord Your God with Your Whole Mind

Scientists tell us that our brain is divided into two hemispheres, each associated with various functions and abilities. We now know that the left brain controls the right side of the body and is responsible for the logical aspects of our lives: math, language, analysis, and so forth. The right brain, on the other hand, controls the left side of the body and is responsible for the more "ethereal" aspects of life such as romance, poetry, art, music, love, and emotion. The fact is, we cannot truly love God with our whole hearts, beings, strength, and minds[80] if we are not engaging the right side of our brain in liturgy! "Ritual makes a very direct appeal to the right brain, that territory of our mind that deals with the irrational, the emotional, and the poetic."[81] Singing is perhaps the most powerful way of tapping into the right brain where we find a myriad of ways to praise and honor God that the left brain cannot fathom. Likewise, God speaks to our whole being. If we focus solely on the spoken word as perceived by the left brain, we are missing out on half of God's communication with us! Without song, it is as though we are trying to listen through only one speaker when God is speaking to us in stereo!

"How I wept, deeply moved by your hymns, songs, and the voices that echoed through your church. What emotion I experienced in them. Those sounds flowed into my ears, distilling the truth in my heart. A feeling of devotion surged within me, and tears streamed down my face: tears that did me good."

(*The Confessions of St. Augustine, Book 9*)

Biblical Foundations of Singing

"Many ancient civilizations, including Judaism, did not always make a clear distinction between speaking and singing. Quite often, the spoken word would take on a lyrical character with rhythmic and melodic features which migrated toward song."[82] This would be logical in an oral tradition that placed less emphasis on other sense imagery such as vision. References to music and singing begin in the Bible as early as the book of Genesis where we find that a descendant of Cain, Jubal, is identified as "the ancestor of all who play the lyre and harp."[83] In fact, the patterns and refrains of the opening chapters of Genesis suggest that the creation story itself was at least in poetic, if not musical form.

Later, we find that Israel often expresses and proclaims her various feelings and experiences through music and song:[84]

- social merrymaking (Exodus 32:17–18)
- dirges and laments (2 Samuel 1:19–27)
- martial noisemaking (Judges 7:18–20)
- songs of warfare (Numbers 21:14–15)
- songs of victory (Exodus 15:1–18)
- acclamations of heroes (1 Samuel 18:6)
- magical incantations (Joshua 6:4–20)
- working songs (Joshua 27:2–5)
- worship (1 Samuel 10:5–6)
- greeting people (Genesis 31:27)
- saying farewell (Luke 15:25)
- at marriages (Jeremiah 7:34)
- at burials (Jeremiah 48:36)
- when people went to war (Judges 30:34)
- when people returned from war (Isaiah 30:32)

In fact, the crucial role of music and singing is illustrated poignantly through the experience of the Babylonian exile when the only proper expression of Israel's devastation is the refusal to sing or play music: "How could we sing the LORD's song in a foreign land?"[85]

To emphasize the role of music and song in biblical history, consider this: many biblical scholars believe that the *oldest* piece of Scripture is the Song of Miriam, Moses's sister. As Scripture records in Exodus 15:1–21, after the crossing of the Red Sea (the pivotal point in Hebrew history), the Israelites sang a song in the Lord's honor. Miriam and other women picked up tambourines and "sang to them: / 'Sing to the LORD, for he has triumphed gloriously; / horse and rider he has thrown into the sea.'"[86]

The role of music in the life and worship of the people of Israel reaches its pinnacle under the rule of David who, as legend has it, played the harp and composed the psalms. Suffice to say, David is responsible for establishing professional temple music. Many of the psalms clearly suggest that the assembly was invited to join in on refrains and responses to the songs led by temple musicians.

"O come, let us sing to the LORD; / let us make a joyful noise to the rock of our salvation! / Let us come into his presence with thanksgiving; / let us make a joyful noise to him with songs of praise!"

(Psalm 95:1–2)

In the New Testament, the Gospel tells us that Jesus and his disciples sang hymns before leaving the upper room for the Mount of Olives, and we need look no further than Paul to find the role of music and singing for the Christian community.

Paul tells us in 1 Corinthians that while there is a place for solo expression, his main concern is for the engagement and prayer of the whole community.[87] Paul tells us in Ephesians to "be filled with the Spirit, as you sing psalms and hymns and spiritual songs among yourselves, singing and making melody to the Lord in your hearts."[88] (Even the book of Revelation tells us that the saints will enter heaven singing songs of praise: "They sing a new song before the throne."[89] To this day, Christian music continues the emphasis that Judaism placed on the vocal word by using musical settings to support texts such as prayers, liturgical texts, Scripture readings, psalms, and hymns.

Music and Singing in Catechesis

It has been said that if you ask a person to tell you his or her three favorite liturgical hymns, those hymns would reveal that person's operative theology, or understanding of the mystery of God. In fact, a popular ice-breaker at retreats is to have people introduce themselves by identifying the liturgical hymns that best capture who they are, how they feel at the moment, and what they believe most strongly about their faith and/or ministry. Liturgical song is a vehicle to express ourselves to God and to form and inform our faith.

"This common, sung expression of faith within liturgical celebrations strengthens our faith when it grows weak and draws us into the divinely inspired voice of the Church at prayer. Faith grows when it is well expressed in celebration. Good celebrations can foster and nourish faith. Poor celebrations may weaken it. Good music 'make[s] the liturgical prayers of the Christian community more alive and fervent so that everyone can praise and beseech the Triune God more powerfully, more intently and more effectively.'[90]"

(*Sing to the Lord*, 5)

Liturgical music is one of the most powerful catechetical tools available to the catechist . . . and one of the most overlooked. Unfortunately, many of our catechetical experiences are bereft of song. Truth be told, if we told all of our catechists that they were required to sing in order to serve in this ministry, we might end up losing 90% of our catechists! Yet, music and song can play a very important part in our catechesis.

As a junior high catechist, I have been very aware of the importance of music in the lives of these young people. Their love for music is obvious, as they enter class with headphones on and iPods blaring, and as they continue to try to sneak their headphones back on during class! To capitalize on the importance of music in their lives, I regularly bring in examples of contemporary music that relate to the theme we are covering. I've used music by the Black Eyed Peas to talk about the Rosary, Linkin Park to talk about faith, and John Mayer to talk about the seven deadly sins, just to name a few. St. Ignatius believed that when teaching, it is important to enter through the door of those whom we teach but to be sure to leave through our own door (that leads to Jesus). When you enter through the door of young people, you will immediately find that music is very important.   ~Joe

If catechesis is truly to be "initiatory" as described by the *General Directory for Catechesis*, that means that we are to gradually introduce would-be disciples of Jesus to the Christian way of life. As Christians, we are a people of prayer and there is no more profound and powerful way to pray than to lift one's voice in song. Sacred song is not some kind of "frosting on the cake" that would be nice to add if possible, it is part of the fabric of Christian living that calls us to love God with our entire hearts, beings, strength, and minds!

Music and Song in Liturgy

As Catholics, we have been singing our liturgies (not just singing at the liturgy) for, literally, centuries. From the earliest days of monasteries for men and women religious, the brothers or sisters would gather many times during the day to "sing the Office"—that is, to chant the psalms, readings, and texts of the Liturgy of the Hours. The Eucharistic liturgy, too, has in its history a period of time when the readings and prayers were sung, not recited. To this day, many remember the Latin chants that permeated the celebration of the liturgy.

Communal Songs

From the first moments of the liturgy, music and song play a most vital part in expressing the praise and thanksgiving that we, by virtue of our Baptism, are called to offer to God. The hymns acclamations, responses, and songs serve many different functions in the liturgy, not the least of which is to make of our prayer a joyful noise to the Lord.

"Participation must also be external, so that internal participation can be expressed and reinforced by actions, gestures, and bodily attitudes, and by the acclamations, responses, and singing.[91] The quality of our participation in such sung praise comes less from our vocal ability than from the desire of our hearts to sing together of our love for God. Participation in the Sacred Liturgy both expresses and strengthens the faith that is in us."

(*Sing to the Lord*, 13)

Among many things, the hymns, acclamations, responses, and songs serve to *unify* the congregation. For example, the opening song or entrance antiphon is meant to do more than simply accompany the opening procession as it makes its way to the front of the church. The opening song is what helps to *gather* the many people present so that we may be unified into the liturgical assembly—the one body of Christ. Think again of the national anthem—the singing of that one song creates *one voice* out of the thousands of individual voices that fill a stadium. The opening song of the liturgy does the same for the group of people who have gathered in the church: it makes *one voice* of us so that we may raise the one prayer of Jesus, the Son, to God our heavenly Father. Once we have been unified into the body of Christ, then, and only then, do we begin our prayer to God.

The communion hymn, or the antiphon, also serves this same purpose. It expresses the unity of the body of Christ which comes about through the very sharing in which we take part at this point in the Mass. It is the one Bread and the one Cup that unifies us and makes us one.[92] We acknowledge and manifest this same unity in the closing hymn. As we began in one voice, so too do we go forth from our celebration. Commissioned in the Concluding Rites, we are then sent out, as the body of Christ to "announce the Gospel of the Lord."

"The Paschal hymn, of course, does not cease when a liturgical celebration ends. Christ, whose praises we have sung, remains with us and leads us through church doors to the whole world, with its joys and hopes, griefs and anxieties.[93] . . . Charity, justice, and evangelization are thus the normal consequences of liturgical celebration. Particularly inspired by sung participation, the body of the Word Incarnate goes forth to spread the Gospel with full force and compassion."

(Sing to the Lord, 8-9)

Prayers and Scripture

The *Constitution on the Sacred Liturgy* notes that it is from Scripture that "psalms are sung; the prayers, collects, and liturgical songs are scriptural in their inspiration."[94] Much of the music that we sing at the liturgy comes from ancient prayers or from the Scriptures. In the Introductory Rites, the Gloria is one example. An ancient prayer which has its roots in the Scriptures, this "song of the angels" is what burst upon the world in response to the great mystery of the Incarnation.[95] We echo that song by singing it on every Sunday (except during Advent and Lent), major feast, and solemnity. On Holy Thursday and on Easter, we ring bells during this song of the angels to make it even more festive. What God calls us to in the Eucharistic feast is too great to not raise our voices in this ancient song of ours.

The Sanctus, or Holy, Holy, Holy, which we sing after the preface to the Eucharistic Prayer, is likewise an ancient prayer that comes from Scripture. As the song that Isaiah heard when he was granted a vision of the heavenly throne,[96] it becomes our song: "And so, with Angels and Archangels, / with Thrones and Dominions, / and with all the hosts and Powers of heaven, / we sing the hymn of your glory, / as without end we acclaim. . . ."[97]

The psalms are perhaps the most obvious pieces of Scripture that are set to music for us to sing. As has already been noted, the psalms are early Hebrew folksongs. They were *meant* to be sung, and they help us to express our faith and belief in the God who calls us around the table.

"The musical tradition of the universal church is a treasure of inestimable value, greater even than that of any other art."[98]

(Catechism of the Catholic Church, 1156)

Litanies and Acclamations

"Lord, have mercy; Christ, have mercy; Lord, have mercy," "Lord, hear our prayer," "Lamb of God, you take away the sins of the world, have mercy on us, grant us peace." All of these are examples of litanies that we sing during the liturgy. Litanies are ancient forms of prayer that find their roots in our Jewish history. The Song of Daniel[99] and many of the psalms, such as Psalm 136, are examples of litanies where there is a repeated refrain or phrase between which are statements of praise, or intercessions. The repetition of the refrain serves as a mantra: "Lord, have mercy," or "Lord, hear our prayer." Our constant singing of the response draws us deeper and deeper into the prayer each time it is repeated.

Traditionally set to music and sung, these refrains offer us a way of praying that can sometimes be lessened when they're simply recited. As in the Litany of Saints, for example, the music adds a certain power to the prayer. Does this mean that if it is not sung and is recited instead, that it is not prayer? Not by any means. As St. Augustine noted, however, "when we sing, we pray twice." Certainly, he recognized the power that music has to fill our prayer with the power of joy and hope.

Much of the same can be said of the acclamations during Mass. The Holy, Holy, Holy; the Alleluia; the Memorial Acclamation (Mystery of Faith); and the Amen are all parts of the Mass that should, ideally, be sung. When done so strongly by the whole community, they have a wonderful way of expressing the prayer that Christ's Body is offering. While they certainly can be recited, the singing of these texts reaches into our tradition and our history in unique ways.

"O sing a new song to the Lord, / for he has worked wonders; / in the sight of the nations / he has shown his deliverance, alleluia."

(Entrance Antiphon, Fifth Sunday of Easter, *The Roman Missal*)

REFLECTION

» Look over a hymnal and select those songs that best express your relationship with God, your outlook on life, or how you feel in this moment.

» Do you take part in the singing of the music that is a part of your parish's liturgical life? If not, why not? If you are a "full-throated" singer during Mass, taking part in all the songs, hymns, and acclamations, consider why this is important to you. See if you can become aware of how the prayers and acclamations may be different when they are recited instead of sung (or the other way around).

» Do music and song ever become part of your own personal prayer? How? If not, what are some ways in which they might?

» Consider how the texts that we sing (whether the texts of certain songs or hymns, or the texts of the sung prayers and acclamations of the liturgy) have shaped or formed your own faith and belief. In what ways has your faith been strengthened by these texts? How have these texts helped to deepen or develop your prayer? What does this say about the formational and educational aspects of music?

» Music has a powerful way of affecting us in worship and prayer. Can you name an experience in which the song made a particularly strong impression on your prayer or worship? What were the circumstances? Who was present with you? Why was the experience so powerful? What might this tell you about the role of music and song in liturgy and prayer?

CHAPTER 10

THE MYSTERY OF SACRED SPACE

Space Matters!

People tease me about my office space. I am what one might call a "pile-er." I make piles. Once I've looked at a piece of paper, a document, a report, or a file, I put it on top of one of many various piles that have accumulated on my desk, the credenza, or the table. If someone were to walk into my office and ask about one of those files or reports, I can go to a single pile in the room and pull it out. Once in a while, I do get confused, and I begin searching in all the different piles and it can be comical to witness. But, I ultimately find it, note where it was, and put it back when I'm done with it.

This system drives many people crazy. They can't believe that I actually know what is in which pile. They say, with strong conviction, that they could never stand to work in such an environment. Yet, it somehow works for me. The piles are arranged in such a way that the system actually serves me well. The space, though apparently cluttered and in a state of disarray, serves my style of working. I can work there because the space is set up according to the way I work.   **~Todd**

When we arrange spaces, form often follows function. Go into anyone's office space and you'll be able to figure out a little bit of how they work, a little of their style of working, or the kind of work they do. Our homes are arranged according to the same principle: the kitchen is set up according to how one works while cooking. The pots are in specific places and the spices are arranged according to a system that serves the cook best. The family room is arranged in such a way that best fits how one relaxes, recreates, or plays. The bedroom is set up to facilitate our own personal patterns and routines of waking, readying ourselves for the day, and sleeping.

Public areas follow the same principles. Malls are built with wide concourses and stores on either side that allow people to look in the windows and wander in and out of stores, thus increasing the possibility that they might find something they would like to buy. Theaters seats are lined up in order to provide the best view of the stage, and theaters use lighting and decoration to draw the eye to what is happening on the screen or stage. Parks often have different arrangements of plants, benches, and lawns in different places that facilitate different experiences: play, exercise, rest, contemplation. Hotels typically have spacious, well-lit lobbies downstairs where people are intended to socialize or conduct business, but long, narrow hallways upstairs where people are intended to head quietly past the rooms of others rather than congregate or socialize.

Form Follows Function

Space, and the way that it is arranged, matters! So much so that when the space ceases to serve the needs of those who use it, changes are made. A very familiar sight on TV these days is the sight of a building being demolished by implosion. Strategically placed explosives are systematically set off by demolition teams, causing the buildings to cave in on themselves and, in one big cloud of dust, disappear from view. In recent years, three types of buildings have been the target of such implosions: public housing high-rises, Las Vegas hotels, and baseball stadiums. Going up in their places are buildings that are designed to better serve their functions. Las Vegas hotels are now being built to serve families and act as indoor theme parks, replacing those that simply had smoke-filled casinos. Public housing high-rises, built like urban prisons, are being replaced by low-rise or scattered site housing to better serve the needs of families and communities. And new baseball parks are, interestingly enough, being built to replace stadiums built just 40 or 50 years ago. Stadiums built in the 1960s and 1970s were intended to hold huge numbers of people in very sterile environments. Built as though from the same cookie cutter, these stadiums, surrounded by vast concrete parking lots, were cavernous and cold, leaving fans feeling as if they were a million miles from the action. It seems that the architects of these buildings forgot a very important idea: the crowd attending a baseball game plays a very important role in the game. As a result, new baseball stadiums are being built to look like "old" baseball parks. Fans sit closer to the action, the game is played on real grass rather than artificial turf, and glimpses of the surrounding neighborhood are visible over the stadium walls. Modern baseball stadium architects have realized that they need to create spaces that make the fans feel like part of the action and that fill people with nostalgia for stadiums of the past. They have come to realize that form follows function.

Taking my two children to their first baseball game at historic Wrigley Field in Chicago seemed like a "sacred" moment for me! I was taking them to the same place that my father took me when I was a child, and his father took him when he was a child. I remember taking the kids down to the wall by the bullpen where the field is within arm's reach and telling them to look at the same grass that Ernie Banks, Hack Wilson, and Tinkers, Evers, and Chance played on decades before. Space has a way of taking on a very special meaning for us to the extent that we refer to certain spaces as sacred.   **~Joe**

These spaces are sacred because of what we *do* in them, because of what *happens* to us in them, or because of what we perceive to be *present* in them. Cemeteries, for example, are sacred to us because they hold the remains of those who are dear to us—it is their final "resting place," we say. Perhaps there is a completely ordinary spot such as a certain section of a park or a certain classroom at your old school that takes on sacred significance for you because it was the place where you first fell in love.

Even though another family may be living there, or even though another house may be standing in its place, undoubtedly when you visit the site of your childhood home, it is as though it is still there, just as you remember it.

Space for an Encounter

For those of us who are people of faith, to call a certain space sacred is to declare that it is somehow determined to be a place where we meet and are engaged with the mysterious and transcendent presence of God. Celtic spirituality refers to these spaces as "thin places," meaning that the "veil" between this world and the supernatural world is very thin in certain sacred locations, thus allowing a unique opportunity for an encounter between God and man. In Scripture, we are told that when Moses encountered God in the burning bush, the Lord told him to remove his sandals for "the place on which you are standing is holy ground" (Exodus 3:5). Note that it was not just that God was present in the space that made it holy. What made it holy was the encounter between God and Moses that took place in that space.

This idea of holy space being the point of encountering God follows throughout the account of the Exodus and throughout the new relationship that was being formed between God and the Israelites. In a dramatic way, the most holy of these encounters between God and Moses took place on the top of Mount Sinai. Amid trumpet blasts, peals of thunder, and billowing clouds,[100] Moses encountered the one and true God whose will was to save the people and set them free. As we know, it was in that encounter that Moses received the Law in the Ten Commandments.

Later in the Exodus experience, as the Israelites are making their way across the desert, that place of encountering God became the meeting tent where the ark of the covenant was kept. "Now Moses used to take the tent and pitch it outside the camp, far off from the camp," the book of Exodus tells us. "And everyone who sought the Lord would go out to the tent of meeting, which was outside the camp."[101]

"Then the cloud covered the tent of meeting, and the glory of the Lord filled the tabernacle. . . . For the cloud of the Lord was on the tabernacle by day, and fire was in the cloud by night, before the eyes of all the house of Israel at each stage of their journey."

(Exodus 40:34, 38)

Later in the Israelites' history, once the people had settled in the promised land, that place of encounter between God and God's people became more permanent.[102] In the building of the Temple, the people of Israel now had a definite space that was designated as *the* space to meet God. The psalmist sings of this in Psalm 132: "'Let us go to his dwelling-place; let us worship at his footstool.' . . . For the Lord has chosen Zion; he has desired it for his habitation: / 'This is my resting-place forever; here I will reside, for I have desired it.'"[103] At the same time, the people of Israel acknowledged that God is not "contained" in the Temple.

"But will God indeed dwell on the earth? Even heaven and the highest heaven cannot contain you, much less this house that I have built!"

(1 Kings 8:27)

For the people of Israel, the Temple served as a representation of all of God's creation with the Temple itself serving as the center of all reality. The Temple was a place of ritual sacrifice and communication with and about God (although the synagogue served as the place for public/communal worship and study). The Temple also served as a symbol of holiness (since it represented the presence of the Holy One on earth) and of community (since it represented God's people). Finally, the Temple was also seen as "the embodiment of God's people's longing for justice, peace and blessing,"[104] a symbol that was intensified by its destruction. To this day, Jewish people still gather in front of the remaining western wall, praying for justice, peace, and blessing.

Christ, the New Temple

For Christians, Christ is now the place in which humans encounter God and the salvation that he offers. The Gospel alludes to Jesus's comparison of himself to the Temple: "Destroy this temple, and in three days I will raise it up."[105] Just as the Temple represented God's presence on earth, for Christians, Jesus represents the fullness of God's presence in physical form. Because of the prominence of the Temple in Jewish thought, early Christians quickly came to see in Jesus's Death an image of the destruction of the Temple. Likewise, Jesus's Resurrection came to be seen as a symbol of its rebuilding. Through the events of Pentecost and the sending of the Holy Spirit, Christians came to see the Church as the Body of Christ. St. Paul helps develop this imagery: "For we are the temple of the living God."[106]

The Temple is still where we encounter God. For us Christians, that Temple is the Church—the People of God, saved through Christ. Peter speaks of the Church, God's people, using this Temple imagery: "Come to him, a living stone, rejected by mortals yet chosen and precious in God's sight, and like living stones, let yourselves be built into a spiritual house, to be a holy priesthood, to offer spiritual sacrifices acceptable to God through Jesus Christ."[107] The Church, as Christ's Body, is where we experience God's presence and saving action.

Liturgical Space

As we saw in Chapter 4, the earliest reference to the Church uses the term *ekklesia*, denoting the sense of a community that is convoked by God for a specific purpose: to do the work or the service for which they were baptized. So in our communities, then, we need space that allows us to do our *leitourgos*. What might that space look like?

Space for Gathering

Early basilicas had elaborate areas where the people gathered before entering the main body of the building to celebrate the Eucharist. These were actually areas of transition, areas that helped facilitate the movement from the busy atmosphere of their lives into the atmosphere of table and communion, the atmosphere of proclamation and thanksgiving, the atmosphere of death and resurrection. It was the space that allowed people to move from the world's time, *kronos*, to God's time, *kairos* (see Chapter 17). These spaces were outfitted with lush plants and trees. They had places to sit, surrounded by fountains that invited a sense of recollection before entering the great banquet hall.

"For where two or three are gathered in my name, I am there among them."

(Matthew 18:20)

These spaces for gathering made great symbolic use of portals and doorways. Our forebears in faith saw a powerful connection to their "passing over" from the daily and weekly pattern of life into the banquet hall of the Lamb. Often such entryways were dark, requiring the eyes of those who entered to adjust—to go through a transition. We carry a sense of that symbolic richness in a few of our present-day rites. The Rite of Baptism for Children, and the Rite of Christian Initiation for Adults, for example, both begin at the door of the church. In a similar experience of transition and "passing over," those who are not yet members of the Body of Christ stand *outside* the gathered church and make a formal request to be admitted, through holy Baptism. The funeral Mass also begins at the door of the church, as the body of the deceased is greeted and sprinkled with holy water. The Rite of Dedication of a Church, too, makes use of this symbolism as it begins with the bishop leading the people to the doors of the church that is to be solemnly dedicated. Once there, the bishop leads the community through those doors for the first time with these words: "Go within his gates giving thanks, enter his courts with songs of praise." Indeed, this too is a moment of transition for the whole parish as the community processes through the doors of their brand new church to celebrate for the first time the rites of the Eucharistic liturgy.

Today, many of our churches are without this vast space for gathering and for transitioning. The *narthex* of the great basilicas gave way to the smaller, more economic vestibule with which most of us are familiar. The purpose, however, is still the same: to provide a space that helps us enter fully into the place of Word and sacrament. It is interesting to note that the church is rediscovering the importance of having this kind of space in which to gather. Today in the United States, whenever a new church building is being constructed, or in the renovation of older church buildings, emphasis is placed upon the value of having such a space for gathering. We recognize the need to provide a space in which we can greet one another, a space in which we can come together and begin to be formed into the liturgical assembly that will celebrate the Eucharist.

Space for Baptizing

During the warm summer months, we hear a great deal about how much water we need to drink to keep from dehydrating. Water is so crucial to our survival as humans. Without water, we literally face death. It's no coincidence then, that the symbol of our dying and rising in Christ is water! Through the waters of Baptism, we have gained eternal life. For this reason, the placement of the baptismal font is central to the design of any church.

"Placing the baptismal font in an area near the entrance or gathering space where the members pass regularly and setting it on an axis with the altar can symbolize the relationship between the various sacraments as well as the importance of the Eucharist within the life and faith development of the members."

(*Built of Living Stones*, 69.5)

My mom once went to visit the church of her childhood after many years of going to a different parish. She found that the church had been significantly remodeled. The thing that caught her attention more than anything was the fact that the old holy water receptacles at each entrance were empty. She said, "Instead of blessing yourself at the doorway, you had to walk to the actual baptismal font that they built within the church near the main entryway." I reminded her that this particular church once located its baptismal font (where I and my eight siblings were baptized!) in a baptistry behind the sacristy. The only access people had to the baptismal waters were the receptacles at each doorway. Now that the place of baptism was in the midst of the main entryway, people could bless themselves with water from the very font in which baptisms are celebrated.   ~Joe

This font of flowing water at the main entryway of the church—where we pass through the doors into the physical structure of the building—symbolizes our passing through the waters into the mystical Body of Christ. This is, in a very real way, another doorway through which we all pass. It is the womb of the church from which are born as members of the People of God, the Church. The space in which this happens needs to be worthy. It needs to be visible, so that the rites involving the font can be easily performed and so that the whole assembly can see and become engaged in the rite.

Space for Listening, Walking, and Responding

"I hope we get good seats!" How often do we find ourselves saying this when we are going to a sporting event or to a show? We want to be in a spot where we can see and hear everything that is going on. We want to be able to call out to the players on the field, or catch a fly ball if it happens to drop into the stands. We want to see, hear, and respond. The same principles should hold true for our worship spaces. Every seat in a church should be a "good seat." Wherever a person sits, he or she should be able to fully listen and respond to God's Word, and should be able to fully engage in the mystery of the Eucharist.

In our places of liturgy, we need a space in which we can do all the various "work" that we are called to do in our worship. We need a space in which we can hear the Word of God proclaimed and a space in which we can respond to that proclamation. We need a space in which we can walk—to the altar for Communion, to the font to renew our Baptism, to the minister for anointing. We need a space that allows us to do the "work" of other liturgical celebrations and rites—space for the celebration of funerals, weddings, and Baptisms, and space for the rites of the Sacred Paschal Triduum (Holy Thursday, Good Friday, and Holy Saturday). The *nave* provides this kind of space in most of our parish churches. The nave is where the chairs or pews are located. *Built of Living Stones*, the most recent statement from the United States bishops on the subject of Catholic art and architecture, speaks of this space noting that "this area is not comparable to the audience's space in a theater or public arena because in the liturgical assembly, there is no audience. Rather, the entire congregation acts."[108]

Space for Gathering Around the Altar

When you have people over to your house for an important dinner, you take special care to set a table that says, "something special is happening here." The meal is not only to be pleasing to the tongue, but is to be pleasing to the eye as well. In any church, when we gather for the Eucharistic banquet, we gather around the table of the Lord, namely, the altar. The altar is the central visual focus of our worship space and "should reflect the nature of . . . the place of sacrifice and the table around which Christ gathers the community to nourish them."[109]

In a very real sense, the altar is the parish community's banquet table of the Lamb. This is the table around which *this* parish gathers to "proclaim the Lord's death until he comes."[110] This is the table around which the parish gathers to offer its praise and thanksgiving to God, uniting it to that of Christ Jesus, who is the one true priest. This is the table around which, as the *Rite of Dedication of an Altar* points out, "the community would come to celebrate their Passover. Therefore the altar is the table for a sacrifice and for a banquet."[111] This is the table to which the parish community comes to receive the Bread of Life and the Cup of Eternal Salvation, to eat and drink the Lord's Supper, to take part in the heavenly banquet. Again, the space for the altar needs to be worthy, visible to all who are gathered in the church, and situated so that all are engaged in the holy action that takes place there.

"At the Eucharist, the liturgical assembly celebrates the ritual sacrificial meal that recalls and makes present Christ's life, death, and resurrection, proclaiming 'the death of the Lord until he comes.'[112] The altar is 'the center of thanksgiving that the Eucharist accomplishes'[113] and the point around which the other rites are in some manner arrayed."[114]

(Built of Living Stones, 56)

Space for Reserving the Sacrament

By the end of the first half-century of our faith tradition, the Christian community began the practice of saving some of the Eucharistic bread after the celebration so that it could be taken to those who were not able to be present because of sickness. This expressed the reality that was professed in faith: in the Eucharist we are united to God, through Christ, and to one another. Reserving the sacrament so that it could be taken to the sick protected the unity of the community that was fractured due to illness. We do the same thing today in our own parishes. Those who are absent are, literally, re-membered to the community through the Eucharist, which is brought to them by ministers of care.

Where is this Eucharist reserved until it is brought to the sick? We call this place of reservation the tabernacle (see Chapter 11, "The Mystery of Sacred Objects"). Over the years, the tabernacle provided not just a place in which to reserve the Eucharist for the sick, it also began to provide a place in which people could meet the Lord truly present in the reserved sacrament. *Built of Living Stones* reminds us, "as the appreciation of Christ's presence in the eucharistic species became more developed, Christians desired through prayer to show reverence for Christ's continuing presence in their midst."[115] The space in which the tabernacle is located provides us with a very special focal point for our prayer and meditation. It is a space that allows us to come before Christ in the Eucharist for adoration and for silent prayer. It is a space that allows us to "learn to appreciate [our] right and responsibility to join the offering of [our] own lives to the perfect sacrifice of Christ during the Mass[116] and [where we] are led to a greater recognition of Christ in [ourselves] and in others, especially in the poor and needy."[117]

Space for Prayer

Catholics are a sacramental people. As such, we find that images and art can assist us in our prayer. Too often, Catholics are accused of worshiping images. The truth is, of course, that we do not worship statues and images. We use them to engage all of our senses in our prayer and to represent various aspects of our faith and devotion. Statues, shrines, and art draw us to prayer and point us in the direction of the mystery of God that cannot be contained in the image itself.

In addition to our communal worship, Catholic churches also provide space for personal prayer and devotion. Shrines to Mary and the saints, sacred icons, the stations of the cross, a stand displaying the sacred oils, and so on—these are all ways of expressing the rich dimensions of our faith and the mystery of God. When we "venerate them," we are paying homage, respect, and reverence for the reality they represent. They, in turn, serve to remind us of the many rich aspects of the Paschal Mystery of Christ as lived out by the saints and, in doing so, actually teach us about our faith. A great deal of substantive catechesis can occur simply by touring a church and studying/reflecting on the sacred images present!

To have space, then, for encounters with these statues and icons, these pieces of art and sacred images allows us to fully express this dimension of our faith. Many of our various devotions include rituals that "involve singing, intercession, thanksgiving and common postures."[118] Our spaces need to allow for these various ways of praying and reflecting.

Devotional prayer is another way for people to bring the very personal concerns of life to God. . . . Sacred images are important not only in liturgical prayer but also in devotional prayer because they are sacramentals that help the faithful to focus their attention and their prayer."

(*Built of Living Stones*, 131)

REFLECTION

» Take a "tour" of your parish church. Identify how various spaces help to facilitate actions in the liturgy.

» Identify and list the spaces in your life where you most frequently encounter God's presence and action. Determine if you consider these spaces "sacred." Identify the spaces in your life where you rarely encounter God's presence and action. Determine what it is that contributes to this lack of encountering God there. Resolve to be more aware of the many circumstances and situations in which God is waiting to be encountered.

» How or in what ways do you encounter God in the space of your parish church? Is there a particular space where you are most frequently drawn? What is that space and why are you drawn there?

» This chapter mentions several images from Scripture and tradition that have been used in reference to the building of the church (a temple, living stones, Mount Zion, holy ground). Is there a particular image that speaks to you? In what ways does it speak to you?

CHAPTER 11

THE MYSTERY OF SACRED OBJECTS

Sacred Objects

I grew up in a family with nine children! I don't know how my mother did it, but she always found a way to provide sumptuous and abundant meals for us every day. At the same time, our meals were not very extravagant. Quite often, Mom's creations were spooned (perhaps shoveled would be more appropriate for some of us!) out of a large army pot placed in the middle of the kitchen table (the dining room table was usually buried under schoolbooks, mail, and games). We ate off paper plates, drank from plastic cups, and used our everyday silverware.

That all changed whenever the holidays came around. On Thanksgiving, Christmas, and other special days, we were given our marching orders: set the dining room table for dinner! That meant removing all of the clutter from the table, giving it a good polish to bring out the beauty of the wood, putting in several leaves to extend the length of the table, and then covering it with a fine tablecloth that was preserved in a drawer. Then came the special silverware and china that we only saw a couple of times each year. Unlike our everyday silverware, which was thrown into a drawer next to the kitchen sink, the special silverware was stored in a drawer in the china closet of the dining room, neatly arranged in a beautiful wooden case that was lined on the inside with a red velvet-like material. Unlike our everyday dishes, which were stacked on a shelf in the pantry, the good china was neatly arranged behind the glass of our china closet. Next came the glasses that were really glass, not plastic like our everyday cups. Finally came cloth napkins instead of paper towels, serving dishes instead of an army pot, and a gravy boat instead of a small pot with a ladle.

Now that we had all of the right objects in place, we were ready to eat a special meal.

~Joe

My sister and brother-in-law have a pair of champagne glasses that they used at their first dinner as husband and wife. They use these glasses only on their wedding anniversary. Each year on that day, they take out those glasses and they drink champagne from them, toasting their day and recalling the event that united them in the bond of marriage. Their special celebration calls for the special champagne glasses.

~Todd

Sacred events and celebrations call for the use of sacred objects. When we gather to celebrate the sacred mysteries of our Lord Jesus Christ, we use many sacred objects that express to us very clearly that we are not participating in an ordinary meal. From vestments to vessels to furniture, the Christian community gathers to celebrate the Eucharist with sacred objects that remind us of the extraordinary food that we are about to receive.

This special attention that we give to the objects used in worship has its basis in the earliest worship experiences of our Jewish ancestors. The building of the Ark of the Covenant, described in the book of Exodus (beginning in Exodus 25) goes into great detail about the specifications regarding these various objects whether they were a table, a veil, a lampstand, or vestments. Later, we find the same attention given to the building of the Temple under Solomon: "Solomon made all the vessels that were in the house of the LORD: the golden altar, the golden table for the bread of the Presence, the lampstands of pure gold . . . the cups, snuffers, basins, dishes for incense, and firepans, of pure gold."[119]

"In accordance with all that I show you concerning the pattern of the tabernacle and of all its furniture, so you shall make it. They shall make an ark of acacia wood. . . . They shall make a table of acacia wood. . . . You shall make a lampstand of pure gold. . . . Moreover, you shall make the tabernacle with ten curtains of fine twisted linen. . . . You shall make a curtain of blue, purple, and crimson yarns and of fine twisted linen. . . . These are the vestments that they shall make: a breastpiece, an ephod, a robe, a chequered tunic, a turban, and a sash."

(Exodus 25:9-10, 23, 31; 26:1, 31; 28:4)

Once again, we may ask, "What's all the fuss?" And once again, when we pause to think of what worship is, namely our efforts to give honor and praise to God, we realize that we need to give special attention to even the smallest detail of our worship. Even the objects we use in worship must serve the purpose of giving praise and honor to God. This does not mean that everything we use in worship must be ornate or inordinately expensive. It simply means that all of the objects we use in liturgy must be appropriate and that such appropriateness is determined by how well the objects serve our purpose of giving God praise and honor. An object becomes a *sacred* object when we somehow encounter the mystery of God in and through it. Something is sacred when it is set aside, or dedicated, for the worship of God. Just as we set aside good silverware and china for special occasions, when we gather to celebrate the Eucharist, we also set aside certain objects that, when used, represent the sacred nature of our gathering.

Sacred Objects Used in Liturgy

In each of our own homes, we have certain objects that we reserve for special occasions. Likewise, when we gather as a Christian community to celebrate the Eucharist, we also have a number of objects set aside for the purpose of worshiping God. Like any family, it is important for us to be familiar with these objects and to know their "story." Let's take a look at the primary sacred objects found in our worship space.

The Crucifix

The cross of Jesus Christ is the most basic symbol found in any Christian worship space. This symbol is so central to our understanding of the mystery of our faith that we have devoted the entire next chapter of this book to it.

Candles

Special meals are often served with candles on the table! When we gather for Eucharist, candles are not merely used for ambiance, but to remind us of the light of Christ that is given to us in Baptism. Jesus referred to himself as the Light of the World. When we celebrate liturgy, candles, especially the paschal candle, dispel the darkness that surrounds us and bathe us in the light of Christ. For this and for other reasons, there is a basic, guiding principle regarding the objects used in our worship— the principle of *authenticity*. If you have the choice between a natural or genuine material and a synthetic material made to look like some natural material, always use the natural material. Real, wax candles are preferred over plastic cylinders that hold oil and are made to look like candles, or plastic candles with electric "flames."

Books

When we gather to celebrate Eucharist, we rely on certain books to assist us in our worship. Our faith tradition loves books! We decorate them and adorn them with symbols and pictures. We carry them in procession. We kiss them and reverence them. We incense them and enshrine them. We recognize the unique way in which God can be present to us and act in our lives through the special readings and prayers contained in these books. Some of the books that we use include:

• **The Lectionary:** We read from this book every time the Body of Christ gathers. This book tells our story—the story of God's action and presence among us. It contains the cycle of Scripture readings proclaimed at Mass.

• *The Roman Missal:* This is the book of prayers that we use every time the Body of Christ gathers to celebrate the Eucharist. It contains the prayers and formulas used by the priest presider.

• **The Book of the Elect:** In this book, we inscribe the names of all those who will be baptized into our faith tradition.

• **The Book of the Names of the Dead:** In this book, we write the names of all those who have gone before us, marked with the sign of faith.

To highlight the importance of these books at our celebrations, it is important that they be visually attractive and impressive. These sacred books are meant to draw our attention to the mystery of God and invite us to give praise and honor.

Vestments

Every Halloween, when kids of all ages put on costumes, an interesting thing happens: they begin to take on the characteristics of the costume they are portraying! They suddenly begin to act like Dracula, wicked witches, or princes and princesses! The truth is that whenever we put on any kind of garment, we tend to act accordingly. At our Baptism, we put on a baptismal garment as our way of professing our call to "put on the Lord Jesus Christ."[120] At our celebrations of the Eucharist, we also have ritual garments, or vestments, that are worn by certain people, not to indicate their stature above everyone else, but quite the opposite: to draw attention away from them personally and toward the inner mystery that the garment or vestment indicates. Among the most common or primary vestments are the following:

- **Alb:** This tunic that wraps around the body with the head as its focal point traditionally symbolized "the human being's spiritual transcendence to a merely physical world."[121] The alb is worn by altar servers, deacons, and priests (as an "undergarment" for the chasuble), and draws attention to their liturgical roles in the sanctuary on behalf of the assembly.

- **Chasuble:** This is the "poncho-like" outer liturgical vestment worn by priests and bishops when celebrating the Eucharist. This outer garment reflects the liturgical season in its color and often includes other artwork that depicts various aspects of the Paschal Mystery.

- **Stole:** This is the primary liturgical vestment of the priest, worn like a prayer shawl. The stole is a sign of the ordained office in the Church.

"Blessed are you, O God, / who through your Son, the Mediator of the New Testament, / graciously accept our praise / and generously bestow your gifts on us. / Grant that these articles, / set aside for the celebration of divine worship, / may be signs of our reverence for you / and helps to our faithful service. / We ask this through Christ our Lord."

(Order of Blessing of Articles for Liturgical Use, *Book of Blessings*)

Vessels

When my wife and I moved into our new home, we discovered a surprise. In a cabinet above the refrigerator we found eight beautiful wineglasses! Apparently, the previous owner unknowingly left these behind. When we finally got in touch with her, she told us to keep them. This was a blessing because we had been without good wineglasses to serve our company. Now, we felt comfortable inviting people over for a more formal dinner celebration because we finally had the right "vessels." When we celebrate the Lord's meal, we also set the table with the proper vessels.

~Joe

Here are some of the most basic vessels used in liturgy:

- **Chalice:** The cup is the only liturgical vessel explicitly mentioned in the Gospel accounts of the Last Supper. The word *chalice* comes from the Latin word *calix*, meaning "cup." From the one chalice, the entire assembly drinks of our Lord's precious Blood. For this reason, one main chalice is consecrated on the altar, perhaps along with other communion cups that are filled in preparation for the consecration. We do not each get our own individual cup to drink from. This would dilute the symbolism of partaking of the one cup, a powerful symbol of our unity. We must also remember the other meaning of *cup* that Jesus uses in the Gospel. In the garden of Gethsemane, Jesus prays that this "cup" may pass him by. Likewise, he uses the same word when two disciples ask if they can be seated at his right and left hands in his kingdom. Jesus replies by asking them if they can drink of the same "cup" as he will. In both of these contexts, Jesus is referring to the cup as a metaphor for commitment. When we drink of the one cup at the Eucharist, we are not only receiving the life source of Jesus through his precious Blood, but we are also expressing our commitment to the mission of this community of disciples. (See Chapter 15, "The Mystery of the Meal.")

- **Paten:** Very simply, the word *paten* comes from the Greek word *patane*, which means "dish" or "plate." The paten is the plate (often more like a bowl and sometimes even a basket) containing the bread that is consecrated into the Body of Christ at Eucharist. Jesus most likely used a common domestic plate when celebrating the Last Supper. The size of such patens varies depending on the size of the assembly as well as on the type of bread used.

- **Ciborium, Pyx, and Monstrance:** When the Eucharist is reserved, it is often placed in a vessel called a *ciborium*, which looks like a chalice but comes with a lid, namely, to preserve the consecrated bread until it is taken to those who are sick or distributed at communion in some cases if too few hosts were consecrated for the number of people present. Other vessels related to the consecrated bread are the *pyx*, which is a small round container used to carry communion to those who are sick, and a *monstrance* (from the Latin *monstro*, meaning to "show" or "reveal"), which is used to display a large consecrated host for the purpose of adoration.

- **Tabernacle:** The consecrated hosts are reserved in a *tabernacle* (from the Latin *tabernaculum*, meaning tent), reminiscent of the Jewish Ark of the Covenant which embodied the presence of God among the people. A burning lamp next to the tabernacle is a constant reminder of the sacramental presence of the Lord in the Eucharist.

- **Thurible:** Since Old Testament times, the use of incense has been integral in worship. Incense was a sign of royalty or a sign of the presence of the sacred. In Isaiah's vision of the heavenly throne, for example, the room was filled with the smoke of incense.[122] Also, since we pray with all of our senses, it is important for us at times to include a sweet-smelling fragrance like incense, which also engages our vision, by rising before us in the same way that we hope our prayers "rise" up to God. The vessel that contains the burning incense is called a *thurible*. The incense is used to bless people, places, and things.

- **Cruets:** When we bring forward the gifts at Mass, we bring forward, along with the paten containing the hosts, a vessel containing wine. Another similar vessel containing water is often on the credence table (the table that holds all those things necessary for the Eucharist but that are not brought up in the Presentation of the Gifts). These *cruets* (from the French *cruette*, meaning a little jug) are usually simple in their design.

- **Aspergillum:** When we enter a church building, we often dip our fingers into a holy water receptacle and bless ourselves as a reminder of our Baptism. Likewise, at Mass, especially during Easter Time, we often renew our baptismal vows all together and are sprinkled with holy water. The *aspergillum* is the instrument (usually a short, metal tube with a ball at the end that allows for the water to be sprinkled) with which the priest or deacon sprinkles the holy water. When this sprinkling is done, it is called an *asperges* rite (from the Latin *aspergere*, meaning to "spray" or "sprinkle").

"Sacred vessels may be in 'a shape that is in keeping with the culture of each region, provided each type of vessel is suited to the intended liturgical use and is clearly distinguished from [utensils] for very day use.'[123]"

(Built of Living Stones, 164)

Growing up as an altar server, I was quite familiar with all of these vessels and learned their proper names and functions until they were second nature. At the time, many of my fellow altar servers would sometimes refer to various sacred vessels as "that thing." The priest in charge of the altar servers did not look kindly upon one of his crew who was unable to use the proper terminology! It is important for us as a worshiping community to be familiar with the objects used at our celebration of the Eucharist. After all, if we are all truly celebrating this meal, then these objects and vessels are being used by us, not just by the priest!   **~Joe**

REFLECTION

» At Mass, pay attention to the meaning and significance of sacred objects. How well do you understand the meaning and significance of the various sacred objects used in liturgy?

» Examine the stories of the construction of the Ark of the Covenant (Exodus 25) and the building of the Temple (1 Kings 7). How do these stories lay a groundwork for our use of sacred objects in our celebration of the liturgy? What sacred objects' significance or meaning do you not understand?

» What special objects do you have/use in your home life and what are their "stories?" Pay special attention to the people who may be connected to them and the previous experiences they represent. What makes them special? How and when do you use them? How do these familiar objects help you to understand the sacred objects that we use in liturgy?

CHAPTER 12

THE MYSTERY OF THE CROSS

How Did the Cross Become Beautiful?

It is hard to remember that the cross, now a familiar symbol of Christianity, was once the means of brutal capital punishment. Today, we use crosses as decoration. We wear them on our clothing and jewelry. We often romanticize the image of the cross by decorating it with flowers or jewels. Children and young people sometimes make the cross "cute," coloring it in bright colors on sheets of paper or as decoration on notebooks or backpacks. This can lead us to forget what it truly means to prominently display a crucifix in each of our churches. It would be as if you walked into a church and saw a large figure of a dead man strapped to an electric chair displayed prominently for all to see. The image, on its own, is not beautiful or comforting; we find beauty and comfort in its message.

"The Cross is the utterly incommensurable factor in the revelation of God. We have become far too used to it. We have surrounded the scandal of the Cross with roses. Our faith begins at the point where atheists suppose that it must end. Our faith begins with the bleakness and power which is the night of the Cross, abandonment, temptation, and doubt about everything that exists!"

(Ronald Rolheiser, *The Shattered Lantern: Rediscovering a Felt Presence of God*)

The crucifix does indeed symbolize ultimate victory. Yet, unlike other symbols of victory that display a powerful, conquering figure who is in control of the situation, the crucifix displays defeat and loss. Jesus conquers death not with the force of an army, but with surrender. Jesus's Passion, Death, and Resurrection are not something that he accomplishes. Rather, he allows it to happen to him. As Richard Rohr reminds us, "We are, after all, the only religion that worships the victim."[124] The meaning of the Cross is that we find salvation only in letting go and entering into the mystery. We find salvation only when we dismiss the idea that somehow we are in control and can do something to earn it. We find salvation when we come face to face with loss and defeat and realize that God has already been there through his only Son who died for us. The crucifix brings us face to face with the real meaning of life which, as Ronald Rolheiser says, is understood more by *not* understanding than by understanding.[125] When we come face to face with ultimate mystery and bow in reverence, trusting that God is somehow at work and present in whatever we are experiencing, we have discovered the meaning of the Cross.

"More than anything else, the Cross says that God can and must be seen in all things, but most especially in the seemingly sinful, broken and tragic things. The place of the supposed worst becomes the place of the very best. The mystery of the Cross teaches us to be prepared to be surprised about how and where God reveals God's heart. It is beyond our control."

(Richard Rohr, *Hope Against Darkness: The Transforming Vision of St. Francis in an Age of Anxiety*)

There is a man I know named Steve who has been living with the HIV virus for 10 years. The main manifestation of the virus has most often been in the form of pneumonia, which began to strike him more frequently and more severely in recent years. One such time I was visiting him in the hospital and he asked me to pray with him. I did so, and we shared a wonderful experience of proclaiming Scripture, praying some intercessions, and praying the Lord's Prayer. After I had prayed a closing prayer, we ended the same way we began: we each blessed ourselves by making the Sign of the Cross.

At that moment, Steve shared a profound and powerful statement of his faith and of how he had begun to make sense of this experience of sickness within the context of that faith. He told me of how he had recently realized that whenever he made the Sign of the Cross he was doing it over the upper part of his body, which was where the virus was doing the most damage. "I trace the cross," he said, "over my lungs, which is where the sickness is. I bless my sickness." In talking more about this revelation, Steve explained that through that experience, he realized that this sickness was not due to God. This was not a punishment. This was not an experience of God not caring that Steve was sick, or an experience of God abandoning Steve. "This is what has happened to me in my life," Steve said, "and I need to bless it. It's part of who I am now. It's part of my life. I cannot bless myself any longer, without also blessing the sickness. And God is right there with me in it all."

God is there with Steve—and with any of us who have suffered pain, or sickness or loss—through it all. For he has been there first, before us.   **~Todd**

The Sign of the Cross

St. Paul called the cross "God's foolishness" and "a stumbling block" and "an absurdity."[126] In ancient as well as in popular lore, the cross has been said to have the power to turn away evil and demons. We carry the cross in procession at Mass. We incense it at different times in our liturgies. Every Good Friday, we gather as a community to reverence the cross—to kiss it, embrace it, and hold on to it.

In medieval times, people referred to the cross as a "brand," much like the owner's symbol that is burned into the flesh of livestock. If you think about it, that is a rather close comparison. The obvious associations of pain and wound aside, the cross can very much be seen as our "brand." What does a brand do? It identifies to whom something belongs. It serves as a claim the owner has on that object. It has the power to separate its wearer from everything else. What a powerful symbol it is for us and for those around us, then, when we begin our common worship together by not just praying before the crucifix in church, but also by tracing the Sign of the Cross on our very bodies. In this one gesture, we turn that symbol into a living action of faith. We are saying that we are the people of the cross! By marking ourselves with this "brand" we are identifying whose we are—reminding ourselves that we are not in control but belong to Jesus Christ, who surrenders himself to the will of the Father.

"I claim you for Christ our Savior by the sign of his cross."

(Rite of Baptism for Children, 79)

Beginning with Baptism, the presider traced the cross on the forehead of each of us who are baptized and said, "I claim you for Christ our Savior." We are claimed for Christ! And this claiming happens over and over throughout our lives, in all circumstances, in all situations. Throughout a lifetime of reminding ourselves to whom we belong, we are claimed over and over again by the one who has been through suffering and death and now waits to return in glory.

"The *sign of the cross*, on the threshold of the celebration, marks with the imprint of Christ the one who is going to belong to him and signifies the grace of the redemption Christ won for us by his cross."

(Catechism of the Catholic Church, 1235)

A rlene is a woman of Hispanic descent. She ministered as a member of the parish's process of parent preparation for infant Baptism. In the first gathering with parents, she often told the story of how throughout her whole life her mother, aunts, and grandmother had the custom of marking the foreheads of her and of her siblings with the Sign of the Cross whenever they were leaving after a visit, or before going to bed, or before going out somewhere. She tells of how the memory of one of them tracing the Sign of the Cross on her forehead with the thumb had stayed with her all her life. She told the parents of how she herself now practices that same form of blessing with her children, and of how they actually have come to expect it. "They know," she says to the new parents, "that they come for a kiss goodbye or good night, a hug, and the blessing. I want them to grow up with that same sense of God's presence that I always had through those blessings."

This point becomes blatantly clear as Arlene finishes by telling the parents that at her son's funeral, before they closed the casket, one final time she reached in and traced the cross on his forehead, just as she had done the day he was baptized. From Baptism in Christ until he slept the sleep of Christian death in Christ, Arlene's son was marked with the sign that promised victory, even in the face of seeming defeat.

~Todd

The cross of Christ proclaims that death and suffering do not have the final word! The cross proclaims that nothing can separate us from the presence of God that comes to us through Christ. No sickness, no loss, no pain, no suffering, no mishap, no crisis, no outside force, no tragedy can separate us from God, nor can any of it have power over us. After all, we belong to Christ! Sin cannot have us. Sickness and disease cannot have us. Not even death can have us. Christ has us! We belong to him!

"Whether we live or whether we die, we are the Lord's."

(Romans 14:8)

Surrender to the Cross

In today's world of the quick fix, we learn to avoid pain and suffering whenever possible. We are blessed to have medical advances today that can reduce or eliminate pain in many circumstances. The result, however, is that most of us do not know what to do with pain when we do encounter it! By its very nature, the cross of Jesus represents pain and suffering, first and foremost. It is no wonder that we have turned the cross into a sentimental symbol of beauty, because otherwise we would have to face up to the reality it represents: pain! It can often seem easier to try to skirt the pain of bearing the cross, rather than accept that pain.

The scandal of the cross is that to all appearances, it represents the abandonment of Jesus by the Father, the one he called *Abba*, or "Daddy." Its scandal in our own lives is the appearance that we have been abandoned by God in whatever unfortunate circumstance we find ourselves. It can seem very unfair when God does not step in and stop the progress of cancer in a loved one, or stop someone from hurting us. Yet, we know it was through the cross that God's salvation was made manifest in Christ Jesus, and it is through the cross that we experience that same salvation. We know that God does not abandon those who belong to him. We know that, in spite of suffering, or pain, or loss, God is still with us and still present to us in the person of Christ. God meets us through Christ in sickness, death, and suffering, promising that none of it will have the final word.

Jesus does not mince words when it comes to the cross. In all three synoptic accounts of the Gospel, Jesus tells us that anyone who wishes to follow him must pick up their cross.[127] What does this mean? It means that if we wish to follow Jesus, we must not run away from the pain and suffering that come with discipleship but must be open to the grace of God that is encountered there. Through pain and suffering, we mysteriously experience transformation and eventually new life.

It is only by being open to this mystery that we can truly surrender—surrender control, surrender the notion that God somehow *wants* this pain or suffering in our lives, surrender the notion that God has abandoned us in our pain, or surrender the idea that we can have new life and salvation *without* the Cross. Then, we can be led to a new awareness of God in our midst. Like Mary, who experienced the pain of her child's death, we are called to treasure all these things in our hearts. We are called to hold on to the mystery of suffering and pain and instead of trying to solve it, trust in God's power, hold it patiently and faithfully, allowing ourselves to be transformed by it.

"O marvelous power of the cross! O ineffable glory of the passion! There we find the tribunal of the Lord, there the judgment of the world, there the power of the crucified! You have drawn all things to yourself, Lord, and when you stretched out your hands one whole day toward a people who did not believe in you and persisted in discrediting you, the whole world acquired the understanding to confess your majesty!

. . . [Y]our cross is the source of all blessings, the source of all graces; through it, from their weakness, the faithful receive strength, from shame, glory, from death, life. Now, in truth, when the array of sacrifices of the flesh have come to an end, the unique offering of your Body and your Blood swallows up all the differences between the victims; for you are the true Lamb of God who takes away the sins of the world, and you accomplish in yourself all the mysteries, so that all the peoples may form a single kingdom, just as all the victims gave way to one sole sacrifice."

(Pope St. Leo the Great, De Passione Domini)

"O God, who willed that your Only Begotten Son / should undergo the Cross to save the human race, / grant, we pray, / that we, who have known his mystery on earth, / may merit the grace of his redemption in heaven."

(Collect, Feast of the Exaltation of the Holy Cross, The Roman Missal)

REFLECTION

» September 14 is the Feast of the Triumph of the Cross. Use the occasion as an opportunity to reflect deeply upon the significance of the cross of Jesus Christ in our lives and in our worship.

» Spend some time reflecting about the idea of being "branded" or claimed by Christ with the Sign of the Cross. Incorporate the action of signing yourself with the Sign of the Cross into your daily experience.

» Reflect upon what it truly means to identify yourself with Christ. Read the letter of Paul to the Philippians 2:6–11 and reflect upon what it means to sign yourself with the Sign of the Cross that Jesus humbly accepted.

» Pay attention to all of the places in which you see a cross displayed or worn on a typical day. Each time you encounter one, pause for a moment to reflect upon how that cross has claimed you for Christ.

» In Baptism, you were marked numerous times with the sign of Christ's cross with the following words repeated: "Receive the sign of the cross . . ." What do these words mean to you? What does it mean that Christ claims you? What does it mean to identify with Christ and to belong to him? How does this sign separate you or set you apart?

» Where in your life are you experiencing, or have you experienced, Christ's cross? How did you, or how might you now, surrender the idea that this cross is a sign of God's abandonment of you in your need? How does surrendering that notion help you to experience transformation?

PART THREE

Proclaiming the Mystery of the Eucharistic Liturgy

CHAPTER 13

THE MYSTERY OF GATHERING

Forming Community

Normally, boarding an elevator is a very mundane and individual experience. While it's true that a group of individuals may gather on an elevator at the same time, there is usually no sense of community. In fact, if someone attempts to talk to the whole group, it is usually seen as an annoyance. People are entering and exiting on different floors and the goal, for most people, is to do so without interacting with other human beings—that is, of course, unless the elevator you are boarding is going to the top of the John Hancock Building in Chicago! Taking the elevator to the ninety-sixth floor of the Hancock building (the second tallest building in Chicago) is a community experience. It is an "introductory rite," so to speak, to the amazing experience of viewing the city of Chicago from the 96th floor. Since everyone on the elevator is getting on at the same time and getting off on the same floor (the elevator is an express with no stops along the way), and since everyone is gathering for the same purpose, there seems to be a natural sense of community on that elevator ride. People from all over the world pile onto the elevator and gradually begin to speak to one another, asking each other where they're from and how long they've been in Chicago. As the elevator rises and ears begin to pop, the conversation takes a humorous turn as people make jokes about the exciting and swift ride. By the time the elevator slows down to make its stop on the 96th floor, people on the elevator have created a unique bond: their common destination turned a typically individual experience into a sense of community. If you were preoccupied and feeling alone before entering the elevator, the brief ride up to the ninety-sixth floor of the Hancock building would no doubt serve as an effective transition, preparing you to open up, not only to the people around you, but also to the spectacular view that will soon change your perspective!

The same holds true of our Eucharistic liturgies. We arrive as individuals but soon realize that we are here to form community. As we enter the church and greet friends and acquaintances (and are greeted by ministers of hospitality or ushers), we slowly begin to put aside our individualism and take on a "corporate" identity. From there, the greeting, the opening hymn and procession, and the greeting of the priest celebrant all begin to form the Introductory Rites of the Mass, designed to prepare us to become one body and one spirit in Christ. "The assembly should *prepare* itself to encounter its Lord and to become 'a people well disposed.' The preparation of hearts is the joint work of the Holy Spirit and the assembly, especially of its ministers. The grace of the Holy Spirit seeks to awaken faith, conversion of heart, and adherence to the Father's will. These dispositions are the precondition both for the reception of other graces conferred in the celebration itself and the fruits of new life which the celebration is intended to produce afterward."[128]

Transition Time

Whenever we invite people over for a dinner party, we tend to engage in some very simple rituals before ever reaching the dinner table. We greet people at the door, exchange hugs, kisses, and handshakes, invite people to sit down in the living room. We offer them a drink and perhaps some snack foods, and engage in lighthearted conversation (often revolving around the weather, traffic, or busy schedules). We do this because we need to transition from one reality to another. It would be awkward to rush our guests directly to the dinner table and begin serving food. We need time to make a transition from business to pleasure, from isolation to relationship, from individualism to community. As a result, by the time we go to the dinner table, we have begun to form a bond with our guests. In the same way, the Introductory Rites of the Mass allow us to make this transition. We come with all of our seemingly secular problems, headaches, joys, plans, anxieties, and preoccupations of everyday life and begin the task of transitioning to a place where all of these can be integrated into the sacred. We do not leave everything at the door. Rather, we bring in all of our baggage and present it to our brothers and sisters and to God who will transform it and us. Likewise, it is important to remember that what we are entering into is mystery. As discussed in Chapter 7, "The Mystery of Reverence," we do not enter into mystery casually. Rather, we do so with a spirit of reverence. To do so requires a transition from the typically casual and informal nature of our everyday lives.

The Introductory Rites

The purpose of the Introductory Rites is to unify the assembly and prepare it to listen and celebrate. We accomplish this through the following steps.

The Gathering of the Assembly

How we gather informally is crucial to how we gather formally. In one sense, this gathering begins before we even get to the church. From the very start of the day we are involved in actions and rituals that will ultimately lead to our being gathered into the Body of Christ, the Church. How we begin the day, how we deal with other family members, what we do during the time of preparation in order to leave for the church—all of this can be seen as part of the experience that gathers us into a liturgical assembly. Gathering is actually a series of events that leads us as individuals through a transition that makes us part of a community.

Save us, O Lord our God! / And gather us from the nations, / to give thanks to your holy name, / and make it our glory to praise you."

(Entrance Antiphon, Fourth Sunday in Ordinary Time, *The Roman Missal*)

As we enter the place of worship before the Mass begins, we are aware of this process of transition. For example, Gothic church architecture assisted people in this task by placing statues of gargoyles and other frightening images on the outside of the church building, while the inside was adorned with images of the angels and saints. The message was clear: entering through these doors was to be a transition from all that distracts us from God to a place where we cannot help but be aware of God's constant presence. Other forms of church architecture included darkened vestibules that required the eyes of visitors to adjust when entering from the bright sunlight outside and transitioning to the stained-glass-filtered sunlight within. Again, the message was clear: a transition is needed. Finally, many Gothic churches included vast gathering areas that helped to facilitate the people's transition as they assembled for the Eucharist (see Chapter 10, "The Mystery of Sacred Space").

As we gather to worship, we greet our brothers and sisters and are often greeted by ministers of hospitality. Such a greeting reminds us that, by virtue of our Baptism, we are not individuals but members of this body gathering here to worship God. Such a welcome communicates to us that we are about to take part in something extraordinary and that our presence is a key element in the experience that is about to unfold. As we enter the worship space, we engage in rituals that assist us in making this transition. We bless ourselves with holy water as a reminder of our Baptism. We make the Sign of the Cross as a reminder that we are "branded" and that we belong to the Lord (see Chapter 12, "The Mystery of the Cross"). As we approach our seat, we either bow to the altar or genuflect to the tabernacle as a sign of reverence to our Lord who is present. We may spend a few moments in quiet meditation preparing ourselves for the celebration or *quietly* chatting with neighbors (out of respect for those who are trying to quietly meditate) as we continue to bond with the members of our community. As we do so, we may notice liturgical ministers making last-minute preparations, such as lighting candles. Just as we might light a candle or place flowers on the dinner table for a party, we take care with the details in our liturgical space.

Welcome

As we prepare to sing the entrance hymn, a commentator often welcomes us to the celebration. This welcome serves several purposes: it is another gesture of hospitality (especially for those new to the community), and it provides an opportunity to make initial announcements, for example, announcing the day of the liturgical year that is being celebrated. All of this serves to lead us into the celebration and to prepare us to listen to God's Word. Other parish announcements may or may not be read at this time as another way of inviting people to take part in the work of the Gospel that continues after we leave the place of worship. Finally, we are invited to sing the entrance hymn (not to "join the choir in singing" since singing this hymn is our responsibility and the choir assists *us* in singing it!) as a first major step toward joining our hearts, minds, and voices.

Entrance Song and Procession

"When the people are gathered, and as the Priest enters with the Deacon and ministers, the Entrance Chant begins. Its purpose is to open the celebration, foster the unity of those who have been gathered, introduce their thoughts to the mystery of the liturgical time or festivity, and accompany the procession of the Priest and ministers."

(General Instruction of the Roman Missal, 47)

You don't have to be Andrea Bocelli to sing at Mass! Singing is a powerfully profound way of allowing ourselves to open up. When we sing "Happy Birthday" or

"Take Me Out to the Ballgame," we are not self-conscious about our singing ability, we simply belt it out! In the same way, singing in church is not meant to be a performance reserved only for those with golden throats. Some choir directors and cantors delight in reminding the assembly that, "If you don't like the singing voice our Lord gave you, turn around and give it right back to him!" We need only to sing loud enough for the person next to us to hear us; we do not need to sing for the whole assembly to hear.

The entrance song, like all songs of the Mass, is not a time filler. All of the songs are sung prayers of praise. St. Augustine is credited with the famous saying, "When we sing, we pray twice." We need not finish singing the moment the priest and ministers reach the altar. Rather, our prayer of praise should continue until all of the designated verses are sung. As we sing, the first of several processions takes place (later we will encounter the Gospel procession, the procession of the gifts, the communion procession, and the closing procession). Processions are an expression of our faith and our beliefs. In some cultures, processions include, in addition to the ministers of the liturgy, dancers, banner-carriers, drummers, or bell-ringers. All of this is to draw our attention to the act of gathering. Processions are not meant to be the shortest distance between two points. Rather, like parades, they go out of their way to create a spectacle, ritually symbolizing the gathering of hundreds or even thousands of individuals into a community of faith approaching the altar of God. Upon reaching the sanctuary, all of the ministers of the altar bow to the altar as the priest and deacon go even further and kiss it. This is called the veneration of the altar, and it is a sign of reverence to our Lord who, we believe, is symbolized in the altar. Because of this, the priest may at times incense the altar as the entrance hymn continues. This is also a sign of veneration and reverence.

The Sign of the Cross and the Greeting of the People

The very first ritual gesture that we perform after the entrance hymn is the making of the Sign of the Cross. In doing so, we express who we are and whose we are (see Chapter 12, "The Mystery of the Cross"). Following this gesture, the priest offers one of the following greetings:

The grace of our Lord Jesus Christ, / and the love of God, / and the communion of the Holy Spirit / be with you all.

or

Grace to you and peace from God our Father / and the Lord Jesus Christ.

or

The Lord be with you.

So why doesn't the priest just say, "Good morning" like a normal person? Because we are participating in a ritual. The ritual of the Mass contains within it a ritual greeting. Actually, these greetings are taken from Scripture. St. Paul used these greetings in his letters. These ritual greetings remind us that we are not just entering Walmart and being greeted by a friendly welcomer. We are being greeted in a manner that proclaims the Lord's presence in our midst. Our response is also part of the ritual: "And with your spirit." The priest celebrant's greeting is rooted in the writings of

St. Paul, and so is our response.[129] Together, then, with the priest, we are acknowledging through ritual language that we are entering into mystery.

The Penitential Act and the *Kyrie, eleison*

Didn't our parents always tell us to wash our hands before coming to dinner? Before we can sit at the table, we need to rid ourselves of that which would interfere with or taint our dinner. In much the same way, the penitential act prepares us to celebrate the Eucharist by acknowledging our sinfulness and praising Jesus for his forgiveness and mercy. This is not meant to be only an examination of conscience, but an acknowledgment of our sinfulness and, most important, an acknowledgment of God's mercy that comes through Christ. Simply put, the Penitential Act reminds us that God is God and we are not! This is a good frame of mind to have as we enter into the Eucharistic liturgy. The Penitential Act can take various forms. One of the most familiar to many people is the *Confiteor*, a communal recognition of sin that begins with the well-known words, "I confess to almighty God . . ." This is followed by the threefold *Kyrie, eleison*, or "Lord, have mercy."

When we think of the word *mercy*, we often picture someone groveling at the feet of some violent, cruel, and ruthless villain, pleading for his or her life to be spared. Are we asking God for mercy only because we are fearful of incurring some violent punishment or retribution for our sins? Certainly not! When we pray, "Lord, have mercy," we are calling on God in the only way we know him: as one who responds to the needs of those who are suffering. We begin the liturgy by admitting that we have done nothing to earn God's favor. It is only through God's compassion and mercy that we are saved.

Another option for the Penitential Act makes use of the same threefold invocation, "Lord, have mercy." It involves three separate short proclamations of praise to Christ, each followed by the response. These proclamations are addressed directly to Christ and announce some aspect of his divine work of salvation and reconciliation among us. For example, we may hear the cantor proclaim, "Lord Jesus, you came to reconcile us to one another and to the Father: Lord, have mercy. Lord Jesus, you heal the wounds of sin and division: Christ, have mercy." To all three of the proclamations, we answer with the invocation asking for mercy. Notice that the invocation is in direct response to the proclamation made about Christ. It is not a response to a petition or intercession. So, it really isn't appropriate to craft penitential rites that name some particular sin of ours, for example, "For the times we have not listened to your voice: Lord have mercy." The emphasis is on Christ, who is directly addressed, not on us or on our sins. Another option, especially during Easter Time, is for the Penitential Act to be replaced with a sprinkling rite. Consisting of a blessing and sprinkling with water, this rite recalls our Baptism, renounces sin, and praises the Lord for his mercy and forgiveness first shown to us in the waters of rebirth.

"In the Eucharistic liturgy and in the daily prayers of her faithful, the Church implores the mercy of God, who does not want 'any to perish, but all to come to repentance.'[130]"

(*Catechism of the Catholic Church*, 1037)

The Gloria

What better response could we make, in the face of God's great mercy, as we were just reminded of in the Penitential Act, than to offer our praise? This is exactly what we do in the Gloria, as we joyfully sing the words of the angels that rang out on that first Christmas night. The Gloria is an anthem that reinforces, in a more joyful manner, what the Penitential Act just accomplished—namely, positioning ourselves where we belong as sinners before a merciful God. Traditionally, the singing (not the recitation, for we don't say songs) of the Gloria signifies more festive and joyful occasions.

The Collect

"Let us pray." What do we do when the priest says those words? Often, we simply watch as the altar server gets up to carry the Roman Missal to the priest so that "he can pray." Actually, when the priest says "Let us pray," we should do just that—*pray*! The moments of silence that follow are meant to allow us to pray so that we may once again acknowledge God's presence and offer our petitions (remember, we leave nothing at the door, but rather carry in all that we have and offer it to God). The words that the priest offers in the Collect are meant to literally "collect" all of our silent prayers into one spoken prayer. Following a defined pattern, the Collect is always addressed to God the Father. It expresses the theme of the liturgy being celebrated through an acknowledgment of something that God has done for us. It always includes a petition regarding what we hope to gain through the celebration of this Eucharist, and finally it invokes the Trinity, asking that the prayer to be granted "through Christ our Lord." To all of this we reply "Amen," meaning that we make the prayer our own.

Are You Ready?

Having engaged in the Introductory Rites, we are now ready to begin the work that we gathered to do, namely, to listen to God's Word, to offer praise and thanksgiving over the bread and wine which become for us the Body and Blood of Christ, and to be sent forth to proclaim the Good News of salvation to others. As we are seated following the Collect, we make the transition from the Introductory Rites to the Liturgy of the Word. Without these rites of transition, we would not be predisposed to hear God speaking to us in the Scripture readings. Having unified our hearts, minds, and voices and having acknowledged God's presence, we are now ready to open our ears so that the Word of God might touch us and transform us.

"[The purpose of the Introductory Rites] is to ensure that the faithful who come together as one, establish communion and dispose themselves to listen properly to the Word of God and to celebrate the Eucharist worthily."

(*General Instruction of the Roman Missal*, 46)

REFLECTION

» Before going to Mass, reflect for a few moments and make a list of the "baggage" that you are bringing with you to Mass: your joys, sorrows, anxieties, problems, desires, and so on. Be aware of the fact that you do not leave these at the door of the church, but bring them in with you and present them to the Lord during the opening prayer.

» On Sunday, be aware of the many events that ultimately lead to your gathering as part of the liturgical assembly. Make a habit of getting to church five to ten minutes before Mass begins to allow yourself the time you need to make the transition needed to encounter mystery.

» How is the opening procession in your parish community's liturgy a spectacle?

» How would you explain the concept of God's mercy to someone? What are examples of God showing mercy in the Old Testament? What are examples of Jesus showing mercy in the Gospel?

» What impact does God's mercy have on your life? In what areas of your life are you most in need of God's mercy? When and how have you experienced God's mercy in your own life?

» What is your routine for hosting a dinner party? How do you allow your guests to make a transition before inviting them to the dinner table? How does this compare to the Introductory Rites of the Mass?

CHAPTER 14

THE MYSTERY OF THE WORD

Stories To Tell

My parents have a theory about me and my brothers and sisters that they believe very strongly and enjoy repeating over and over: "We find out more things that you've done, which we've never known about, just by listening to you talk and tell stories when you all get together." What they're referring to is probably familiar to most families. It's a plain, simple fact that whenever a family gets together, they tell stories. Some begin with "remember when you did . . ." and others with "remember when you got caught doing . . ." My brothers and sisters and I love it! We start laughing and remembering and soon get caught up in it. Stories that have long since been forgotten trigger memories that come rushing back to everyone. We relive those experiences and situations again and the power of the stories seems to overtake us.

~Todd

If you really want someone to know who you are, tell him or her your story. If you want to really know someone else, ask to hear his or her story. Every one of us has our own story that tells who we are and where we come from. They tell why we are the way we are and they tell how we came to be that way. Individual people have stories, families have stories, and groups have stories. They are one significant way through which we identify ourselves.

The power of story was dramatically portrayed in the groundbreaking book *Roots* by Alex Haley. It demonstrated the power of one particular family's story, and how the retelling of it helped to give a sense of self-identity to each generation that heard it. From the capture of Kunta Kinte in Africa and his sale into slavery in 18th-century America through the years of the Civil War and the post-slavery era, the telling of the family's story helped to give shape to how they understood themselves. It was a source of strength and a means of support for them through struggle and adversity. It provided a context to allow them to understand themselves, and it helped to give voice to the hopes and dreams they had as a family, as members of an oppressed people, as individuals. Indeed, the story of one family's "roots" gave them a basis from which to move forward with hope and courage.

Scripture is Story

As Christians, we too have our stories, namely our Scriptures. Like any family that passes its story from generation to generation, we tell our stories every time we gather together. Like any family, when we, as Christians, tell our stories, we relive them and are strengthened by them. When we read these stories aloud, we are reminded of who we are and of whose we are. These stories remind us of who God is and, in telling them over and over again, our identity as a people of faith is shaped more and more.

These are the holy stories of our salvation. They are the stories of our relationship with God from the very beginning of time, when "the earth was a formless void and darkness covered the face of the deep."[131] Scripture tells of salvation history—the saving actions of God throughout time. These stories are ancient. Even before they were written down, they were passed from generation to generation so that no one would forget the wondrous acts by which God made us, claimed us as his own, and saved us, again and again.

These are the sacred stories of Adam and Eve, of Noah and the ark, of Abraham and Sarah, and of Jacob and Joseph. These are the stories of Moses and Miriam and the ten plagues in Egypt. These are the stories of the Exodus and the crossing of the Red Sea, of the Ten Commandments and the everlasting covenant God made with his people. These are the stories that recount the journey to the Promised Land and the struggles of the Chosen People. They are the stories of the prophets and their continual challenges to the people to remain faithful to the covenant. These are the ancient stories of God's promise to send the Messiah who would bring salvation to the ends of the earth, and these are the accounts of God's fulfillment of that promise in the person of Jesus of Nazareth, the Son of God, the Christ. These are the accounts of Christ's teachings, miracles, suffering, Death, and Resurrection. These are the stories of Christ's early followers, the Apostles. They recount the beginnings of the Church and its spread throughout the world. They tell of the promised return of Christ, in glory, to bring about the everlasting kingdom and reign of God.

These are our stories. They remind us where we have come from and where we are going as God's holy people. They forever hold before us the covenant of God, established first with his Chosen People and then ultimately with all who would believe in his Son, Jesus Christ. Indeed, the Scriptures are the story of our salvation.

"The liturgical celebration and participation of the faithful receive outward expression in actions, gestures, and words. These derive their full meaning not simply from their origin in human experience but from the word of God and the economy of salvation, to which they refer. Accordingly, the participation of the faithful in the Liturgy increases to the degree that, as they listen to the word of God proclaimed in the Liturgy, they strive harder to commit themselves to the Word of God incarnate in Christ. Thus, they endeavor to conform their way of life to what they celebrate in the Liturgy, and then in turn to bring to the celebration of the Liturgy all that they do in life."

(Introduction, *Lectionary for Mass*, 6)

Proclaiming the Story: The Living Word

One of the hallmarks of the revision of the Church's rites (including the celebration of the Eucharist) was the rediscovery of the importance of the Word of God and the importance of its proclamation whenever the Church gathers. In all of the revised rites, this is reflected in the Liturgy of the Word. Every celebration of the sacraments, every rite, every order of blessing, every liturgy, has some format of a Liturgy of the

Word. The result is the wonderfully powerful reality that we don't do anything as a people of faith before we first hear the Word of God proclaimed.

Remember that *liturgy* comes from a Greek word that means "the work of the people." That work begins with the act of listening to the story proclaimed. Likewise, the work of baptizing, marrying, reconciling, confirming, anointing—all of the sacramental liturgies—begins with the work of listening to the proclamation of part of the story. We need to proclaim the saving acts of the Father, through Christ, for those saving acts of God that have brought us to the moment of whatever sacrament or rite we are celebrating.

"The many riches contained in the one word of God are admirably brought out in the different kinds of liturgical celebration and in the different gatherings of the faithful who take part in those celebrations. This takes place as the unfolding mystery of Christ is recalled during the course of the liturgical year, as the Church's sacraments and sacramentals are celebrated, or as the faithful respond individually to the Holy Spirit working within them."

(Introduction, *Lectionary for Mass*, 3)

In the *General Instruction of the Roman Missal* we find this principle expressed: "when the Sacred Scriptures are read in the church, God himself speaks to his people, and Christ, present in his word, proclaims the Gospel."[132] When the Scriptures are proclaimed in the midst of the Body of Christ, gathered for liturgy, they are never meant to be a simple recounting of what once took place a long time ago. When the Scriptures are proclaimed in the liturgy, they are the living Word of God.

This understanding of God's Word comes to us from our Hebrew ancestors. The Hebrew word *dahbar* means "word," but it also means "deed," "action," or "thing." The Word of God is dynamic and active. Recall the very first story in the Scriptures, the story of creation. The recounting of the seven days of creation is marked by a familiar, poetic pattern: God says something, and so it comes into being. God says, "Let there be light," and so there is light.[133] This pattern of God speaking the universe into creation carries throughout the Scriptures. When God speaks, something happens. When God promises something, it comes to be. When God speaks the covenant, it is. When God promises salvation, then those to whom God spoke the promise are saved. We Christians believe that in Christ, God continues to speak, act, and thereby bring about the salvation that he promised. Furthermore, we believe that in the Church, Christ continues to speak and to act. One way we experience that continued presence and action of God in Christ is through the proclamation of the living Word found in the Scriptures.

"For as the rain and the snow come down from heaven, / and do not return there until they have watered the earth, / making it bring forth and sprout, / giving seed to the sower and bread to the eater, / so shall my word be that goes out from my mouth; / it shall not return to me empty, / but it shall accomplish that which I purpose, and succeed in the thing for which I sent it."

(Isaiah 55:10–11)

"In the hearing of God's word the church is built up and grows, and in the sign of the liturgical celebration God's wonderful, past works in the history of salvation are symbolically presented anew. . . . Whenever, therefore, the church, gathered by the Holy Spirit for liturgical celebration, announces and proclaims the word of God, she is aware of being a new people in whom the covenant made in the past is perfected and fulfilled."

(Introduction, *Lectionary for Mass*, 7)

Recall that God's Word *does* something. It is not passive. It has an effect on those who hear it. We noted earlier that the Word of God has the power to shape us and to form us. It also has the power to transform us, to make us anew! Our role is to allow that to happen.

Logos: The Very Presence of God

In the first verses of John's account of the Gospel, we read, "In the beginning was the Word, and the Word was with God, and the Word was God."[134] A few verses later, we read that "the Word became flesh and lived among us, and we have seen his glory, the glory as of a father's only son, full of grace and truth."[135] This is how John's account of the Gospel begins to speak of Christ: as the eternal Word that existed before the creation of the world—*logos*, the identification of Christ as the embodiment of the active, living Word of God that accomplishes that for which it was sent. This deep philosophical and theological concept is best understood when we consider that it refers to Christ who, as the Word of God, reveals the fullness of God. As the Word of God, Christ reveals who God is: Creator, Father, Healer, Savior, and Redeemer. As the Word of God, Christ reveals what God is like: merciful, slow to anger, rich in kindness, just, and righteous. As the Word of God, Christ reveals what God does: forgives, makes whole, strengthens, re-creates, remembers, and promises. As the Word of God, Christ reveals what God wants: justice, compassion, righteousness, mercy, humility, and right relationships.

"[T]he liturgical celebration, founded primarily on the word of God . . . becomes a new event and enriches the word itself with new meaning and power. Thus in the Liturgy the Church faithfully adheres to the way Christ himself read and explained the Sacred Scriptures, beginning with the 'today' of his coming forward in the synagogues and urging all to search the Scriptures."

(Introduction, *Lectionary for Mass*, 3)

As the Word of God, Christ reveals the fullness of God's presence to us. In the liturgy, as an action of the risen Christ, that revelation of God continues. For it is in the liturgy that the fullness of Christ's presence is revealed to us. As we have already seen, one way that Christ's presence is revealed is in the proclamation of Scripture at liturgy. As the *General Instruction on the Roman Missal* asserts, "in the readings . . . God speaks to his people,[136] opening up to them the mystery of redemption and salvation, and offering them spiritual nourishment; and Christ himself is present through his word in the midst of the faithful."[137] Indeed, in the Liturgy of the Word we are reminded, once again, of what God has done for us, and what God, through Christ, is doing for us right now. (For more on this, see Chapter 19, "The Mystery of Christmas Time.")

Structure of the Liturgy of the Word

First Reading

The Liturgy of the Word begins immediately after the Collect, or the opening prayer, of the Mass. Once we have been gathered into a liturgical assembly by the gathering hymn and the Introductory Rites, we are ready to do the work of hearing the Word. Once we are seated and settled following the Collect, the reader or lector approaches the ambo—the table of God's Word. Then, with a clear and deliberate voice, the reader or lector proclaims the First Reading.

Except during Easter Time, when all the readings at Mass are taken from the New Testament, this First Reading comes from the Old Testament. Perhaps it is from one of the prophets or from the Pentateuch (the first five books of the Bible—what our Jewish brothers and sisters refer to as the "Books of Moses," or "The Law"). Perhaps it is from the history of the Hebrew people: from the Chronicles, or the books of Samuel, or the books of Kings. Whatever its source, this First Reading begins to give us the theme or the focus that the Liturgy of the Word is to take. With the end of the reading, the lector proclaims to the liturgical assembly that this is, indeed, "the word of the Lord." How else can we respond but to humbly and simply say, "Thanks be to God"?

Responsorial Psalm

As the reader or lector leaves the ambo, the cantor begins to makes his or her way to the same table of the Word. From there, the cantor will lead the assembly in singing the psalm response. Since the ambo is the table of God's Word, it is most appropriate that this be the place from which the psalm—a piece of Scripture—is sung. Although the psalm may be recited, that option is only a last resort used if there are no music ministers present at the Mass. The psalms are, first and foremost, meant to be *sung*. We respond to God's Word by singing the very songs used by the people of Israel over many centuries. The psalms are ancient Hebrew songs expressing praise, thanksgiving, longing, lamenting, sorrow, and more. We respond to God, who spoke to us in the First Reading, by lifting our voices in song. The psalms are actually more along the lines of what we might call "folk songs." They were written to be sung, not recited. The psalms are not simply pieces of Scripture that the Church sometimes sings. Rather, the psalms are songs that the Church sometimes recites (as at some experiences of daily Mass, when there is no cantor to lead singing). We sing them on Sundays because that is what we're supposed to do.

Second Reading

After the psalm, another lector or reader proclaims the Second Reading, taken from the New Testament. This reading comes from one of the epistles (letters of instruction or guidance to the early Christian communities), from the Acts of the Apostles, or from the book of Revelation. In this reading, if it comes from one of the epistles, the teachings of the Apostles to the early Christian communities are once again proclaimed. Giving direction in how to live a life in Christ, these readings expound on what it means to be a disciple and how we are to conduct ourselves as Christ's follow-ers. If the reading comes from the Acts of the Apostles, we are given a glimpse of the history of the earliest days of the Church after Pentecost. The struggles and graces of the early Church are often mirrors of our own struggles and graces as we strive to live the way of Christ. If the reading comes from the book of Revelation, we hear of the great prophetic vision that describes the fulfillment of the reign of God: the new heavens and new earth that will be established when Christ, the Lamb of God, returns in glory.

Gospel

After the Second Reading, we once again raise our voices, this time in the great song of praise to the Risen One: the Gospel Acclamation. Whether it is "Alleluia" or the Lenten acclamation of "Praise to you Lord Jesus Christ," the Gospel Acclamation is a song that calls us to our feet in reverence and honor for the Gospel. In many parishes, the Book of the Gospels is used at this point in the liturgy. Taken from the altar, where it was placed after being carried in the opening procession, the Book of the Gospels is again processed in the midst of the liturgical assembly. Held high in procession (remem-ber, processions are meant to be a spectacle, not the shortest distance between two points!), it is carried to the ambo, where Christ will once again speak to his disciples.

As the people stand, the priest or deacon begins the familiar formula: "The Lord be with you" to which we respond, "And with your spirit." After we are told which account of the Gospel the selection is from, we respond "Glory to you, O Lord" while making a small sign of the cross with our thumb on our forehead, lips, and breast (symbolizing our desire that the Word of God be in our minds, on our lips, and in our hearts). Then, a selection of one of the four accounts of the Gospel is proclaimed. "The reading of the Gospel is the high point of the Liturgy of the Word. For this the other readings, in their established sequence from the Old to the New Testament, prepare the assembly."[138] Once again, we respond to this gift of God's Word: "Praise to you, Lord Jesus Christ."

Homily

In 1982, the United States Bishops' Committee on Priestly Life and Ministry of the National Conference of Catholic Bishops wrote a document on preaching to the peo-ple of God. In particular, it addressed the preaching of the homily in the context of the Eucharist. *Fulfilled In Your Hearing* is an exhortation to all those who are charged with breaking open the Word of God. A wonderful piece of instruction and teaching, the document calls for preaching that stems directly from the Word proclaimed and that feeds and nourishes those who are present.

It is in the homily that the "today" of the Scriptures is connected to the "today" in the lives of those who have gathered to celebrate the liturgy. The homily does not attempt to simply explain Scripture but "to interpret the human situation through the Scriptures"[139] The homily seeks to connect the living, active Word of God to the very circumstances and situations in which the people of God find themselves on any given Sunday. It is in the homily that the Word of God spoken "today" is connected to the faith, the joys, the struggles, the hopes, the sufferings of those who long to find in their midst the presence of the One who will make them whole. It is in the homily that we find reason to give thanks and praise in the Eucharist that will follow. Liturgical preaching, which seeks to transform rather than just inform, is *vital* to the celebration of the Sunday Eucharist, so vital that the *General Instruction on the Roman Missal* notes that, "On Sundays and Holydays of Obligation there is to be a Homily at every Mass that is celebrated with the people attending, and it may not be omitted without a grave reason."[140] Liturgical preaching does not simply preach about Jesus, but "is, rather, an experience of the personal presence of God as the church worships."[141]

"In the Eucharistic celebration the homily points to the presence of God in people's lives and then leads a congregation into the Eucharist, providing, as it were, the motive for celebrating the Eucharist in this time and place."[142]

(Fulfilled in Your Hearing: The Homily in the Sunday Assembly, p. 23)

The Creed and the Prayer of the Faithful

Whenever people emerge from a theater where they have just witnessed an outstanding performance, they can't help but to describe the experience to others. In their attempts to describe the performance, express their excitement, and convince others to attend, people search for the right combination of words in response to their experience. The Creed, or the Profession of Faith serves as a way "that the whole gathered people may respond to the Word of God proclaimed in the readings taken from Sacred Scripture and explained in the homily."[143]

Like those people coming out of an outstanding performance, we cannot help but burst forth in praise of what we have just heard in the readings and homily. Just as the liturgical assembly will give its assent to the Eucharistic prayer in the "great Amen," so, too, do the people give their detailed assent, in the words of the Creed, to all that has been proclaimed in the Liturgy of the Word. "I believe," we say, in the Father who has just been revealed to us. "I believe," we say, in the Christ who has just spoken to us. "I believe," we say, in the Spirit whose presence makes what we have heard, *living words.* "I believe," we say, in the Church that has preserved these words, has guarded them, and kept them, from one generation to the next. "I believe" in the Church that these words call us to be. Yes, I believe!

At the same time, the Creed further proclaims our story of salvation. While we have just heard some select stories from our salvation history, we summarize the whole story in short form through the Creed. We assert our faith in God, who has extended salvation to us throughout all of history. That faith is further demonstrated when, before the God who has just been revealed, we bring our needs and concerns through the general intercessions of the Universal Prayer or Prayer of the Faithful.

These prayers of petition, like all prayers, are a response to God. Because God has first acted with such power, mercy, and compassion, we respond by asking for more! If, in the Liturgy of the Word, the "today" of which the Scriptures speak is made present in the here and now, if Christ's assertion holds that "today this Scripture has been fulfilled in your hearing,"[144] then the Prayer of the Faithful, or the Universal Prayer, is indeed our response. If we have heard his voice and have not hardened our hearts, then the only proper response is to open our hearts and lay bare the prayers that lie within them. For, in revealing his presence to us today, God already knows those prayers.

There is also another element to the Prayer of the Faithful. In interceding through Christ, for the Church, for the world, for all who suffer and are oppressed, and for the local community, we are exercising the priestly character of our Baptism. In short, we intercede because that is part of our duty and responsibility as baptized members of the Body of Christ. With Christ, the One True Priest, as our head, we fulfill our duty as members of that priestly body to offer intercession. To pray for the world and for all humanity is what we were baptized to do!

This should call into question the "usual" format that our parish uses for the intercessions. By the way they are crafted and prepared, is it obvious that these are the needs of your parish that are being brought before God? Do they truly voice the prayers and concerns of your community, reflecting the real needs and hopes of the people of your parish? Are they "canned"—that is, simply "lifted" from a liturgy resource or missalette—or is there thought and preparation to their development during the week before Sunday? How are they crafted and worded? Do they reflect our belief that God can still act among us and change our lives? Do we believe that our prayers have an effect on the Church, the world, and the local community? How is that reflected in this part of the Liturgy of the Word?

In his pastoral letter on the liturgy to the people of the Archdiocese of Los Angeles, Cardinal Roger Mahony described the intercessions in a most powerful and direct way. This is, he wrote, the time when we "stand before God and demand to be heard."[145] If we truly believe that God hears our prayers and if we truly believe that God has the power to act in our world, in our communities, and in our lives to answer those prayers, then our intercessions will, indeed, come from our hearts and accurately reflect our faith and hope as we give voice to them. It is only then that we will be able to properly lift up our hearts to the Lord in the next part of the Mass, the Liturgy of the Eucharist.

REFLECTION

» Familiarize yourself with the books and the texts that are used for the celebration of the Liturgy of the Word during the Sunday Mass. Examine a Lectionary and the Book of the Gospels and discover what the appearance and beauty of these books say about how we regard the Word of God in our Church.

» One way to more fruitfully prepare for the proclamation of the Word of God on Sunday is to read and reflect upon the Scriptures before Sunday. Reserve some time during the week to quietly read the readings that are given for the coming Sunday. Reflect on how the Scriptures are speaking to you now, at this time in your life.

» Be mindful of how you "hear" the Word of God each Sunday. How attentive are you during the readings and the homily? Do you connect your profession of faith to what you hear in the readings and homily each week? Are you aware that during the intercessions you are exercising your baptismal duty to pray hard to God for the needs of your parish and local community?

CHAPTER 15

THE MYSTERY OF THE MEAL

Staples of Our Lives and Our Worship

The smell of baking bread is one of the most comforting smells. For many, it triggers a host of childhood memories and feelings. The scent of baking bread fills every room of the house and spreads a blanket of comfort and warmth. The smell of wine is different, but no less stirring. It is sweet, and some will say that the scent has a weight to it: "It has a light scent," they say, or "Its aroma is heavy." Sometimes the aroma is pungent with the hint of alcohol or fermentation. In the thoroughly fast-paced, contemporary culture of the United States, we sometimes overlook the simple joys that can come from something as common and as "everyday" as bread and wine. And yet, there is something deep within us that identifies with this "staff of life" and this "blood of the grape." No meal is complete without bread being placed on the table, and if the reason for gathering is at all festive, you can bet that someone will bring the wine. Bread and wine have a history that is as old as humankind. In many cultures, past and present, their value is so recognized that they are used as money: they are something with which to barter. They are seen as some of the necessities of life. They hold permanent places in the routines and rituals of our lives.

"Following the example of Christ, the church has always used bread and wine with water to celebrate the Lord's Supper. The bread for celebrating the Eucharist must be made only from wheat, must be recently made, and, according to the ancient tradition of the Latin Church, must be unleavened. By reason of the sign, it is required that the material for the Eucharistic Celebration truly have the appearance of food. . . . The wine for the celebration of the Eucharist must be from the fruit of the vine,[146] natural, and unadulterated."

(*General Instruction of the Roman Missal*, 320–322)

Every week, these are the gifts that we bring to the altar to be blessed, broken, and then shared by the community. These are the items we use to symbolize our lives and the work of our hands, our thanks and praise to God, and our very selves. They are gifts from God, which we turn around and offer back to God for the Church, the world, our local community, and for those who have died. Fruit of the earth and work of human hands, they are products of our labor and our lives. We bring them, along with ourselves, and ask God to transform them into the presence of Jesus, the Christ. We ask the Father's love and active presence in Jesus to be as common and as "everyday" as the bread and wine. We do all of this every Sunday in the Liturgy of the Eucharist at Mass.

Structure of the Liturgy of the Eucharist

The Preparation of the Gifts

When we give a gift to someone, we never expect to have that gift given back to us! Yet, each week, that is exactly what happens at the Sunday Eucharist. Perhaps that is not quite accurate. Though we do present our gifts at the Eucharist, and though we do expect to have returned to us that which we have given, it must be added that what we give and what we have returned is not at all the same gift.

In the Preparation of the Gifts, gifts are brought to the altar and gifts are given for the needs of others. In the early church, this was the time when the members of the community presented bread and wine, brought from their homes to be shared with the liturgical assembly. The early church collected food and other items for the poor and for the needs and maintenance of the community at this time.

"The offerings are then brought forward. It is a praiseworthy practice for the bread and wine to be presented by the faithful. . . . Even though the faithful no longer bring from their own possessions the bread and wine intended for the liturgy as was once the case, nevertheless the rite of carrying up the offerings still keeps its spiritual efficacy and significance."

(*General Instruction of the Roman Missal*, 73)

In the giving of these gifts, we hand over to God more than just our financial resources for the community. We hand over to God more than the bread and wine, which are to become for us the Body and Blood of Christ. In addition to all of this, we hand over to God our very selves. For in the presentation of the gifts, we bring all that we have, all that we are dealing with at that moment, all that is going on in our lives, and all that we are as God's people. Along with our financial gifts and the bread and the wine, we offer ourselves to God, to be prayed over. In our prayer we ask that we, along with the bread and the wine, will be transformed into the presence of Jesus Christ in our world, our communities, and our families.

When we present the gifts during this rite, we do so in faith and trust that God will "accept the sacrifice . . . / for the praise and glory of his name, / for our good / and the good of all his holy Church."[147]

"Blessed are you, Lord God of all creation. . . ." So begins the Liturgy of the Eucharist. This ancient form of praying, known as the *Berakah*, comes from our Jewish forebears. It is a prayer that blesses God for what God has so lovingly and graciously given us. This form of prayer was a standard part of any meal prayer, and it is used to this day by our Jewish brothers and sisters. In particular, this prayer is part of the Jewish Seder and scholars believe that it most certainly would have been part of the prayers Jesus used at the meal which we know as the Last Supper. We, too, use this ancient blessing to begin the great meal of the Eucharist.

"Blessed are you, Lord God of all creation, / for through your goodness we have received / the bread we offer you: / fruit of the earth and work of human hands / it will become for us the bread of life. / . . . / . . . we have received / the wine we offer you: / fruit of the vine and work of human hands / it will become our spiritual drink."

(Preparation of the Gifts, *The Roman Missal*)

The Eucharistic Prayer

After the Preparation of the Gifts, the priest invites all those present to pray with him, to lift up their hearts to the Lord. This is the preparation for the great prayer to follow, the Eucharistic Prayer. The *General Instruction of the Roman Missal* calls this the "high point of the whole celebration."[148]

Now, some people take this to mean that the Eucharistic Prayer is the most important part of the Mass. This is a misconception. The Mass has no "most important part." The liturgy as a whole, taken and understood as one prayer from start to finish, is the "most important part." This single prayer, however, the longest prayer of the whole liturgy, is that around which the other parts of the Mass are situated. All that comes before the Eucharistic Prayer prepares us for it. The Introductory Rites shape us into one body in order to pray it. The Liturgy of the Word tunes our minds, hearts, and souls to God's saving actions in our world so that we can properly celebrate the Eucharist, which is itself the *next experience* of God's saving action in our lives. The Universal Prayer, or Prayer of the Faithful, and the Preparation of the Gifts further prepare us to celebrate the mystery of Christ's presence in the Eucharistic elements— the bread and the wine. All these aspects of the liturgy help us to pray with the priest, who offers this great prayer of praise of thanksgiving in our name.

Recall that the word *eucharist* comes from the Greek, meaning "thanksgiving." Indeed, that is at the heart of this prayer. The preface to the Eucharistic Prayer helps to prepare us for this by noting some aspect of God or of his presence and action in our world for which we are thankful. Here we remember that we are to give thanks to God our Father. The preface calls us to unite our thanks and praise to that of the angels and saints, who are already and forever singing at the heavenly banquet table. Fittingly, every preface ends with the wonderful acclamation that calls the liturgical assembly to proclaim, "Holy, holy, holy Lord God of hosts. . . ." (see Chapter 9, "The Mystery of Song," for a more detailed discussion of the Holy, Holy, Holy).

The Eucharistic Prayer itself is a combination of many parts that all work together to form a single, beautiful whole. Once we have recalled our need to give thanks to the Father for all that we have and for all that he has done, the prayer then moves to ask God to continue showing that same power and glory. The prayer asks God to send the Holy Spirit upon the gifts that we have brought to the altar. This part of the prayer is called the *epiclesis* and it shows us the transforming power of God's Spirit. Just as "in the beginning" the Spirit transformed chaos into the created world, so now do we call upon God to send the Spirit and to transform our gifts into the presence of Jesus, the Christ.

Only a few of our official liturgical prayers have this consecratory element to them. In addition to the Eucharistic Prayer of the Mass, the prayer that is said over the sacred chrism is also a prayer of consecration. In this prayer, the bishop of a diocese asks God to send the Spirit over the chrism and to make of it a sign of Christ's presence and action among us. In a similar way, the blessing of water from the Easter Vigil is a prayer of consecration. In that prayer, the priest asks God to send the Holy Spirit upon the water of the font, giving it the "grace of [God's] Only Begotten Son."[149] In all these prayers, we ask that the Holy Spirit transform whatever is being prayed over, that it may become a vehicle for God's action and presence through Christ.

At this point in the Eucharistic Prayer we remember the action and words of Jesus on "the night he was betrayed."[150] Reciting the words of institution, the priest takes the bread and the wine, and, once again, the promise is given that "this is my Body" and "this is my Blood." Once again, we are called to "do this in memory" of the One who offered everything he had to the Father: his thanks, his praise, his trust in God's faithfulness, and his very life. Such an act, such a remembrance, can only be followed by joyful acclamation! For this reason, the Eucharistic Prayer calls for the liturgical assembly to proclaim the mystery of our faith—that "When we eat this Bread and drink this Cup, / we proclaim your Death, O Lord, / until you come again." The prayer continues by recalling the actions of Jesus by which we have been saved: his life, his Death, and his Resurrection. This part of the prayer is very much like a profession of the most basic elements of our faith: those things that we believe about Jesus that make us his followers, his disciples, his brothers and sisters. This is the *anamnesis* of the Mass, the recalling or remembering of our salvation through Christ. We recall how Jesus suffered, died, and rose again.

After this, the Eucharistic Prayer once again calls upon the Holy Spirit to come and act among us. We pray that through this memorial, the Spirit may come upon the whole gathered liturgical assembly, as well as the whole Church. As we pray for Christ's presence in the sacred elements on the table, so do we pray for Christ's presence in us. As we offer, through the prayer said by the priest, this "sacrifice of praise,"[151] we do so for the Church, the pope, our own bishop, and our priests, together with all the people who have been claimed by Christ, the spotless Lamb.

"The Priest . . . associates the people with himself in the Prayer that he addresses in the name of the entire community to God the Father through Jesus Christ in the Holy Spirit. Furthermore, the meaning of this Prayer is that the whole congregation of the faithful joins with Christ in confessing the great deeds of God and in the offering of Sacrifice."

(*General Instruction of the Roman Missal*, 78)

The intercessions follow the offering as we pray for the Church, for the peace of the world, for the dead, and for all those who are gathered around the table of the Lord. Then, the concluding doxology marks the formal end to the Eucharistic Prayer. We acknowledge that in all that has been prayed and done "through him, and with him, and in him, / O God, almighty Father, / in the unity of the Holy Spirit, / all honor and glory is yours, / for ever and ever." *Doxology* is a word that refers to any prayer that explicitly gives glory and praise to the Triune God, as does, for example, the traditional prayer of the Glory Be. Indeed, the Eucharistic Prayer gives God glory and praise. We give our assent to this offering and to all that has been prayed up to this point in the prayer through the final acclamation, the Amen. "Yes," we say, through our Amen, "so be it! So be this prayer. So be all that has been prayed here in our names."

Which Prayer To Use?

Parish liturgy committees spend a great deal of time preparing for special liturgies. There are long discussions about what music to use, or how to prepare the environment. When the time comes to choose which Eucharistic Prayer to use, however, the discussion often comes to a halt. Somehow, the idea of looking at the many options for the Eucharistic Prayer, identifying their differences, seeing what is emphasized in each one, and choosing the one that best fits the celebration just doesn't occur to us. Yet, each one of the options for the Eucharistic Prayer is different in terms of wording, imagery, and flow. Though they all have the basic elements described above, there are times and celebrations in which one may be better suited than the others.

Before the Second Vatican Council, when the liturgical rites and texts were revised, there was only one prayer used at Eucharist throughout the whole Catholic Church. The council fathers, however, recognized the need for other prayers to be available for use. As a result, there are now many approved Eucharistic Prayers for use around the world. Here in the United States, there are ten approved prayers. Four of these prayers—Eucharistic Prayers I, II, III, and IV— are the ones usually chosen for Sundays. Each one has its own style and character.

Eucharistic Prayer I, known as the Roman Canon, is the one prayer that was used prior to the Second Vatican Council. The longest of the four, it is often used for special, solemn occasions.

Eucharistic Prayer II is the shortest of the four prayers, and it is based on an ancient prayer from the beginning of the third century, known as the Prayer of Hippolytus, a Roman priest.

Eucharistic Prayers III and IV were new compositions that were created after the Council. They are actually a culling of various prayers that were used throughout our Church's history. Prayer IV includes a beautiful summary of the key elements of salvation history. In a sense, it has a built-in profession of faith that makes this prayer ideal for use at Masses where initiation is being celebrated.

In addition to these four prayers, we have three Eucharistic Prayers for use at Masses where the liturgical assembly is made up primarily of children. While they are full Eucharistic Prayers, they have been written in a style and language that is easily understood by children and in which they can be especially engaged. There are also two Eucharistic Prayers for reconciliation, which are appropriate for use when that particular theme is emphasized in the Mass being celebrated—for example, during the season of Lent or during a retreat.

Finally, the most recently approved Eucharistic Prayer for use in the United States is a prayer that is called "Eucharistic Prayer for Use in Masses for Various Needs and Occasions." This Eucharistic Prayer has four prefaces from which to choose and is for use when the Mass is being celebrated for various circumstances of Christian life, for the needs of the whole world, and for the needs of the Church, both local and universal.

Often, a careful reading of these prayers will help determine which would be best to use in a particular celebration. They are not, however, simply the "domain" of the liturgy committee, or of the parish leadership, or of the priest. As people of faith who hear these words every Sunday, week to week, season to season, and year to year, we all are invited to become familiar with them. Although they are the prayers voiced by the priest on Sunday, they could be used for personal meditation and preparation during the week as we get ready for each Sunday. As part of our personal prayer life, we might more easily connect to the prayer when it is prayed on Sunday, in our name and in the name of the whole Church.

The Communion Rite

The sharing of communion, which began in the Eucharistic Prayer, reaches its fullness in the Communion Rite. Like the Eucharistic Prayer, this rite is actually made up of many elements, all of which prepare us to approach the table of the Lord to receive the Bread of Life and the Cup of Salvation.

The Lord's Prayer

In this experience of God's saving action and presence here and now, we stand as a people, assembled by the God whom Christ called "Abba," or "Daddy." In the spirit of sons and daughters, we pray for sustenance and forgiveness. In the Lord's Prayer, the one prayer that unites us with all those who are called Christian, we acknowledge that, like Christ, we are completely dependent on God. We ask for bread—daily bread as well as the Bread of Life. We ask for forgiveness and pray for the strength to forgive those who "have sinned against us." Finally, we ask to be delivered from all that threatens to separate us from the love of God, the fullness of which is shown in the very Eucharist being celebrated.

The Rite of Peace

Next, we turn to one another and share the peace for which we have just prayed, the peace that foreshadows the kingdom for which we have just prayed. Peace seems to be a rare commodity these days. The news is constantly filled with the national and international experiences of anything but peace. Peace is one of the most basic characteristics of the reign of God. Isaiah the prophet says that peace will identify God's reign when it is finally established, and peace shall reign on God's holy mountain.[152] In the Gospel accounts of the events of the Resurrection, Jesus's first words to the Apostles who were hiding were, "Peace be with you." Today we certainly do long for peace in our hearts, in our families, in our communities, and in our world. God's love and the peace that comes from it are the basis for this rite, which precedes our sharing in the Eucharist. We turn to one another and, with whatever gesture we use, whether a handshake, embrace, or a kiss (which was the initial gesture called for in the early days of our history), we share the words, "Peace be with you." The words we say to each other during this rite are the exact words Jesus used in the Gospel. Once again, the liturgy calls us to be Christ to one another. In this rite of sharing the peace of Christ, the Church follows the words of the Master who said, "So when you are offering your gift at the altar, if you remember that your brother or sister has something against you, leave your gift at the altar and go; first be reconciled to your brother or sister, and then come and offer your gift."[153] Only after we have shared a portion of the peace that is promised in fullness are we ready to approach the table of the Lord and share in the meal.

Fraction of the Bread

In the Acts of the Apostles, the celebration of the Lord's Supper is actually referred to as "the breaking of the Bread."[154] It is in this action that the early church identified the Eucharist, and it is this action today that is one way we express our belief in the unifying power of the Eucharist. As the Body of Christ is one body made up of many parts, so is the Eucharistic Body of Christ one, though broken into many parts. The wine, too, is shared and "poured out . . . for many." During the Fraction of the Bread, the Lamb of God is sung. The text from this litany comes from the Gospel according to John and recalls John the Baptist's identification of Jesus as the Lamb of God, alluding to the customary offering that was made at the Temple.[155] A "spotless lamb" was sacrificed in atonement for sins during the Passover. John's allusion is, for Christians, the identification of Christ as the final offering that would bring complete atonement in his self-offering on the cross. We sing this litany still, calling upon the spotless Lamb to have mercy on us and to grant us peace. Likewise, we recall the story of the Exodus when the people of Israel were saved by the blood of the lamb.[156] When we refer to Jesus as the "Lamb of God," we are not describing him as being cute and cuddly. Rather, we are invoking the imagery of an innocent man who was the victim of a bloody and violent execution, knowing that our salvation was made possible by the blood of the Lamb. Then begins the great procession to the table. The liturgical assembly, after recognizing their great need for the Lamb who was slain[157] calls out, "Lord, I am not worthy / that you should enter under my roof, / but only say the word / and my soul shall be healed." This acclamation of the assembly recalls the centurion whose faith, as a Gentile, was the impetus for Jesus's healing of his servant.[158] We, too, acknowledge that we could never be truly worthy of such a gift given as that of Christ himself. And yet, calling upon the mercy of God, which alone can make us worthy (justified), we are able to approach the table.

The Communion Procession

We as Catholics are a Eucharistic people. Since the very beginning of our faith's tradition, we have been a people for whom the Lord's Supper was a distinguishing action. For the first years of the church, in fact, members of the community would attend services at the synagogue on Saturday (remember, the first Christians were Jewish), and then on Sunday, the Lord's Day, they would gather again for the meal. As we noted earlier, the Acts of the Apostles records that the first members of the church "devoted themselves to the apostles' teaching and fellowship, to the breaking of the bread and the prayers."[159] In later generations, once Christianity became separated from its Jewish roots, Eucharist—that is, being admitted to the table of the Lord and sharing with the community in the Body and Blood of Christ—was the culminating experience of initiation into the faith. People were fully initiated only when they were finally admitted to share at the table. This is how distinguishing the sacred meal is for us.

The importance is not lost today. The Rite of Christian Initiation for Adults (RCIA) still highlights the centrality of the Eucharist for adults entering the faith. The documents of the Second Vatican Council emphasize how the Eucharist is the very source and summit of our Christian life. This experience is at the very heart of our lives as baptized members of Christ's Body. It is the summit of our work, our prayer, and our relationships with God and with one another. At the same time, it is the source that empowers us to maintain and develop our relationships and our individual Christian lives.

The Eucharist still defines who we are. We are the people who, Sunday to Sunday, week to week, season to season, and year to year, walk to the table and, with all that we are and all that we have, stretch our hands out to receive the Bread that brings us salvation. We are the people who take the Cup and, recalling Christ's words to the disciples who vied for position in his kingdom, dare to drink the cup that Christ drinks.[160]

The procession to the table is the very icon of our spiritual life. We are, forever, on a pilgrimage to the heavenly banquet. Our whole life is a metaphor for that one great journey upon which our Baptism sets us. Beginning there, in the waters of death and new life, our journey of spiritual growth and development is found in the constant returning to the table each week. There we are nourished and sustained in this journey, and there we see a foretaste of what is ours for all eternity. The communion procession mirrors our whole life of faith. Eating the Bread of our salvation, and drinking from the Cup, we take part in the Lord's Last Supper, which he shared with his closest disciples on the night before he died.

When We Eat This Bread and Drink This Cup

"Then [Jesus] took a cup, and after giving thanks he gave it to them, saying, 'Drink from it, all of you; for this is my blood of the covenant, which is poured out for many for the forgiveness of sins'."

(Matthew 26:27–28)

Taking communion from the cup has been part of our tradition's meal since the very beginning of the Church. In the first centuries of the church's history, to eat and drink, in the name of the risen Lord, was one of the most identifying characteristics of the Christian community. Neglecting to take from the cup bordered on heresy in the early Christian community. While the early church always invited the assembly to partake of the cup, as time went on, the practice declined. By the end of the 16th century and the Council of Trent, reception from the cup was so infrequent that the Church decided to withhold communion from the cup for the assembly entirely. It was during the Second Vatican Council that we regained our sense of what it means to have our words more closely match our actions (the liturgy refers to "our spiritual food and drink"[161]). The revision of the rites included a return to the practice of sharing from the cup for all who are present at the liturgy. Through our Baptism, we are called to be the community that eats and drinks with the risen Lord.

"Holy Communion has a fuller form as a sign when it takes place under both kinds. For in this form the sign of the Eucharistic banquet is more clearly evident . . ."

(*General Instruction of the Roman Missal*, 281)

At the same time, receiving the sacrament of the Eucharist is an expression of our communion with Christ, with one another, and with the Church and its mission. As we have seen, to eat of the one Bread is to express our unity as the one Body of Christ. To drink from the Cup is to express our commitment to the Church's mission. In the Garden of Gethsemane, Jesus prayed, "My Father, if it is possible, let this cup pass from me; yet not what I want but what you want."[162] In the same way, when we come forward to drink from the Cup to receive the life of Jesus, we are also expressing our commitment to the mission of the Church. It is no accident that within a few minutes of receiving from the Cup, we are sent forth to carry out the mission with the words, "Go in peace glorifying the Lord by your life."[163]

Of course, we have to remember to take responsibility for ourselves and for others in community. This would mean that anyone with a contagious condition, for example, would prudently refrain from the Cup until he or she was healthy again. It is important to note that the Centers for Disease Control, in Atlanta, Georgia, has never reported the communion cup as a source of disease transmittal. Studies have shown that there is more possibility of passing germs from handling a missalette than from drinking from the cup! "As often as you eat this bread and drink the cup," Paul writes, "you proclaim the Lord's death until he comes."[164] Our participation in the full meal aspect of the Eucharist ensures this proclamation: in both our eating and our drinking.

The communion procession ends after everyone has returned to his or her seat, and the priest has returned to the chair. The *General Instruction of the Roman Missal* notes that at this time a period of silence is observed for prayer and reflection on what we have just dared to do. It is interesting that this directive can often be overlooked in some parishes. We often get so caught up in our own battle with the clock that we miss just this opportunity that the rite offers us. Often the state of the parish parking lot dictates the schedule and timing. Not only do we have the option for silent prayer, but the rite also allows for the singing of a communal song of thanksgiving at this point. Since the liturgical assembly has just finished the hymn or song that accompanied the communion procession in most parishes, however, the option for silence seems to make sense here.

Prayer after Communion

At the end of this period of silence, the Communion Rite comes to a close with the priest praying the Prayer after Communion. Short and concise in its structure, this prayer asks of God that the sacrament just celebrated might have some effect on those of us who have shared in it. We pray that this Eucharist may bear fruit in our lives and in the life of this community. May we truly become what we receive: the broken Body of Christ, poured out for the sake of the world. Amen.

REFLECTION

» Consider your own participation in the Liturgy of the Eucharist. See how each element connects to your own life of faith. Resolve to be especially mindful to the praying of the Eucharistic Prayer and identify which parts of this great prayer speak the loudest to you in your own faith journey.

» What are ways in which you connect your own life to the different elements of the Liturgy of the Eucharist?

» How would you describe your understanding of the bread and wine being transformed into the Body and Blood of Christ at the Eucharist? How do you refer to the consecrated elements of the Eucharist: do you still call it "bread" and "wine," or do you refer to it as the Body and Blood of Christ? (This is not meant to be a "trick question." How we refer to the consecrated elements says something about what we truly believe.)

» When you go to Mass, you are taking part in something that, at one time in our Church's history and even still today in some parts of the world, would condemn someone to death. What does this mean for you now, at this point in your life?

» How "present" are you to the various elements of the Liturgy of the Eucharist? In this part of the Mass, are you aware of your part in the prayer? Do you take part in the acclamations and responses with enthusiasm and conviction? Do you understand that the priest is voicing the prayer in the name of the whole Church, which includes you?

CHAPTER 16

THE MYSTERY OF DISMISSAL AND DISCIPLESHIP

A Minor Rite with Major Implications

In its simplest form, the Concluding Rites of the Mass can be accomplished with a minimum of 34 words, a Sign of the Cross, a procession, and a song. All told, this simple rite can come and go in the blink of an eye, literally taking little more than 60-90 seconds.

> Priest: **The Lord be with you.**
>
> People: **And with your spirit.**
>
> Priest: **May almighty God bless you, the Father, and the Son, and the Holy Spirit.**
>
> People: **Amen.**
>
> Priest: **Go forth, the Mass is ended.**
>
> People: **Thanks be to God.**
>
> (Concluding Rites, *The Roman Missal*)

So why devote an entire chapter to something so seemingly insignificant? Simply because there is nothing minor or insignificant about being sent forth on a mission from God. For fans of classic comedy films, that phrase, "on a mission from God," conjures up images of Dan Aykroyd and John Belushi in *The Blues Brothers*.[165] In that movie, Jake and Elwood Blues tirelessly (and hilariously) struggle to raise money to save an orphanage because, as they are fond of saying, they are "on a mission from God."

In a very serious and literal way, we Catholics are on a mission from God—a mission that was bestowed upon us the day we entered the waters of Baptism. As disciples of Christ, we are entrusted with proclaiming the Good News to the ends of the earth. Each time we gather for the Eucharist, we are renewed, instructed, fortified, challenged, and commissioned to carry out this mission. The Concluding Rites, although brief and simple, are the punctuation mark that sends us forth so that we might resume "good works, praising and blessing God."[166] The Concluding Rites of the Mass need not be elaborate since the preceding rites, specifically the Liturgy of the Word and the Liturgy of the Eucharist, very clearly, adequately, and eloquently articulate our mission. Like runners who have prepared thoroughly for a race through drills and strategy sessions, we need only to hear, so to speak, the sound of "on your mark, get set, go!" in order to know exactly where our feet should be taking us next.

Mission: Possible

In the classic TV and movie saga, *Mission: Impossible*,[167] Mr. Phelps, the main character and leader of the Impossible Mission Force, was the regular recipient of a recorded message. The voice on the recording would identify in detail the task they were being assigned. The voice would then say, "Your mission, should you decide to accept it, . . ." followed by a description of the complex strategies to be followed in order to defeat the evil forces at work. Finally, after all the complex details (including the famous "this tape will self-destruct in five seconds"), the voice simply said, "Good luck, Jim." With those simple concluding words, the real work of making an impossible mission possible began.

In much the same way, the Concluding Rites at Mass send us forth with a few simple words to begin the real work of undertaking what may seem like an impossible mission: bringing the Good News of Jesus into every aspect of our lives and world. Like the *Mission: Impossible* tape that dissolves in smoke when the message is concluded, leaving no trace of itself behind, our ritual celebration of the Eucharist "dissolves" as we are dismissed from a now-empty altar, leaving no external trace of the bread and wine that only moments earlier was before our very eyes. Filled with the Body and Blood of Jesus and "armed" with the Good News, we set forth to proclaim our firm belief that with God, all things are possible!

Unlike the Impossible Mission Force, who concealed their identity in order to accomplish their goal, we boldly reveal our identity as disciples of Christ. We leave in unison, knowing that without one another's support and strength, this mission would indeed be impossible. We leave with a song of praise on our lips, announcing for all who would hear that we are indeed on a mission and that we will indeed overcome all obstacles.

"Go!"

If you look closely at the last words said by the priest or deacon in the Concluding Rites, you will not find the words "Let us go" but only "Go forth." This final utterance is not a suggestion or invitation to be considered by those present but, rather, a command, a mandate, an imperative. We were told very clearly that the work of the Body of Christ has only begun here in church. The bulk of the work of the people is now to take place in the streets, neighborhoods, villages, towns, cities, workplaces, and communities of our world. We are "on assignment."

The following story illustrates this sense of mission. A priest was once taking a group of children on a tour of the church. At one point, he asked the young people to point out what they thought was the most important location in the church, hoping to use the opportunity to explain the altar, the tabernacle, and so forth. Before anyone else could raise a hand, a young man blurted out, "The exit sign!" The priest, somewhat perturbed by what he thought was a wisecrack, invited the young man to explain why he thought the exit sign was so important. Without hesitation the boy replied, "Because that's where we're supposed to take the Gospel!"

With this in mind, we are indeed dismissed to carry out our mission. In fact, the very word *Mass* is derived from the Concluding Rites. In Latin, the priest or deacon says, "*Ite, missa est!*" which means, literally, "Go, (the assembly) is dismissed!" It is this word *missa* that gives us the word *Mass*. In other words, when we say that we are going to Mass, we are saying that we are going in order to be dismissed! We are truly a people who are being sent; ambassadors, as it were, to borrow a term from St. Paul[168] and from the world of diplomacy. In fact, when we say in the Creed we are "one, holy, catholic and apostolic church," we must recall that the word *apostolic* means not only that we trace our roots to the apostles, but also that we count ourselves among "those who are sent."

It would seem that the Concluding Rites of the Mass are quite important if the word *Mass* itself emerged from the act of dismissal. The exits of our church buildings are the crucial portals through which we pass in order to begin the real work of the Gospel: the transformation of the world, in Christ, through the power of the Holy Spirit. How we leave will determine the extent to which we will truly carry out our mission. The Concluding Rites consist primarily in "the Dismissal of the people by the Deacon or the Priest, so that each may go back to doing good works, praising and blessing God."[169]

Every Second Counts

Here's some classic sports history: during the 1990s, the Chicago Bulls enjoyed a dynasty amassing six championships under the leadership of Michael Jordan and Scottie Pippen. In the middle of that championship run, Michael Jordan retired for the first time. In their first year without Jordan, the Bulls enjoyed a great season and made it deep into the playoffs, only to eventually bow out. During one crucial playoff game before their elimination, the Bulls had the ball with 1.8 seconds left on the clock and a chance to win the game with one final shot. Everyone, including Scottie Pippen, figured that Scottie would get the ball. When coach Phil Jackson announced that, instead, the ball would go to teammate Toni Kukoč, Pippen vehemently protested. When his protest went unheeded, Pippen took himself out of the game to the dismay and anger of his coach and his teammates. Kukoč hit the winning shot, but the damage to Scottie Pippen's reputation had been done. By separating himself from the rest of the team and acting independently, Pippen damaged what had been seen as a tightly knit unit, and had shown great disrespect for his teammates. You wouldn't think that leaving 1.8 seconds early could cause so much damage, but in a basketball game, it can be quite dramatic.

What about leaving Mass early? When it comes to the end of Mass, we sometimes find ourselves and others leaving at all different times without giving it a second thought! "What's the big deal?" we may ask. "I'm just trying to beat the crowd to the parking lot!" Leaving the church after Mass is not like leaving a theater or stadium after a show or event. It is a ritual action. The problem is that, when we take it upon ourselves to leave as soon as we have received Communion, or before the Concluding Rites and Closing Song are finished, we are diminishing the value of this ritual action by separating ourselves from the "team" and breaking up our unity. Certainly, there are times when our early departure is justified. Sometimes a member of the family feels unwell, or there are important travel arrangements that cannot be changed. If we are simply leaving, however, because we think the "important" parts of the Mass are over, or because we're trying to get out so that we can be first, we are showing a lack of respect and reverence for the liturgy as well as for the assembly. As those who are in communion with one another and with our God, we leave from our liturgy as a people, shoulder-to-shoulder, united in our mission, and united in our love for one another. We leave with a song on our lips so that as we go forth to carry out this mission, we do so while giving praise to God.

God's Blessing Sends Us Forth

In *Fiddler on the Roof*,[170] each of Tevye's daughters, one by one, seeks his blessing as they embark upon a life of marriage based on love, not on the traditional arrangement of a matchmaker. Without Tevye's blessing, they feel paralyzed, unable to continue with their lives unless they know they are in good favor with their father. The Concluding Rites of the Mass provide each and every one of us with the same opportunity to embark on our journey, knowing that it is with our Father's blessing that we are sent forth. Although very brief, the blessing at the end of Mass is crucial to our transition from the work we have done at liturgy to the work we will do in the world. It is important to know that, if we are being sent forth to do God's work, we indeed have God's blessing!

To be blessed is the wish of every human heart. We all desire to achieve a blessed state. Too many people go through their lives regretting that they never felt they had their parents' blessing. A blessing, however, is something that comes from outside of ourselves. A blessing necessarily involves a benefactor (one who imparts the blessing) and a recipient (one who receives the blessing). In Scripture, blessings often are obtained through a mediator who goes between the benefactor and the recipient. In fact, in order to better understand just what a blessing is and does, we need to look more closely at Scripture.

> Praise God from whom all blessings flow!
> Praise Him all creatures here below!
> Praise Him above ye heavenly host!
> Praise Father, Son and Holy Ghost!
>
> ("The Old Hundredth")

In the Old Testament, we encounter the notion of blessing in the very first chapter of Genesis. As God creates the heavens and the earth, he blesses first the natural world and then, most importantly, human beings. The creation story tells us that God's favor has been bestowed upon us and upon our world since the very beginning of time. Throughout the Old Testament, the tradition of passing on God's blessing fell to the father of the family, like in *Fiddler on the Roof*. This blessing was much more than simply "best wishes." A blessing in the Old Testament was efficacious, meaning that the very utterance of the words was expected to bring about or accomplish what they were saying. In other words, once the words passed the lips of the father, the results were inevitable.[171]

The idea of God's blessing also involved the notion of God's covenant beginning with God's promise to his people. This promise was, however, conditional: if the people obeyed, the promise or blessing would be renewed or sustained. At the same time, this blessing was still considered unearned—a gift of grace bestowed freely by God out of divine generosity. If, however, the people were unfaithful, then God's blessing was to be withdrawn. Thus, during times such as the Exile, the people of Israel knew that their only hope was repentance and adherence to the covenant so that God's blessing could once again become a reality in their lives.

Throughout the Old Testament, God's blessing is manifested in its most obvious form through material prosperity. In the New Testament, however, we encounter a shift in our understanding of God's blessing. In Jesus, blessedness is seen as a spiritual state for those who are living in the kingdom of God (those who are doing God's will). God's blessing is seen less as material prosperity and more as a spiritual inheritance. The focus is less on a chosen nation but instead on those who do the will of God.

"[While Jesus was speaking], a woman in the crowd raised her voice and said to him, 'Blessed is the womb that bore you and the breasts that nursed you!' But he said, 'Blessed rather are those who hear the word of God and obey it!'"

(Luke 11:27–28)

In the context of our liturgy, we continue to see God's blessing as a most powerful prayer. Through God's blessing, we come to know that God's power and favor are being placed at our disposal for our safety and well-being. This sense of God's blessing comes through the many options available for the Final Blessing of the Mass. Though we have cited the most concise option here, the liturgy actually offers a host of other forms to use. The Solemn Blessing is an extended form that consists of three short blessings or invocations that pick up on a particular aspect of the liturgical occasion (a solemn feast, like Pentecost or All Saints) or season (Advent or Lent). To each of these individual blessings, we respond with our "Amen," and the blessing ends with the familiar, "And may the blessing of almighty God, / the Father, and the Son, and the Holy Spirit, / come down on you and remain with you for ever."[172]

The other form of blessing that may be used is what is called a Prayer over the People. It actually consists of a short collect prayer (see Chapter 13, "The Mystery of Gathering") that the priest prays over the people before the blessing. The prayer used in this blessing always includes a short intercession that recognizes our dependence upon God, our faith in God's care, and God's concern for us. For each of the kinds of blessings, other than the simple form, there is a formal invitation given by the deacon or the priest: "Bow down for the blessing." The priest then extends his hands out over the people as the blessing is sung or said.

Though there may be various forms, the result of God's blessing is always the same: we are not only strengthened and reaffirmed, but our identity as disciples of the Lord is both renewed and intensified. Our "Amen" is not simply a religious "thank you" or a spiritual punctuation mark. It is our humble and solemn acceptance of this blessing and the profound favor and awesome responsibility that comes with it. In this blessing, God's favor is made known and its effect is irrevocable: we are sent forth with a powerful reminder that what we are about to do is not our work but God's—achieved not through our own power, but through God's. God's blessing is freely given and humbly accepted, and it carries a great responsibility. Knowing that all of this profound meaning is packed into those few words uttered before we head for the exits might make us think twice about just where we are going and what we are to be doing when we go through those exits!

Sent Forth to Do What?

"What are we supposed to do?" These words are often heard by schoolteachers from students who weren't paying attention when directions were being given. In the same way, many of us sometimes leave church after Mass without a clear understanding of what it is we are being sent forth to do. Whether the result of our own lack of attention or liturgy done poorly, we occasionally pass through the church exit with no real sense of direction. Just how do we "announce the Gospel of the Lord"[173] and where do we go to do that?

In his first Apostolic Exhortation, *Sacramentum caritatis*, Pope Benedict XVI wrote of the Dismissal Rite of the Mass, noting that "the People of God might be helped to understand more clearly this essential dimension of the Church's life, taking the dismissal [of the Mass] as a starting point. In this context, it might also be helpful to provide new texts, duly approved, for the prayer over the people and the final blessing, in order to make this connection clear."[174] In light of this assertion, two new texts for the Dismissal were added to the Concluding Rites in the Third Edition of *The Roman Missal* (the only changes not directly related to a closer translation of the Latin). The first was "Go and announce the Gospel of the Lord," and the second was "Go in peace, glorifying the Lord by your life." Both of these texts do well to highlight the point of the Dismissal. We are sent! It is not an option! We are to announce the Gospel of the Lord and we are to glorify the Lord by our lives! One cannot miss the imperative in this charge, the commissioning that is part of our dismissal!

In the document *Evangelii Nuntiandi*, Pope Paul VI very clearly states that "[the Church] exists in order to evangelize."[175] The *General Directory for Catechesis* echoes this statement when it reminds us that evangelization "must be viewed as the process by which the Church, moved by the Spirit, proclaims and spreads the Gospel throughout the entire world."[176] If we as a Church exist in order to evangelize, then it is clear that we are being sent forth from Mass to do just that: to evangelize. This means that we are to bring "the Good News into all the strata of humanity, and through its influence [transform] humanity from within and [make] it new."[177] Ultimately, evangelization is about conversion: our conversion (transformation) and the conversion of society through the power of the Holy Spirit. The US Bishops, in their document *Go and Make Disciples: A National Plan and Strategy for Catholic Evangelization in the United States*, laid out three very clear goals for Catholic evangelization:

• "To bring about in all Catholics such an enthusiasm for their faith that, in living their faith in Jesus, they freely share it with others."[178]

• "To invite all people in the United States, whatever their social or cultural background, to hear the message of salvation in Jesus Christ so that they may come to join us in the fullness of the Catholic faith."[179]

"To foster gospel values in our society, promoting the dignity of the human person, the importance of the family, and the common good of our society, so that our nation may continue to be transformed by the saving power of Jesus Christ."[180]

What does all of this mean? It means that when we are told to go at the end of Mass, we are being sent forth to (among other things)

- live our lives with an openness to conversion and renewal in Jesus;

- deepen our prayer life and learn more about our faith (especially Scripture) so that we can enthusiastically share our faith in Jesus with others;

- foster a greater openness and appreciation for physical, mental, and cultural diversity;

- be more welcoming to others;

- develop skills of sharing our faith with others in our homes, neighborhoods, and workplaces;

- actively invite others to the Catholic faith;

- become involved in ecumenical activity (reaching out to other Christian denominations);

- proactively reach out in service and charity to those in need; and

- become more involved in areas of public policy, the media, and the economy in order to shape and transform society's values.

"May the world of our time, which is searching, sometimes with anguish, sometimes with hope, be enabled to receive the Good News, not from evangelizers who are dejected, discouraged, impatient, or anxious, but from ministers of the Gospel whose lives glow with fervor, who have first received the joy of Christ, and who are willing to risk their lives so that the Kingdom may be proclaimed and the Church established in the midst of the world."

(Evangelii Nuntiandi, 80)

When we are sent forth from the liturgy, we are sent forth with an attitude to have and a job to do. Our attitude is to be one of enthusiasm and joy, and our job is to cooperate in God's ongoing creation and change the world! Notice how the bishops' call to evangelize leads us directly to involvement in catechesis! In order to share our faith, we need to better understand it and be able to articulate it to others. In a sense, evangelization can be likened to sowing the seeds of faith while catechesis can be likened to nurturing the seeds of faith. If you're going to plant seeds, be sure to water them! Nourished by the Eucharist in our liturgy, we are sent forth in the Concluding Rites with gratitude and joy to renew and deepen our faith and share it with others so that our lives and our world may be transformed through the power of the Holy Spirit. That's quite a powerful mandate from the Concluding Rites, which can be completed in under 90 seconds while using only 34 words!

» Closing hymns, like all church hymns, express some of our deepest beliefs. Using a hymnal, look at the words to several closing hymns and reflect upon the words and what they tell us about our exit from worship.

» Begin an "Ite!" journal! When you get home after Mass, simply jot down, in your own words, what you consider to be the "assignment" facing the Church in the coming week and the contribution you can make in your own life. Consider the Scripture readings, preaching, music, and liturgical actions you have just been a part of at Mass.

» What kinds of rituals are part of your exits, goodbyes, and farewells (consider home, family, work)? How do these compare with the Concluding Rites of the Mass? What part of the Church's mission do you feel most passionate about?

» What does it mean to you personally to be sent forth from the liturgy with God's blessing? What does Scripture teach us about blessings?

PART FOUR

Proclaiming the Mystery of the Liturgical Year

CHAPTER 17

THE MYSTERY OF TIME

Time is of the Essence

How appropriate that we began our initial work on this chapter, "The Mystery of Time," on that day in October when we change our clocks to fall back an hour! This yearly ritual heightens our awareness of the role that time plays in our lives. If the importance of time can be measured by the number of clocks we have in our homes, then time is certainly an absolute priority in our lives. Personally, I counted twenty clocks that needed changing in my home, including clocks on my DVD player, computer, microwave and other electronic appliances, wall clocks, wristwatches, and car dashboard clocks! In earlier times, most households had only one clock to judge time by. In today's fast-paced society, we have clocks all around us, reminding us constantly that we have so much to do and so little time to do it in. Time is, indeed, of the essence. For many of us, time has become a source of stress as we rush from one commitment to another with one eye always on the clock.

Time as Sacred

In the opening chapter of the book of Genesis, we see that time is an integral part of creation. In making the heavens and the earth, God created time and blessed it along with all of creation saying, "Let there be lights in the dome of the sky to separate the day from the night; and let them be signs and for seasons and for days and years."[181] The creation story goes on to show how God designated one of those days as Sabbath— that is, as a time for simply being instead of doing. Later, in the story of the Exodus, God includes observance of this sacred time as one of the Commandments given in the covenant. The placement in the Decalogue of this requirement to observe the Sabbath gives it a gravity that parallels the proscriptions against killing, stealing, or lying. God's command to keep holy the Sabbath day involves much more than our obligation to attend church. The Third Commandment is a recipe for spiritual wellbeing, reminding us to observe and honor the sacredness of time by setting aside one day each week to simply be. "Be still," the psalmist counsels us, "and know that I am God!"[182]

"And on the seventh day God finished the work that he had done, and he rested on the seventh day from all the work that he had done. So God blessed the seventh day and hallowed it, because on it God rested from all the work that he had done in creation."

(Genesis 2:2–3)

When time and its passing become stressful, we've forgotten that, as Christians, we believe time to be something that is sacred. The mystery of the Incarnation, the mystery of God breaking into our world as one of us, sanctifies every aspect of creation, including time. "All time belongs to him," we pray on Holy Saturday night, "and all the ages."[183] As we prepare the paschal candle with these words, we are reminded that indeed the clock does not have ultimate power over us. "For you laid the foundations of the world / and have arranged the changing of times and seasons," we hear in the preface to the Eucharistic Prayer.[184] Not even time passes without God's consent and blessing.

> Christ yesterday and today
> the Beginning and the End
> the Alpha
> and the Omega
> All time belongs to him
> and all the ages
> To him be glory and power
> through every age for ever. Amen.
>
> (The Blessing of the Fire and Preparation of the Candle, the Easter Vigil, *The Roman Missal*)

In our fast-paced society, we tend to lose sight of the fact that time has a rhythm and a pattern. All too often, we fail to recognize that time is fluid—it ebbs, flows, and winds around us, charged with the presence and holiness of God. It is this sacred sense of time that pervades our liturgical year and provides us with a cyclical rhythm and pattern within which we encounter Jesus.

Heaven's Time

Time takes on a very different sense in the context of liturgy and worship than it does in our ordinary daily lives. A good example of this can be found in the worship experience of our Eastern Orthodox brothers and sisters. In their understanding, when we enter into liturgy, *kronos*, which is passing time—time that we mark with clocks and watches—is suspended. At that point, *kairos*, which is eternal time or "heaven's time"—stretching back into the past without ceasing and at the same time into the future without ceasing—breaks into our time. *Kairos* is time that can't be marked. It is time that does not pass. In a very real sense, when we enter into worship, we "go on God's clock" which has no past and has no future, just the "eternal now," the holy and sacred moment in which we are worshiping. In this sacred time, heaven and earth are united . . . there is no separation.

"The Church . . . through the liturgy of the hours . . . consecrates to God the whole cycle of the day and the night. The purpose of the liturgy of the hours is to sanctify the day and the whole range of human activity. When the Church offers praise to God . . . it unites itself with that hymn of praise sung throughout all ages in the halls of heaven; it also receives a foretaste of the song of praise in heaven, described by John in the Book of Revelation, the song sung continually before the throne of God and of the Lamb."

(*General Instruction of the Liturgy of the Hours*, 10, 11, 16)

This rhythm and pattern of the eternal now has always been kept by the Church. Our ancestors in faith marked time's passing with prayer. Gathering at the start of the day, they consecrated it to God, asking God to bless the passing of the day and its events. Then again, as evening would begin to fall, the end of the day was marked with thanksgiving and praise to God. The approaching night was blessed and the request was made for protection and safety. The Church continues to mark time in this fashion in its celebration of Morning Prayer and Evening Prayer, as well as other liturgical prayers at different hours of the day.

This rhythm of days flows into the pattern of weeks, and the weeks flow into seasons. Within this flow, the Church marks the passing time with a cycle of seasons and special feasts. This celebration of the feasts and seasons forms the liturgical year: Advent and Christmas Time lead us through winter and into Ordinary Time. From late winter and into the spring, our calendar gives us the cycle of Lent, the Sacred Paschal Triduum, and Easter Time. This takes us into Ordinary Time again through summer and fall, which ultimately leads us to the great Solemnity of Our Lord Jesus Christ, King of the Universe, which marks the beginning of another winter and the end of the liturgical year. The Lectionary—the book from which the readings are proclaimed at Mass—provides us with a semi-continuous reading of the books of the Bible. It is arranged in a three-year cycle in which the readings of each year are dominated by a specific synoptic Gospel text: Year A, the Gospel according to Matthew; Year B, the Gospel according to Mark; and Year C, the Gospel according to Luke. As a result of these patterns, we are led through the time that orders our celebrations and our prayers. From year to year, we live out this pattern that the Church has established.

On the surface, this may seem like a repetitive cycle that we simply go through every year, entering each particular season the same way we entered that season last year, only now we're just a year older. "This Christmas is like last Christmas," we may say. But this is exactly what our liturgical year is *not*. Each season is different from the year before. We are not the same people we were last year. God has been active in our lives since then, in ways in which he has never been active before. Our God is waiting to meet us in ways in which we've never experienced him. God's "eternal now" is always beckoning us to experience him in different and wondrous ways. This calls for a certain openness that allows us to meet God in a new way. Every year, we are called to enter into each of our grace-filled liturgical seasons again, as if for the very first time.

At the Heart of It All

At the very heart of our liturgical year, we find the lifeblood that flows through every season, every feast day, every celebration: the life, Death, and Resurrection of Christ. From season to season, the Paschal Mystery of Christ is the context, the backdrop, and the basis for our celebrations. It's almost as if each season is a different pair of glasses through which we see the Paschal Mystery. This is easy to grasp during Lent, the Sacred Paschal Triduum, and Easter Time, when the Passion, Death, and Resurrection of Christ are so central to the readings. It may be a bit more difficult, however, to see the Paschal Mystery during Advent and Christmas Time, when the readings focus on Jesus's infancy and the beginnings of his public ministry. Yet, it is during these seasons that we look at the Incarnation and the events of Bethlehem as the birth of One who was born to die, and in his dying to destroy death and save the world from everything that separates us from God. The whole liturgical year is a journey of immersing ourselves into the Mystery of Jesus Christ, shaping us more and more into the image of Christ, a process that began with our Baptism.

Keeping the Days

We all know people whose lives absolutely revolve around their calendars. They don't do or plan anything until they've first consulted whatever electronic device they're carrying in their purse or pocket. Other people use their calendars in a different way. They mark the birthday, Baptism day, wedding anniversary, and so on of every person they know. They make sure that they never miss a saint's feast, and that if someone they know is having surgery or a job interview, they have the day marked in their calendar so that they can reach out with an encouraging note or a prayer. The way that each of these types of people regards the calendar is striking. For the first, the calendar is a burden. For the second, the calendar is a wonderful ordering of what they consider important in life. Instead of letting the calendar control them, these people use their calendars as tools to enrich their lives and their relationships with God and others. For them, the calendar is a treasure chest of memories and celebrations, all of which have colored their lives and have given them a context and meaning.

This is how we Catholics approach our liturgical calendar, which not only gives us the seasons of the year (Advent, Christmas Time, Lent, the Triduum, Easter Time, and Ordinary Time), but also marks the people and events that are important to us as a people. The people and events that we celebrate in our liturgical calendar are those that have shaped us and formed us into the people we claim to be. They are part of what gives us our identity as Christians and as a people of God. These celebrations of people and events help us to understand ourselves and help others to understand us.

At the same time, these feasts of people and events do not overshadow the integral role of the Paschal Mystery. These feasts, Holydays of Obligation, and solemnities of the liturgical year mark and celebrate the life, Death, and Resurrection of Christ as it has been lived out in the lives of his holy ones, the saints. Through the faith of the Church, we believe that Christ's Paschal Mystery is seen and celebrated in those people whose lives have mirrored Christ's in some unique and wondrous way. These are the feasts and solemnities of the different seasons and of Ordinary Time. These days are called *ordinary*—not in the sense of "common" or "routine," but rather in the sense of "ordered," "numbered," or "counted." Remember, because of the Incarnation, no time is "ordinary"—all time, all seasons, and all ages are charged with the glory of God. All time is holy and all seasons are sacred because of the coming of our God in Christ!

"For everything there is a season, and a time for every matter under heaven:
a time to be born, and a time to die; / a time to plant, and a time to pluck up
       what is planted;
a time to kill, and a time to heal; / a time to break down, and a time to build up;
a time to weep, and a time to laugh; / a time to mourn, and a time to dance;
a time to throw away stones, and a time to gather stones together; / a time to
       embrace, and a time to refrain from embracing;
a time to seek, and a time to lose; / a time to keep, and a time to throw away;
a time to tear, and a time to sew; / a time to keep silence, and a time to speak;
a time to love, and a time to hate, / a time for war, and a time for peace."

(Ecclesiastes 3:1–8)

REFLECTION

» Take inventory and reflect on of all the ways in which your parish community observes and celebrates the particular liturgical seasons (environment and art, traditions, celebrations, and so forth).

» Begin every day by naming the season or feast day that is being celebrated. Include it somehow in your prayer time.

» Find ways to keep the seasons of the liturgical year in your own home. Find traditions that help to "mark" each season. For example, keep an Advent wreath and light its candles each day of the season, or keep holy water in your home during the fifty days of Easter Time and use it to bless yourself and your family each day. Use the Scripture readings of the day to guide your prayer. Keep a liturgical calendar in your home in a place where you will notice it regularly. Note on it the passing of the feasts and seasons.

» How do you or can you prayerfully prepare to plan and celebrate each liturgical season so that it is truly different from last year?

» How can you bring the notion of "heaven's time" into your daily life? In what ways can you instill a sense of time being sacred in your lived experiences?

» How does each liturgical season speak to our ever-deepening conversion and initiation into the Paschal Mystery of Christ? How does the liturgical calendar shape our faith journey? How has your growing faith in Christ affected your view of creation, your view of the passing seasons, and your view of time?

» How have you experienced time as sacred? Assess your observance of the Sabbath day. What are you doing or can you do to set aside sacred time each week to simply rest in God's presence? Do you mark any part of the day or night with prayer? How? How do you keep the various seasons of the liturgical year? Which season is your favorite? Why?

CHAPTER 18

THE MYSTERY OF ADVENT

The Themes of Advent

The First Two Weeks: Longing and Waiting for the Second Coming of Christ

How many of us pray for the end of the world? How many of us actually look forward to the end of time? How many of us consciously long for the moment when all time will cease and the reign of God will fully be in our midst? Chances are that not many of us normally do any of this. Somehow, to think of actually wishing for the end of time is to think of people we would label as "crackpots," namely, the kind of people who stand on street corners, yelling and hollering, or walking around with placards that read: "Repent! The end of the world is coming!" None of this usually sits very well with us, and so it would not be surprising if no one admitted doing any of these things. Yet, during Advent, we enter a season of our Church's liturgical year, half of which is devoted to the very idea of looking forward to "the end of time." Just look at some of the words from the Advent liturgies:

- "Lord Jesus, you will come in glory with salvation for your people."[185]

- "[Christ] will come again in glory / to judge the living and the dead."[186]

- "We proclaim your Death, O Lord, / and profess your Resurrection / until you come again."[187]

- "Therefore, O Lord . . . / . . . as we look forward to his second coming."[188]

- "We remember Christ's Death / . . . / as we await his coming in glory."[189]

Every year, Advent reminds us that part of being a Christian is to keep one eye focused on the now, and the other eye focused on that final day. The idea itself sounds very attractive—to see the end of life as we know it now, with all its pain, suffering, trials, and struggles, and to have it all (including ourselves) be made anew. How appealing it is to imagine having everything engulfed and surrounded by the fullness of God's love to the point that it literally becomes a new creation! When thought of that way, it doesn't seem too scary! We could all use this in our lives: to spend some time thinking about—no, actually longing for—that re-creation that God's love will bring. That's what Advent is, and that is something that we could all pray for!

"Beware, keep alert; for you do not know when the time will come"

(Mark 13:33, Gospel for the First Sunday of Advent, Year B)

Very simply, Advent is about God's promises to always be with us. More than that, it is about God's faithfulness to those promises. We need only look at two Advent characters to understand this: Mary, the Mother of Jesus, and Zechariah, the father of John the Baptist.

In Mary's *Magnificat*[190] she says, in reference to her bearing the Holy One of God, "He has helped his servant Israel, in remembrance of his mercy, / according to the promise he made to our ancestors, to Abraham and to his descendants for ever."[191] Just 16 verses later, Zechariah follows these words of Mary in his canticle of praise to God.[192] "Thus he has shown the mercy promised to our ancestors, / and has remembered his holy covenant, / the oath that he swore to our ancestor Abraham, / to grant us that we, being rescued from the hands of our enemies, / might serve him without fear, in holiness and righteousness before him all our days."[193] These Advent voices celebrate the promises that God has made to us: God's promise to live among his people, God's promise to show mercy to his people, and the promise that God made to Abraham and Sarah. "I will make of you a great nation, and I will bless you, and make your name great, so that you will be a blessing."[194] The day is coming, the prophet Isaiah says, when God will fulfill those ancient promises he made!

Like Mary, Zechariah, and countless others after them, we recognize Jesus as the fulfillment of God's ancient promises. Jesus is God's mercy! Jesus is the embodiment of God's promise to be with us. Advent is not a time for us to pretend that we are waiting for the baby Jesus to be born. That amazing event has already happened! Advent is the season to remember God's ancient promises. It is the season to see anew the fulfillment of those promises in Jesus the Christ, and to renew our faith in the promise that Christ will return in glory to reign over us, and over all creation.

> "Grant your faithful, we pray, almighty God,
> the resolve to run forth to meet your Christ
> with righteous deeds at his coming,
> so that, gathered at his right hand,
> they may be worthy to possess the heavenly Kingdom.
> Through our Lord Jesus Christ, your Son,
> who lives and reigns with you in the unity of the Holy Spirit,
> one God, for ever and ever"

(Collect, First Sunday of Advent, *The Roman Missal*)

The Second Two Weeks: Preparing to Celebrate the Incarnation

In the last days of Advent, the final days before the great feast of Christmas, anticipation usually builds. Final plans are made, last-minute preparations get under way, and that "one last gift" still needs to be bought. Excitement is high, and maybe even some anxiety begins to creep in. You may find yourself saying, "I'm not going to make it," whatever "it" is.

That same urgency can be found in the liturgies that mark the last days of Advent. The prayers and the readings echo the urgency that many of us feel as Christmas approaches. We pray, "Grant that your people . . . / may be ever watchful for the coming of your Only Begotten Son, / that . . . / we may hasten, alert with lighted lamps, / to meet him when he comes."[195] What a perfect prayer! In the midst of loose ends and unfinished plans, we pray a simple prayer that we might be ever watchful and the hope of the season not be lost on us. This could be just what many of us need to get through it all. In the Advent Gospel readings, Mary and Joseph are repeatedly told by God's angels that, in the face of all of the confusing and stressful things that are happening in their lives, they are not to be afraid. The readings and the images of the second half of the season all have this same element of peace and calm in the midst of anxiety and fear. The shepherds are at first frightened and startled. They receive the same greeting: "Do not be afraid."[196] These are words for all of us, in the later days of the season, as we quickly approach the great feast of Christmas Time.

> "The angel said to her, 'Do not be afraid, Mary, for you have found favor with God.'"
>
> (Luke 1:30, Gospel for the Fourth Sunday of Advent, Year C)

"Peace on earth" is a familiar phrase during Christmas Time. Biblically speaking, peace on earth is not simply the absence of violence or confrontation. Rather, peace, or *shalom*, is that reality that occurs when heaven and earth become united in the hearts of people. Peace is what occurs when humanity and divinity become one; when everything "fits," is connected, or makes sense. Peace is the result of reconciliation, when that which is broken or disconnected becomes reconciled or reunited. Through the Incarnation, God has reconciled the world to himself. Peace has been given to us once and for all. We need only to allow it into our hearts.

So, if the fear and anxiety start to build in the last days of Advent, we are in good company. Our faith calls us to stand in the face of such obstacles and to remain firm in our conviction that Christ is more powerful than anything that threatens to keep us from him. Joseph and the shepherds, wise men and women, and simple folk are all given the same hope-filled prayer: "Peace and tidings of great joy!" God's nearness in Christ shines to us as bright as a star in the dark night sky. Surely, it brings glad tidings!

The Symbols of Advent
Light in Darkness

Whenever June 21 rolls around, my wife, Joanne, sighs a little sigh of lament. While it is the longest day of the year, she always reminds me that, from this point on, the days will be getting shorter. She can't wait for December 21 when the winter solstice reverses the trend! For most of us, this may not be a big deal, but many people suffer from a condition known as Seasonal Affective Disorder Syndrome (SADS), which causes people to suffer various degrees of depression and anxiety due to light deprivation. By the time November and December roll around, those of us in the northern hemisphere wake up and go to work in darkness and come home in darkness! Medical experts have determined that people suffering from SADS need to be exposed to significant amounts of very bright light to make up for the loss of sunlight. It seems that the effects of light and darkness are very real, and not just the imaginings of children who fear shadows and dark corners! ~Joe

During Advent, we anticipate the light of Christ coming to dispel the darkness of sin. Just as the world around us reaches its darkest depths, we Christians recall how

Jesus, the light of the world, came to dispel the darkness of sin, and we eagerly await his second coming when darkness will give way to a light that will never fade. In our Advent liturgies, the themes of light and darkness surround us and remind us that our time of walking in darkness will end when we invite Jesus to come into our lives!

"The people who walked in darkness have seen a great light; / those who lived in a land of deep darkness— / on them light has shined."

(Isaiah 9:2)

Waiting and Keeping Watch

Let's face it, nobody enjoys being made to wait! Think of the time you've spent waiting at doctors' offices, auto mechanics' shops, in lines at the supermarket, or at the bank. None of these times of waiting are very fun. So why should we feel good about waiting during Advent? It is true that Advent is a season of waiting. It is not the type of waiting mentioned above, however. It is not idly hanging around and watching the seconds tick off the clock while we twiddle our thumbs awaiting some mundane event. Advent waiting, as opposed to empty waiting, is full of joy and anticipation because of what (who) it is we are waiting for.

I remember waiting for the call from Michigan when my younger sister and her husband were expecting their first child. This was the first time one of my siblings was to have a baby, so it also happened to be my first experience of being an uncle. Then it happened: the phone rang. "Hi! It's Dad . . . your sister had the baby!" Inside, I instantly became still: my heart, which had quickened at the sound of the phone ringing, had now seemed to stop. I distinctly remember holding my breath. In the stillness of my body, the anticipation and the expectation were overwhelming.

~Todd

How many of us, in various different circumstances, can say that we've experienced a time of waiting that was full of hope and anticipation? Think of waiting rooms in the hospital. Think of airports just after the plane has landed and you strain to spot someone special walking through the security point. Think of that "perfect job" and the call that came through with the result of the interview. Think of that one, long moment right after the proposal of marriage. These are moments of Advent waiting. These are moments when anticipation and expectation dominate. These are moments that wonderfully convey the sense of this liturgical season. During Advent, we are like children knowing that their birthday is coming around and they're going to get presents and have a party. We feel like we do on Thanksgiving Day when the turkey is in the oven and our home is filled with the aromas of a pending feast. We long for the moment to arrive when our celebration will reach its climax. We do not spend the time waiting for that meal in sadness and sorrow, but rather in joyful preparation, knowing that family and friends will be arriving and conversation and laughter will fill our homes.

So, just what are we joyfully waiting for during Advent? Again, we are not waiting for the baby Jesus to be born. The Incarnation has already filled our world with the Word made flesh. And yet, we are indeed preparing for the celebration of the feast of the incredible Incarnation at Christmas. At the same time, we wait for the coming of the kingdom in its fullness. Likewise, we confidently and joyfully anticipate the second coming of Jesus Christ that we proclaim each time we celebrate the Eucharist: "We proclaim your Death, O Lord, / and profess your Resurrection / until you come again."[197]

"When the Church celebrates the *liturgy of Advent* each year, she makes present this ancient expectancy of the Messiah, for by sharing in the long preparation for the Savior's first coming, the faithful renew their ardent desire for his second coming."[198]

(Catechism of the Catholic Church, 524)

This type of waiting is better described as a longing. It is a desire that we long to have fulfilled. Advent waiting is less like the kind of waiting we do at the laundry as we wait for the spin cycle to finish and more like the kind of waiting we do during a pregnancy as we nurture the life already conceived and anticipate with great joy the life that is yet to be born. It is a time when we keep watch, moving through our lives with eyes wide open, knowing that hints of the fullness of God's kingdom are all around us if we have the eyes to see them. At Mass, after we pray the Lord's Prayer, the priest proclaims, "we await the blessed hope and the coming of our Savior, Jesus Christ."[199] We do not wait in ignorance, hoping that some vague "good thing" will come along. We wait with a hope that is secure in knowing that Jesus, our Savior, will return. With each setting sun (which happens earlier and earlier each day during Advent), Christians watch hopefully for Jesus Christ to be revealed in the dawn of each new day! In a world that is often hopeless, Christians need to spread hope. Christians need the liturgies of Advent to reignite our hope, which is grounded in faith and leads to love.

Christ will come again in glory, and right now we are living in that one, long, seemingly eternal moment right before it happens. Will we know it when it happens? Are we truly and actively waiting for that moment? Do we strain to catch a glimpse of that approaching glory? Do we hold our breath, sure that "This is it! This is the moment"? In the darkness of the winter nights of Advent, is the stilled hush quiet enough so we can hear the Master approaching? These are Advent moments in our lives.

"It is good that one should wait quietly / for the salvation of the LORD."

(Lamentations 3:26)

The Advent Wreath

It is said that the custom of the Advent wreath began when wagon wheels were brought indoors as the days of winter got shorter and shorter and the darkness began to come earlier and earlier. Once inside, these wheels would be decorated with evergreens. People would put candles on the wheels, making them beacons of greenery that would stand in the shadows of the deepening winter. The light and greenery proclaimed that the earth had not seen the last of spring, and that the sun would return and would once again warm the land and the tired people who longed for its return. That's one story behind the Advent wreath. Whatever the "true" story may be, it's hard to imagine preparing for Christmas without one! Nothing captures our hopes and fears at this time of the year better than the Advent wreath: a beautiful, full, green circle that never ends, but rather turns into itself (much like our seasons turn into one another and symbolize the cycle that is life) and lights that get progressively brighter as the winter nights get longer. They shine with a brightness that promises fulfillment of all our hopes and longings. The dark, rich colors of the candles speak of a darkness that is not quite complete. After all, it's not a blackness that graces our evergreen circles. It's a mixture of purple and pink—colors of morning—the colors of the sky just before dawn, just before the sun comes over the horizon. Go out early, before the sun comes up, one clear, cool winter morning. Look at the sky. Notice the mixture of purples, blues, and pinks. Notice that to the west, the sky is still the dark of night. Notice that as you move your focus east, where the rising sun approaches, the colors get lighter: more purple and blue. Keep watching and you'll see, right before the sun actually breaks over the horizon, a rose or pink hue become visible: the color of the sky immediately before daybreak! There's a reason for our colors on this circle of life and light!

During Advent, our liturgies are especially graced with the wreath of light. As we praise God, we will light one more candle on the wreath, emphasizing the great need we have for Christ's light to penetrate our world's darkness. Only Christ, we say, can completely save us. That is our faith and we proclaim it loudly every time we light the candles and pray for God to be with us.

"Lord God, / let your blessing come upon us / as we light the candles of this wreath. / May the wreath and its light / be a sign of Christ's promise to bring us salvation. / May he come quickly and not delay. / We ask this through Christ our Lord"

(Blessing of the Advent Wreath, Book of Blessings)

The Advent Liturgy

Advent Violet

The *General Instruction of the Roman Missal* tells us, "Diversity of color in the sacred vestments has as its purpose to give more effective expression even outwardly whether to the specific character of the mysteries of faith to be celebrated or to a sense of Christian life's passage through the course of the liturgical year."[200] Typically, white symbolizes the presence of the Risen Christ in the Church and in his saints. Likewise, throughout the liturgical year, other colors are used to express the various manifestations of Christ's presence.

During Advent, a form of violet is used that differentiates this season from Lent. The violet of Advent is a bluer tone (more suggestive of the darker late autumn skies) while Lent maintains a royal violet that is more reddish, specifically suggesting the penitential spirit of Lent. Both shades of violet, however, suggest the kingship of Jesus that is celebrated in both seasons: during Advent we joyfully anticipate the coming of our king in his fullness, while during Lent, we commemorate how that kingship was achieved through the suffering, Death, and Resurrection of the King of Glory!

The Absence of the Gloria

While Advent is indeed a joyful season, by comparison, it does not have the same level of exuberance with which Christmas will follow. For this reason, we dispense with the singing of the Gloria during Advent, not because Advent is a "downer" season, but simply to create a contrast—in the same way that we withhold the Alleluia during Lent so that its proclamation at Easter will be even more profound. Simply put, we dispense with the Gloria during Advent because "absence makes the heart grow fonder!" When Christmas comes along, the singing of the Gloria will be all the more festive.

The O Antiphons

O Wisdom, O holy word of God, you govern all creation with your strong yet tender care: Come show your people the way to salvation. (December 17)

O Sacred Lord of ancient Israel, who showed yourself to Moses in the burning bush, who gave him the holy law on Sinai mountain: Come stretch out your mighty hand to set us free. (December 18)

O Flower of Jesse's stem, you have been raised up as a sign for all peoples; kings stand silent in your presence; the nations bow down in worship before you: Come let nothing keep you from coming to our aid. (December 19)

O Key of David, O royal Power of Israel, controlling at your will the gate of heaven: Come, break down the prison walls of death for those who dwell in darkness and the shadow of death, and lead your captive people into freedom. (December 20)

O Radiant Dawn, splendor of eternal light, sun of justice: Come, shine on those who dwell in darkness and the shadow of death. (December 21)

O King of all the nations, the only joy of every human heart; O Keystone of the mighty arch of man: Come and save the creatures you fashioned from the dust. (December 22)

O Emmanuel, king and lawgiver, desire of the nations, Savior of all people: Come and set us free, Lord our God. (December 23)

(Antiphons for the *Magnificat* during Evening Prayer, *Liturgy of the Hours*)

The O Antiphons provide us with a wonderful opportunity to pray in the days approaching Christmas. We look forward to them every year as we enter the second half of our Advent journey. Every year, we begin praying them on December 17, the day that marks the liturgy's change in tone and mood as we enter the second half of the Advent season. From this point on, we focus more closely on the quickly approaching celebration of God's coming in our history—God's Incarnation in the person of Jesus.

The antiphons themselves come from the Church's celebration of Evening Prayer during these last days of Advent. Each evening, beginning with December 17, one of the antiphons is prayed before the singing of the *Magnificat*, Mary's canticle. Dating back to the 7th century, we know these wonderful prayers through the most familiar of all Advent hymns, "O Come, O Come Emmanuel."

Taken all together, the O Antiphons are overwhelming for us as each verse calls upon God to "Come!" Taken individually, each one seems to touch upon a different element or aspect of creation. All of creation is infused and imbued with the presence of the Divine: the winds of wisdom called the "breath of the most high;" the fire of the burning bush from which the Sacred Lord spoke; the trees of God's creation from which life sprouts in the form of Jesse's stem; the rocks, metals, and ores that form both walls and gates; the splendor of light that was the first of God's creation; all nations and every individual human heart; and even time itself, is sung in this ancient hymn. All of it culminates and reaches its highest point in the wonderful crescendo of the last verse that recognizes the great mystery, which is almost too much for words: Emmanuel, God-with-us, you are the desire of all nations! Come and set us free!

"Beloved, now is the acceptable time spoken of by the Spirit, the day of salvation, peace and reconciliation: the great season of Advent. This is the time eagerly awaited by the patriarchs and prophets, the time that holy Simeon rejoiced at last to see. This is the season that the church has always celebrated with special solemnity. We too should always observe it with faith and love, offering praise and thanksgiving to the Father for the mercy and love he has shown us in this mystery."

(Reading from a pastoral letter by St. Charles Borromeo, bishop, from the Office of Readings for Week 1 of Advent, *The Liturgy of the Hours*)

REFLECTION

» Reflect upon experiences of waiting, longing, and anticipation for joyful events. Reflect upon the role of hope in waiting and how such hope is tied to faith and love.

» Use this Advent as an opportunity to reflect upon the anticipation that is building within you as you continue to enter more deeply into the Paschal Mystery. Consider how this period of joyful longing is "practice" for becoming a disciple of Christ.

» Use the O Antiphons for your own prayer during the final days of Advent. Beginning on December 17, pray a verse each day as we prepare to celebrate the great gift of God's presence among us: Emmanuel! (The O Antiphons, which are the Alleluia verses for December 17 through December 24, can be found in the revised Lectionary or on the Internet).

» How can light and darkness be integrated into your personal celebration of Advent?

» How can Advent serve as a "training ground" for Christians to practice the art of spreading hope to a world that needs it desperately? Where in your community is hope most urgently needed? How can you bring hope to these areas?

» What are your experiences of waiting? Read the following Scripture passages: Psalm 27:12–14; Psalm 37:7; Proverbs 20:22; Is 33:2; and Isaiah 40:31. What does it mean to you to wait for the Lord or to wait on the Lord?

» What do you think of when you consider the end of the world? How does Advent's consideration of the end times help us in the present times?

CHAPTER 19

THE MYSTERY OF CHRISTMAS TIME

Dangerous Territory

We are about to venture into dangerous territory. To even think about "messing with" the images and emotions surrounding society's celebration of Christmas could be taking one's life into one's hands! In our society, the commercial element of the holiday bursts into our public consciousness sometime between Labor Day and Thanksgiving. Similarly, in our culture, much is made of the emotional element, fueled by Scrooge and Jimmy Stewart, Nat King Cole and Burl Ives, "Home for the Holidays" and "White Christmas." It is important, however, to realize that, in the midst of the tinsel, lights, mall traffic, sales, Black Fridays, Cyber Mondays, and party after party, there is a profound and terribly meaningful mystery, namely, the Incarnation (see Chapter 2, "The Mystery of Jesus"). At the heart of this celebration of Christmas (or as the liturgical calendar refers to it, "The Nativity of the Lord") is the powerful mystery that God so desired to be one with us that God became one of us.

The Themes of Christmas

A Season, Not a Day

We do well to explore the riches and treasures that the whole season of Christmas offers us. From the late afternoon of Christmas Eve to the evening of the Feast of the Baptism of the Lord, the whole season of Christmas Time is one that holds a host of elements and celebrations. Marking the birth of Christ is only one aspect of that season. Granted it is the way the season begins, amid carols and crèches at Midnight Mass. That is not the note upon which the season ends, though. In between those two points, the season calls us to be mindful of the whole scope of what Christ's coming into our world means for us as his followers. In the liturgies and themes of this season, we find diverse and sometimes conflicting images: wedding banquets and flights into exile, angelic messages given in dreams and the nightmare of children slaughtered, lights that shine in the darkest places and prophecies of hearts pierced by a sword. All of it expresses our belief that the birth of Jesus the Christ has set the world on its end.

In our last chapter, we noted that Mary's *Magnificat* and the Canticle of Zechariah speak of the Messiah's coming as something that ushers in a new way of seeing our life and the way it is lived in this world. "The dawn from on high shall break upon us," sings Zechariah, "to give light to those who dwell in darkness and in the shadow of death."[201] Likewise, Mary sings of how the mighty are cast down and the lowly are raised, how the hungry are filled with good things and the rich go empty away.[202] In the birth of the Lord, the world is turned upside down, never again to be the same! Christmas Time points to the difference that God's presence and action make in our world.

The Marriage of Heaven and Earth

Some things are just too important, too big, to celebrate in a single, solitary day. Think of a marriage. Since there is just too much to celebrate in a single day, there is a honeymoon: an extended period of time immediately after the wedding day that continues the celebration of the marriage event. In the same way, the Church celebrates a type of honeymoon immediately following Christmas Day. It's called the Octave of Christmas, and it celebrates the marriage between heaven and earth, the marriage between God and humanity. Lasting eight days (*octo* is Latin for "eight"), this "honeymoon" consists of liturgical feasts that mark this great marriage. From Christmas Day until the Feast of Mary, Mother of God (January 1), the Church honeymoons!

Since the earliest days of the Church, Jesus has been imaged as the bridegroom and we, the Church, as the bride. "For as a young man marries a young woman, / so shall your builder marry you, / and as the bridegroom rejoices over the bride, / so shall your God rejoice over you"[203] In Christmas Time, the Church celebrates the great marriage feast between God and God's people. In Jesus, we are wedded to God; bound in a union that can never be broken. So, we celebrate. We honeymoon. We take eight days to bask in the wonder of this marriage, this bond, this covenant of love. We take eight days and we celebrate the great mystery of it all.

"I will take you for my wife for ever; I will take you for my wife in righteousness and in justice, in steadfast love, and in mercy. I will take you for my wife in faithfulness; and you shall know the LORD."

(Hosea 2:19–20)

Hodie: Today

A traditional Latin carol sings, "*Hodie, Christus natus est!*" ("Today, Christ is born!"). The Mass During the Day on Christmas makes this same assertion: "Grant, O merciful God, / that, just as the Savior of the world, born this day. . . ."[204] Christmas is a celebration of *hodie*, or today. When does this wedding between heaven and earth take place? When is Christ born? When does the Savior come? The answer of Christmas is: today! We do not celebrate Christmas as a past event. It is not as if we are marking the birthday of a long deceased person. In celebrating Christmas, we are celebrating the fact that today God has acted in the world! Today God has "broken in upon us," as Zechariah sang, and has sent the Savior to set us free. Today we have seen our salvation and the fulfillment of God's ancient promises.

"O God, who on this day / revealed your Only Begotten Son to the nations / by the guidance of a star, / grant in your mercy / that we, who know you already by faith, / may be brought to behold the beauty of your sublime glory."

(Collect for the Solemnity of the Epiphany of the Lord, *The Roman Missal*)

This element of Christmas as *the day* has been hinted at during the Advent season. In fact, the very First Sunday of Advent sets the stage for the day of the Lord that Christmas marks. On that First Sunday of Advent, the prophet, in the First Reading of all three cycles, speaks of "the day" or speaks of the plea for God to act now:

- Year A: "In days to come, the mountain of the LORD's house / shall be established . . ."[205]

- Year B: "O that you would tear open the heavens and come down"[206]

- Year C: "The days are surely coming . . . when I will fulfill the promise I made to the house of Israel and the house of Judah"[207]

Christmas Time heralds that today is "the day" of which the prophets wrote. Today is when God rends the heavens and comes down to us in the person of Christ. Today, God has remembered the ancient promises. Today, now, is when God is acting to establish the kingdom of heaven.

Ironically, it is not only at Christmas that we celebrate *hodie*, or today. Actually, we believe this about every Eucharist we celebrate. Whenever we gather to proclaim the Scriptures, intercede as members of the baptized, offer bread and wine along with our very lives, and celebrate Communion with Christ Jesus among us and within us, we celebrate *hodie*, or today. God's eternal now breaks into our world and into our lives whenever the sacred liturgy is celebrated.

Epiphany

All of Christmas Time is really a celebration of epiphany. *Epiphany* means "to show," as in an appearance. The whole season proclaims that, in Christ Jesus, God is "shown," or made manifest. Quite simply, Christmas celebrates that, in Christ, God has appeared to us. The structure of Christmas Time itself illustrates this. Made up of three "moments," Christmas Time marks the manifestations (note the plural) of Christ. The whole of Christmas is contained in these three moments. It is not only that Epiphany is a Christmas celebration, but, in a very real sense, all of Christmas is a celebration of Epiphany.

The celebration begins in the silence and darkness of Christmas Eve. This silence, along with the waiting and anticipation that have marked Advent, is broken with the singing of the Gloria. This, the song of the angels, ushers in the first Christmas celebration. "We joyfully welcome / your Only Begotten Son as our Redeemer," we pray in the Collect.[208] The readings for this Mass echo the Gloria as we hear of the angels who proclaimed the birth of the Promised One: "I am bringing you news of great joy for all the people: to you is born this day in the city of David a Savior, who is the Messiah, the Lord."[209] At the very start of the season, then, we recognize and celebrate the manifestation of Christ as the one Isaiah spoke of: "He is named Wonderful Counselor, Mighty God, / Everlasting Father, Prince of Peace."[210] Throughout the liturgies of Christmas, we will hear, again and again, of this first epiphany of Christmas: "in the mystery of the Word made flesh / a new light of your glory has shone upon the eyes of our mind."[211]

The second "moment" of the season is really the high point, marked by the actual Solemnity of the Epiphany of the Lord, which is celebrated on the Sunday after the Octave. In the East, the day of Epiphany was the original celebration of Christ's birth, and it was ascribed to January 6. The East still celebrates this feast on that day. We in the West mark the solemnity with the image of light and celebrate it as a further manifestation of God's glory in Christ. Indeed, on this day, we hear in the Gospel about the Magi who were led by a star, a light in the darkness, to the Christ child. The story points to the image of light in this day's celebrations and further reveals the identity of the child. The gifts of the Magi show that they recognized who this infant really is. The gold and frankincense symbolize the royal character of Christ the King, and the myrrh, which was a costly ointment used in burial, points to Christ's identity as the Savior who would die for us. Our Church's most ancient understanding of the Solemnity of Epiphany expresses our belief in the full revelation of Christ. In the second half of the first millennium, the liturgy of Epiphany celebrated more than just the visit of the Magi. It also celebrated two other "epiphanies" of Christ: the miracle at the wedding feast in Cana and the baptism of the Lord. Both of these events, along with the visit of the Magi, were for the early church epiphanies of Christ's identity. Interestingly, the Order of Evening Prayer for the solemnity of Epiphany still maintains the connection to the earliest celebrations of this feast, where all three "revelations" are remembered: "Three mysteries mark this holy day: today the star leads the Magi to the infant Christ; today water is changed into wine for the wedding feast; today Christ wills to be baptized by John in the river Jordan to bring us salvation."[212]

The final "moment" of Christmas Time is the Feast of the Baptism of the Lord. It is in the account of the Lord's baptism that the Gospel notes the "revelation" celebrated in this day's liturgy: "And a voice from heaven said, 'This is my Son, the Beloved, with whom I am well pleased.'"[213] This is another epiphany that unfolds our experience of the Word made flesh. This epiphany, however, is not meant to be watched and admired from afar. Rather, the Collect reminds us that we are "reborn of water and the Holy Spirit,"[214] and since we share in the same baptism of Jesus that led to his mission, our Baptism leads us also to share in his mission. As Christmas Time ends, ushering in a new year, we are called to follow the Light of the Nations as our mission unfolds and takes shape. For some, it will undoubtedly lead to the cross. For all of us, it will be a sharing of Jesus's relationship to God, so that we may "be inwardly transformed / through him whom we recognize as outwardly like ourselves."[215]

A Year of Grace

Christmas Time takes us into a new calendar year. For the Church, it is a continuation of the new liturgical year that began with Advent. The celebration of Christmas poses two questions to us: In the new year of grace, how and where will God enter our days? How will God fulfill the ancient promises in our lives? Christmas Time calls us to be mindful of the many ways in which God acts in our lives—the many ways in which God reveals himself and his love for each of us. In the first weeks of the new year, we are asked to pay attention to the many ways in which God "breaks into" our world, into our relationships, and into our individual lives. This is exactly what we celebrate at Christmas: in Christ Jesus, God fulfilled the ancient promise. In Jesus, we have seen the living God!

Although Christmas Time ends with the Feast of the Baptism of the Lord and Ordinary Time begins the next day, we cannot forget what we have experienced during the Christmas season. God's breaking into our world and into our lives means that nothing can ever be the same again! Like the Magi, who returned home by a different route, we must go into this new year of grace by a different route. Our lives are forever changed because of all that has been made known to us. The liturgy of the Feast of the Baptism of the Lord isn't a door that closes the feast of Christmas. Rather, it is more like a door that opens into the rest of the new year, the light of the feast spilling out in front of us to show us the way.

The Symbols of Christmas
Light in the Darkness

When I was young, my family used to go "house looking" during the Christmas season. My parents and all of us kids would pile into the van after dinner, when the darkness had sufficiently fallen and there was no light left in the winter sky, and would drive up and down streets, looking at Christmas lights. We would drive all over our neighborhood, go over to the next subdivision, and even travel to the next town looking at lights. We'd do this for the whole evening, sometimes getting home just in time to go to bed. We loved to look at the houses, the trees, the store windows, and the yards, all filled with beautiful, twinkling, radiant lights!

Looking back at it now, I can't help but wonder, what were we looking for? What was pulling us, tugging at our curiosity and sense of wonder? For what were we searching? What is it that causes us to travel in search of lights? What is it that summons our imagination, our senses, our hearts and our dreams, and calls us to set out?   **~Todd**

On the Solemnity of the Epiphany of the Lord, we hear, "May God, who has called you / out of darkness into his wonderful light, / pour out in kindness his blessing upon you."[216] In the Collect of the Vigil Mass for the same day, we pray, "May the splendor of your majesty, O Lord, we pray, / shed its light upon our hearts."[217] The prophet Isaiah tells us in the First Reading, "Lift up your eyes from all around and see; they all gather, they come to you,"[218] drawn by the light. The Gospel according to Matthew tells us that "there, ahead of [the Magi], went the star that they had seen at its rising, until it stopped over the place where the child was."[219] The image of light, and the power it has to draw people, is a main touchstone in our faith tradition and in our liturgies. It is also a primary symbol of Christmas Time. Light is a statement of faith for us, and we use it to express our belief in the Incarnate Christ, and in all the grace that comes to us because of our faith.

Darkness can be dangerous! Once, when I had turned off all the lights and gone to bed, I heard my son Mike (he was about fifteen years old at the time) get up to go to the washroom. As he felt his way through the darkness, I heard a loud *bang*! He had walked right into a wall, thinking it was a doorway. He assured me he was fine and went to bed. But the morning light revealed a huge bump on his forehead that reminded him that darkness is indeed dangerous!   **~Joe**

Christmas is the Feast of Light; a light that dispels all darkness. From Christmas Eve, through the celebration of the Epiphany, to the Feast of the Baptism of the Lord, we celebrate the light that is not overcome by the danger of darkness. Christ appears as the Light of the World, and Christ manifests the love our God has for us.

Christmas Trees and Evergreens

There are myriad stories as to the origin of the Christmas tree. Whether they are rooted in the "Paradise Trees" that were part of the morality plays of the Middle Ages or come from different cultural attempts to ward off the bitter winter by bringing an actual tree inside so that it does not die in the snow and ice but remains "evergreen," they are standard elements of our Christmas celebrations. Though they are not, in the strict sense, a liturgical symbol, they are, nonetheless, symbols of life in the dreary dark of winter. Their lights do shine forth in that darkness, offering to us images that are culled from our faith tradition and that speak to us of Christ, who is ever present in our lives and in our world, and who is ever shining in the darkest parts of both.

In his book, *Starlight: Beholding the Christmas Miracle All Year Long*, John Shea eloquently writes of the Christmas tree as something that connects earth to heaven.[220] Describing the "Christmas village" that circles the base of many a seasonal tree, he notes the star-like lights that rise above the village in the branches of the tree. These star-lights in the branches are crowned with the angel that heralds "tidings of great joy." The Christmas tree truly symbolizes and manifests, in a most concrete and profound way, the marriage bond between heaven (the stars and angels) and earth (the village) that we celebrate at Christmas.

"Lord God, / let your blessing come upon us / as we illumine this tree. / May the light and cheer it gives / be a sign of the joy that fills our hearts. / May all who delight in this tree / come to the knowledge and joy of salvation. / We ask this through Christ our Lord."

(Blessing of a Christmas Tree, *Book of Blessings*)

Whether it's the evergreen of the decorated tree, or the wreath that once encircled the Advent candles, the greenery of Christmas speaks of the hope and promise of the season. Undaunted by the natural cycle, warming our homes and our hearts, these testimonies to a promised return of spring and summer can carry us through the darkest days of the year and into the light that is promised in Christ Jesus.

The Liturgies of Christmas

The Return of the Gloria

The *Universal Norms on the Liturgical Year and the Calendar* notes that, "After the annual celebration of the Paschal Mystery, the Church has no more ancient custom than celebrating the memorial of the Nativity of the Lord and of his first manifestations."[221] Nowhere might this be more obvious than in the collection of music, hymns, carols, and songs that accompany our celebration of the Nativity. No other season has such an anticipated and expected repertoire attached to it. Perhaps that is why the Gloria is so important at the Christmas liturgies. Not only have we not sung it for the four weeks of Advent prior to Christmas, but it is also, as we noted in the last chapter, the song of the angels during the night of Christ's birth in Bethlehem. For these reasons, the return of the Gloria speaks wonderfully of the spirit of these liturgies. Joy and peace are the root of this song, and we are called to sing it exuberantly. Remember, today Christ is given to us as Savior of the World, now as before, and always for ever. So indeed, "Glory to God in the highest, / and on earth peace to people of good will."[222]

Companions of Christ

During the days immediately after Christmas, the Church not only celebrates the Incarnation, but it also celebrates feasts and memorials of those who help to reveal Christ and the Gospel that Christ came to give. The saints and holy ones whose days we celebrate during the octave give a sense of Christmas that most people don't have during the holiday. These saints were known during the middle ages as "Companions of Christ." They were martyrs and visionaries, slaughtered children and assassinated archbishops. They point to the paschal character of Christmas Time.

The very next day after the Great Feast, we celebrate the feast of Stephen, the first martyr, who was stoned to death for his belief in Jesus as the Messiah. On the 27th, we celebrate the feast of John the Apostle and Evangelist. John was exiled for the message of Christ and his Gospel. On the 28th, we mark the feast of the Holy Innocents, commemorating the slaughter of the children of Bethlehem by order of Herod. Finally, on December 29, four days after Christmas, we celebrate the optional memorial of Thomas Becket, the archbishop of Canterbury who was killed in the cathedral during Evening Prayer.

Why this sense of death and martyrdom immediately after Christmas? Why the red vestments after the gold and white of the Masses of Midnight and Christmas Day? Because, at the heart of Christmas (as at the heart of every season and feast of our liturgical calendar), we find the only real reason for our celebration: our redemption in Christ's Passion, Death, and Resurrection. This is not meant to squelch the joyful song of the angels. It is, however, a reminder that, without the backdrop of Holy Thursday, Good Friday, and the night between Holy Saturday and Easter, Christmas just doesn't make sense.

Though images of the crèche and the holy family tend to dominate, the liturgies of Christmas are never far from the realization that this child was born to die for us. The light of the Christmas candles is the light of the paschal candle. The readings of the Christmas Masses keep this tension in mind and make clear the connection of Christmas to the Paschal Mystery. Paul reminds us in the Second Reading for the Mass during the night on Christmas that it is Jesus, "who gave himself for us that he might redeem us from all iniquity and purify for himself a people of his own who are zealous for good deeds."[223] In the Mass during the day on Christmas, Paul again reminds us of this child's destiny: "When he had made purification for sins, he sat down at the right hand of the Majesty on high."[224] Even the Gospel for the Mass during the day points us from Bethlehem to Jerusalem: "He came to what was his own, and his own people did not accept him."[225]

Scripture scholars tell us that the infancy narratives are actually a telling of the whole Gospel story in miniature. Elements of rejection in the evil plotting of an anxious and fearful Herod and the irony that foreigners, and not his own people, recognize the promised king, all come together in these stories to foreshadow the events on Calvary Hill. Even when the child is recognized by his own people, in the characters of Simeon and Anna, the shadow of the cross falls across the scene in the prophecy to Mary: "This child is destined . . . to be a sign that will be opposed . . . and a sword will pierce your own soul too."[226]

Some of the most loved and cherished Christmas songs hold this tension of the child destined for the cross. The next time you sing "What Child is This?" pay attention to the fourth verse: "Nails, spear shall pierce him through / the cross he bore for me, for you." Likewise, note the fourth verse of "We Three Kings": "Myrrh is mine: its bitter perfume / Breathes a life of gathering gloom; Sorrowing, sighing, bleeding, dying / Sealed in the stone cold tomb."

"In the liturgical year the various aspects of the one Paschal Mystery unfold. This is also the case with the cycle and feasts surrounding the mystery of the incarnation (Annunciation, Christmas, Epiphany). They commemorate the beginning of our salvation and communicate to us the first fruits of the Paschal Mystery."

(Catechism of the Catholic Church, 1171)

An old adage reminds us that "the wood of the crib is the wood of the cross." That should not put a pall over our Christmas celebration. It is, rather, a profound statement of our faith. "For God so loved the world that he gave his only Son, so that everyone who believes in him may not perish but may have eternal life. Indeed, God did not send the Son into the world to condemn the world, but in order that the world might be saved through him" (John 3:16–17). Indeed, we are reminded of this tension every time we gather for the Eucharist when we recall the Paschal Mystery of Christ's birth, his life among us, his Passion, and his Death. We never pretend to not know the end of the story, and so we stand together around his table and proclaim as Church: "We proclaim your Death, O Lord, / and profess your Resurrection / until you come again."[227]

REFLECTION

» Be mindful of the whole season of Christmas. Celebrate it in its fullness, from Christmas Eve, through Epiphany, all the way to the Baptism of the Lord. Be mindful of all the elements that make up this season.

» Read through the wonderful stories of Matthew and Luke's infancy narratives. Focus on recognizing Christ's mission from the very start of his life on earth. Raymond Brown's book, *An Adult Christ at Christmas Time* is a wonderful guide for an understanding of these powerful stories of the Gospel.

» Strive to come to an understanding of the season of Christmas as it is celebrated in the midst of the Church. Focus and reflect on the ways in which Christmas challenges your growth in faith and your life in the "marketplace." Pay attention to the mysteries of the faith that are opened up for you in your understanding of this season.

» Strive to mark Christmas Time as a celebration of Christ's various manifestations. Think of ways you can keep, in your home, not only Christmas, but also the feast days that remember the "companions of Christ," Epiphany and the Baptism of the Lord.

» How do the symbols of Christmas and the elements of the Christmas liturgies speak to your own faith right now? Which symbols or elements touch you the most? In what ways do you use these symbols or liturgical elements for your own prayer and reflection?

» How do you understand the reality of the Paschal Mystery (Jesus's suffering, Death, and Resurrection) as the basis of Christmas? Does the backdrop of Good Friday enhance your own understanding of Christmas? How? Does it challenge your understanding of and celebration of Christmas? In what ways?

» When and where are you aware of the various "comings" of Christ in your own life right now? Where do you find God "breaking into" your life, the world as you experience it, your relationships, and in your own journey of faith?

» The coming of Christ at Christmas provides the door to the rest of the year. Having celebrated the coming of God in Christ, nothing can be the same! How will that be manifest in your own life this year?

CHAPTER 20

THE MYSTERY OF ORDINARY TIME DURING WINTER

The Themes of Ordinary Time during Winter

Is Ordinary Time "Boring Time"?

Following the Feast of the Baptism of the Lord, we return to Ordinary Time. There are two stretches of Ordinary Time in the liturgical year. The first period is between the end of Christmas Time and the beginning of Lent. The second period of Ordinary Time stretches from the end of Easter Time through the end of the liturgical year, ending with the beginning of Advent and the start of a new liturgical year. Ordinary Time is one complete season that is "interrupted," so to speak, by Lent, the Sacred Paschal Triduum, and Easter. For our purposes, it is helpful to treat these segments of Ordinary Time as two installments (see Chapter 24, "The Mystery of Ordinary Time in Summer and Fall"). Thus, we turn our attention here to Ordinary Time in winter, that brief period of up to ten weeks between Christmas Time and Lent.

"Ordinary Time"—it sounds rather unexciting, doesn't it? In fact, in grad school, my friends and I used to laugh, calling this season "Boring Time" because, so we thought, there are no big feasts to get ready for or to celebrate. Actually, the title "Ordinary Time" can be misleading. In the Church's liturgical year, the term "ordinary" doesn't mean "stagnant," or "routine," or "uneventful" as it may imply. It actually refers to the Latin term *ordinal*, which means "counted." This simply means that this season between Christmas and Easter is "counted time"—time that is marked as we leave one season and approach another.

"Besides the times of the year that have their own distinctive character, there remain in the yearly cycle thirty-three or thirty-four weeks in which no particular aspect of the mystery of Christ is celebrated, but rather the mystery of Christ itself is honored in its fullness, especially on Sundays. This period is known as Ordinary Time."

(*Universal Norms on the Liturgical Year and the Calendar*, 43)

If we were to be true to ourselves as Christians, if we were to be true to the Christmas season celebrated just prior to this season, then there is no such thing as "ordinary" time. All of time is special. All of time has been marked by the life, Death, and Resurrection of Christ. "All time belongs to [Christ]" we say, praying over the paschal candle in front of the Easter fire on Holy Saturday night.[228] All of time is changed because Christ's coming has redeemed us and made all things sacred.

That festive air with which we celebrate the seasons is meant to continue into every aspect of our lives, every one of our relationships, and every celebration, Sunday to Sunday, week to week, and day to day. The return to Ordinary Time, then, is extraordinary for us Christians. It is the time for us to proclaim him whom we have seen: to "proclaim [his] death . . . until [he comes] again."[229]

The Beginning of Jesus's Public Life and Ministry Among Us

At Christmas, we encounter Jesus as a baby. Within a few weeks, the Gospel presents an adult Jesus as he begins his public ministry. The problem is that it appears the Gospel (and the liturgical year, for that matter) is presenting a chronological account of the life of Jesus. This, of course, is a misunderstanding of the nature of the Gospel as well as of the liturgical year. The Gospel is not a biographical or chronological account of the life of Jesus. Rather, it is a proclamation of faith, intended to invite us into an encounter with the Risen Lord. In the same way, the liturgical year is not a week-by-week reenactment of the life of Jesus, but a journey of faith, inviting us into the Paschal Mystery of Christ.

As we enter into Ordinary Time in winter, the Gospel and the liturgies invite us to follow Jesus as he begins his public ministry. Throughout all of Ordinary Time, this journey will continue on, progressing to the fulfillment of the kingdom in the final days (see Chapter 24, "The Mystery of Ordinary Time in Summer and Fall"). During these winter weeks, however, we are invited to encounter Jesus as he introduced himself to the world at the beginning of his ministry. Each year, Ordinary Time in Winter calls us back to the excitement of the initial proclamation of Jesus: "The time is fulfilled, and the kingdom of God has come near / repent, and believe in the good news."[230]

During Ordinary Time in winter, each cycle of readings takes us back to the beginnings of Jesus's public life and ministry among us. In Year A (with readings from the Gospel according to Matthew), Jesus announces the nearness of God's kingdom and paints a portrait of it through his Sermon on the Mount. In Year B (with readings from the Gospel according to Mark), we are introduced to the authoritative teaching of Jesus and challenged to ask the same question being asked by people in the Gospel stories: "Who is this man?" In Year C (with readings from the Gospel according to Luke), we walk with Jesus as he begins his ministry in Galilee, fulfilling the prophecy of Isaiah. Though all three cycles take a slightly different path, these Gospel readings of Ordinary Time in winter propel us forward into a journey of faith through which we enter more deeply into the Paschal Mystery of Christ.

The Living Out of the Paschal Mystery

In Charles Dickens's *A Christmas Carol*, a reformed Ebenezer Scrooge assures the spirit, "I will honor Christmas in my heart and try to keep it all the year."[231] During Ordinary Time in winter, we, too, have the opportunity to honor the reality of the Christmas message that we have just celebrated and keep its spirit "all the year." During Christmas Time, we celebrate the entrance of the Paschal Mystery of Christ into our world through the Incarnation. The weeks following Christmas Time challenge us to live out the fullness of that Paschal Mystery. The reason we celebrate the birth of Christ in the first place is because we believe that his "message" (his teaching, miracles, life, Death, and Resurrection) brings us salvation. We encounter the initial proclamation of this message in Ordinary Time in winter, a message that, through our Baptism, we have promised to honor and keep "all the year."

What does it mean to do this? It means living as though we truly believe that we are blessed to be poor, to mourn, to be meek, to hunger and thirst for justice, to be merciful, to be clean of heart, to be peacemakers, and to be persecuted for the sake of righteousness. It means to live as though we truly believe that we are the light of the world, turning our other cheek, loving our enemies, and praying for our persecutors. It means to live as though we truly believe that Jesus has power over unclean spirits, sickness, and sin. It means living as though we truly believe that, in Jesus, we possess good news for the poor, liberty for captives, sight for the blind, and freedom for the oppressed.

These Sundays of Ordinary Time in winter challenge us to make the message we celebrate at Christmas more than some kind of annual pageant. They call us to live as though we truly believe that the child, born to us at Christmas, came to bring us a "grown-up" message that we are to live and keep "all the year."

The Symbols of Ordinary Time in Winter

The Weekly Celebration of the Eucharist in Its Fullness

All too often, we liturgists and catechists lament what we consider to be the lack of a theme or focus for Ordinary Time. We tend to find it easier to delve into Lent's violet and practices of fasting, praying, and giving alms. We find it easier to light the candles of our Advent wreaths and listen to Isaiah and John the Baptist. Unfortunately, we sometimes fall into the trap of thinking that Ordinary Time has no focus, no theme, and no symbols, aside from the color green.

The truth is that Ordinary Time focuses less on the climactic manifestations of Jesus the Christ (as emphasized during Christmas and Triduum/Easter and their seasons of preparation, Advent and Lent) and more on the person and message of Jesus of Nazareth and the living out of that message through the lives of the disciples and saints. We do not endure Ordinary Time, waiting for the "important" liturgical seasons to arrive so that we might finally focus on the "meat" of the Gospel. Rather, we dedicate every single Sunday of the liturgical year as a day to enter into the Paschal Mystery of Christ. By counting these Sundays (remember, "ordinary time" means counted time), we are literally designating them as the Lord's Day. These are not simply days to rest and refrain from work, but days to proclaim the arrival of a new era initiated by the Paschal Mystery of Christ. In essence, then, the primary symbol of Ordinary Time is the weekly celebration of the Eucharist on Sunday!

With this in mind, it is important to remember that before there was any sense of a liturgical year, before there were any seasons or feasts, before there was even a Christmas or an Easter, there was simply Sunday. It is the original feast day for us Christians: the Lord's Day, the Day of Days, the Eighth Day, the Day of New Creation that has begun this new era of Christ. The weekly remembrance and celebration of Sunday predates any annual celebration that ultimately found its way into our calendars. It is the basic foundation out of which flows every other solemnity, feast, memorial, or season. It is no wonder, then, that it is our primary focus during Ordinary Time.

Ordinary Time does not need to be cluttered with invented signs and symbols to fill up the space that was filled by Advent wreaths, crèche scenes, Lenten crosses, empty tombs, and statues of the risen Lord surrounded by lilies. Quite simply, Ordinary Time calls us, or rather, challenges us, to celebrate our weekly Eucharist to the fullest. It calls us back to our roots, in a sense, and gives us the opportunity to mark our first feast.

"Participation in the communal celebration of the Sunday Eucharist is a testimony of belonging and of being faithful to Christ and to his Church. The faithful give witness by this to their communion in faith and charity. Together they testify to God's holiness and their hope of salvation. They strengthen one another under the guidance of the Holy Spirit."

(Catechism of the Catholic Church, 2182)

By focusing on the initial proclamation of the Good News by Jesus as he began his ministry, Ordinary Time in winter invites us to make a fresh start in our efforts to make each Sunday's celebration of the Eucharist extraordinary.

While the various segments of Ordinary Time do emphasize certain themes—winter focuses more on the beginning of Jesus's ministry, in the summer we focus on discipleship, and as winter approaches anew we focus more on the end times—that focus is more loosely conceived than that of Advent, Christmas Time, Lent, the Triduum, and Easter Time. While the reformers of the Missal and the Lectionary (following the Second Vatican Council) could have developed very tightly focused themes for various periods of Ordinary Time, they chose to keep the season's focus more flexible. The wisdom of this is to avoid "dictating" what the Gospel is to say to us through the course of a liturgical year and to allow the Holy Spirit to speak to us through the Gospel and the season of Ordinary Time.

In short, this models how we encounter God. We do not decide the terms of the relationship. We do not control how God comes to us. Rather, God initiates the circumstances and terms and we respond. Through our weekly celebration of the Eucharist, we respond by proclaiming the presence of the risen Christ until he comes again in glory. We respond by giving thanks. We respond by being sent forth to proclaim the Good News of salvation to others through our daily living. In short, making our weekly Sunday celebration of the Eucharist *extra*-ordinary is the best way to do justice to Ordinary Time.

The Cycle of Nature

During Advent and Christmas, the connection between the liturgical season and the cycle of nature around us is quite evident. As the world around us grows darker and darker, we celebrate the coming of the Light of the World by lighting the candles on our wreaths and illuminating Christmas trees. Likewise, during Lent and Easter, as winter gives way to the new life of spring, we celebrate the new life of the Risen Christ.

What about Ordinary Time? The truth is we continue to take our cues from the cycle of nature as we move into Ordinary Time during winter, and eventually into Ordinary Time during summer and fall. During these winter weeks after Christmas, we continue to observe the victory of light over darkness as the length of daylight grows longer. As the light is taking hold in the world around us and nature struggles to come out of its winter sleep, the liturgies of Ordinary Time during winter celebrate the emergence of the Good News of Jesus Christ upon the world scene.

As the weeks unfold, the Gospel of Jesus gradually begins to take hold in a world that struggles to awaken from its "spiritual winter." Although winter lingers all around us, we don't give in, but, rather, hold out hope for an early spring. Likewise, during Ordinary Time in winter, we recognize that, despite the celebration of Christmas, evil and violence continue to linger in the world around us. In the face of this reality, however, we don't give in, but continue to proclaim the same hopeful message that the angels proclaimed at Christmas: "Glory to God in the highest heaven, / and on earth peace among those whom he favors!"[232] With each Eucharist, we give thanks for the continuing victory of light over darkness that began with the Incarnation celebrated at Christmas.

For some, the connection of Ordinary Time to the cycles of nature may seem too subtle: the seasons of Advent, Christmas Time, Lent, Triduum, and Easter Time seem to more vividly and powerfully connect liturgy with the cycles of nature. We need to realize, however, that, like nature, our liturgical seasons have a natural ebb and flow. At times, the seasons of nature have peak moments: the extraordinary colors of autumn, the dramatic loss of light and warmth of winter, and the explosion of new life in spring. For the most part, though, the cycles of nature move along at a pace that is more gradual. Like a marathon runner who needs to pace himself or herself for periodic bursts of speed along the way, the cycles of nature and our liturgical seasons also "pace themselves." During Ordinary Time in winter, we slow down the pace, in a sense, so that we can continue to take in the immensity of Christmas and prepare for the intensity of Lent. The pace of Ordinary Time in winter sets the stage for the season of Lent that will soon follow. Liturgically, we cannot maintain the intense "pace" of seasons such as Advent, Christmas Time, Lent, Triduum, and Easter Time throughout an entire year. Entering into the Paschal Mystery is a marathon, not a sprint!

The Liturgies of Ordinary Time in Winter

Feasts and Memorials of the Saints and Martyrs

What was the most difficult class that you ever took? Most of us can recall sitting through a class that challenged our ability to comprehend the subject matter. When a teacher or professor presents material that seems beyond our grasp, we can react in one of two ways: we can drop the class or, we can ask him or her, "Can you give me an example?"

During the liturgical year, we are grappling with a subject that is indeed very difficult to grasp: the Paschal Mystery. When confronted with the overwhelming reality of the Paschal Mystery of Christ and our call to discipleship, we can scarcely take it all in. On the one hand, we can respond by simply "dropping the course." We can give up, walk away, and latch on to simpler, more concrete forms of self-gratification. Or, we can ask the age-old question: "Can you give me an example?"

"From the Church, [the Christian] learns the *example of holiness* and . . . discovers it in the spiritual tradition and long history of the saints who have gone before him and whom the liturgy celebrates in the rhythms of the sanctoral cycle."

(*Catechism of the Catholic Church*, 2030)

The Church knows that the Paschal Mystery of Christ is a profoundly challenging concept to grasp. For that reason, the Church provides us with examples to help us understand what the Paschal Mystery of Christ "looks like" when "ordinary" lives become infused with the extraordinary power of the Paschal Mystery. During Ordinary Time in winter, the Church invites us to begin reflecting upon some remarkable examples of "ordinary" people whose lives were profoundly changed by the extraordinary power of the Paschal Mystery. By celebrating the feasts and memorials of the saints and martyrs, we are provided with "illustrations" of the Paschal Mystery in the lives of real people. Through their lives and deaths, we are privy to examples of what it truly means to surrender to the will of God and to enter into mystery. We learn, from their example, what it means to be disciples of Christ.

During these weeks between Christmas and Lent, we come to know the truth of the Gospel through the examples of people like:

- St. Anthony, Abbot (January 17)
- St. Fabian, Pope and Martyr (January 20)
- St. Agnes, Virgin and Martyr (January 21)
- St. Vincent, Deacon (January 23)
- St. Francis De Sales, Bishop and Doctor of the Church (January 24)
- St. Angela Merici, Virgin (January 27)
- St. Thomas Aquinas, Priest and Doctor of the Church (January 28)
- St. John Bosco, Priest (January 31)
- St. Blaise, Bishop and Martyr (February 3)
- St. Scholastica, Virgin (February 10)

Like kids who emulate their NBA heroes when playing basketball at the playground, we, too, emulate the heroes of our faith, as we learn from the examples of the lives of the saints and martyrs and attempt to put the Good News of Jesus Christ into practice.

"In the cycle of the year, as she celebrates the mystery of Christ, the Church also venerates with a particular love the Blessed Mother of God, Mary, and proposes to the devotion of the faithful the Memorials of the Martyrs and other Saints."

(*Universal Norms on the Liturgical Year and the Calendar*, 8)

The Light Continues to Grow: The Feast of the Presentation of the Lord

And you thought that lighting candles was only for Advent wreaths and the Easter Vigil! During Ordinary Time in winter, as we continue to celebrate the growing light of each day in nature, we also celebrate the growing light of Christ that is emerging and taking hold all around us. On February 2, the Church celebrates another feast of light: the Presentation of the Lord, also known as Candlemas, or the blessing of candles. On this day, Scripture recounts the story of "the blessed day / when Jesus was presented in the Temple by Mary and Joseph. / Outwardly he was fulfilling the Law, / but in reality he was coming to meet his believing people." The Scripture story tells us of how Simeon and Anna, led by the Spirit, "came to the Temple . . . [and] / enlightened by the same Spirit, / they recognized the Lord / and confessed him with exultation."[233]

In the same way that God revealed the Light of the World to Simeon and Anna, the Church prays that the Light of Christ will fill the hearts of all believers. To symbolize this, the faithful gather with candles that are lit and blessed with the following prayer: "sanctify with your blessing these candles, / which we are eager to carry in praise of your name, / so that, treading the path of virtue, / we may reach that light which never fails."[234] Throughout the year, these blessed candles are used in our homes and parishes as signs of deliverance, proclaiming Jesus as "a light for revelation to the Gentiles, / and for glory to your people Israel."[235] As winter wanes and hope for spring emerges, we gather in the house of the Lord, like Simeon and Anna, to recognize the light of the nations in the breaking of the bread, so that we may go forth and proclaim him with joy throughout the year.

"Forty days have passed since we celebrated the joyful feast / of the Nativity of the Lord. / Today is the blessed day / when Jesus was presented in the Temple by Mary and Joseph. / . . . / So let us also, gathered together by the Holy Spirit, / proceed to the house of God to encounter Christ. / There we shall find him / and recognize him in the breaking of the bread, / until he comes again, revealed in glory."

(Introductory address, the Feast of the Presentation of the Lord, *The Roman Missal*)

REFLECTION

» Respect the natural ebb and flow of the liturgical seasons and lessen the intensity during Ordinary Time during winter. Allow yourself to take a breather between Christmas and Lent and refrain from imposing any heavy practices for this season. Instead, review some basic practices in relation to Sunday worship such as reverence, responses, and so on.

» Take advantage of Ordinary Time in winter to focus on the lives of the saints who are celebrated during this time. Be sure to commemorate the various feasts and memorials by looking up some background on the saints and martyrs who are being remembered.

» Be sure to mark the Feast of the Presentation of the Lord/Candlemas (February 2) by acquiring candles that you will use in your home throughout the year for prayer and bringing them to church to have them blessed. If you are unable to attend yourself, ask a friend to have them blessed for you.

» The Gospel readings of Ordinary Time in winter focus on the beginnings of Jesus's public ministry. First impressions are very important, and Jesus obviously made quite a first impression. What do you find most attractive about the message being proclaimed by Jesus? What is the most challenging?

» How do you observe Sundays? How do you prepare for the celebration of Sunday Mass? What can you do to make your participation in Sunday Mass more complete?

CHAPTER 21

THE MYSTERY OF LENT

The Themes of Lent

Ash Wednesday: Calling Us to Remember

Broadway musicals almost always begin with a rousing overture. In order to get the show off to a good start, the overture sets the tone for the show and gives a hint of what is to come. Ash Wednesday serves the same purpose for Lent. By focusing more closely on Ash Wednesday, we come away with a better understanding of what the entire period of Lent is all about.

L ate one night, in the summer of 1990, I got a call from my younger sister. She had just talked to my parents who were in upper Michigan, where they were staying at our family's cabin. There had been a terrible forest fire and the cabin itself was burned to the ground. Not only was the cabin gone, but so were 20 square miles of forest, as well as many other homes and buildings.

I was reminded of that fire one December when I went home to see my family (my parents now live there after rebuilding). During the weekend, we built a bonfire in the middle of the snow and gathered around it after a day of sledding. It was while collecting wood for the fire that we all noticed our hands. Everyone's hands were black—literally covered in soot and ash that still lingered from the fire. Then we noticed the same blackness on our clothes and our boots. It was on our scarves from when we had brushed against trees and my brother even had some smeared on his face. Suddenly the fire that happened almost seven years before became very much a part of the present. The ash that now marked our hands and our clothes was calling us to remember.

~Todd

On Ash Wednesday, ashes call us, as a community, to remember. While being marked with them, we are called to remember that we "are dust, and to dust [we] shall return." These words are not meant to be a blow to our dignity or self esteem, saying that we're nothing but dirt. Rather, they call us to remember that, though we are dust, God's love breathes life into us. God alone sustains us. Without God, we are dust. These words and these ashes call us to recognize the folly of trying to go it alone as we struggle to "get it right"—with ourselves, with each other, and with our God. They call us to remember and practice the ancient disciplines of prayer, fasting, and almsgiving. They call us to remember that we are a people who are always in need of redemption, who are broken, and who continually struggle to pick up the pieces.

The ashes that are smeared on our foreheads also call us to remember something else. Put in the shape of a cross, the ashes also call us to remember that our God is gracious and merciful, "slow to anger, and abounding in steadfast love, and ready to relent from punishment."[236] If they remind us that we are a people in need of salvation, the ashes also call us to remember that our God has promised "on a day of salvation I have helped you."[237] If they remind us that we are a broken people, the ashes also call us to remember that our God wants nothing more than to make us whole. If they remind us of how we fall short in our plans, our hopes, or our dreams, they also call us to remember that now is the acceptable time, and that now is the day of salvation.[238] Each Ash Wednesday, we intentionally mark ourselves with ashes, and we remember. We remember personally, as well as communally, that our God always invites us to return to him. God, who is always faithful to what he has promised, will be the one to make us whole.

> "O God, . . . / . . . be pleased to bless these ashes, / which we intend to receive upon our heads, / that we, who acknowledge we are but ashes / and shall return to dust, / may, through a steadfast observance of Lent, / gain pardon for sins and newness of life / after the likeness of your Risen Son."
>
> (Blessing of Ashes, *The Roman Missal*)

The Joy of Lent: Repentance

"Rejoice, Jerusalem, and all who love her. / Be joyful, all who were in mourning; / exult and be satisfied at her consoling breast."[239] These words begin the Entrance Antiphon for the Fourth Sunday of Lent, traditionally known as Laetare Sunday. *Laetare* is Latin for "rejoice." Laetare Sunday has always been a day in the midst of Lenten penance and abstinence to highlight the anticipated joy of Easter. Though we no longer designate this day as Laetare Sunday, it is still the one Sunday in the season of Lent when the priest wears rose-colored vestments.

So why did we stop designating the Fourth Sunday of Lent as Laetare Sunday? Well, if we look at the first Preface to the Eucharistic Prayer given for the season of Lent, we may find a clue: "For by your gracious gift each year / your faithful await the sacred paschal feasts / with the joy of minds made pure. . . ."[240] Lent is a "gift," and we await with "joy"? Somehow, "joy" and "Lent" do not seem to be words that belong in the same sentence! Aren't they contradictory? We tend to think that Lent is a time for somberness and serious self-denial, not for rejoicing and gladness! Perhaps it is this common misconception of Lent that contributed to the rethinking of Laetare Sunday and to the ultimate decision to no longer separate it from the rest of the season since all of Lent is a joyful season!

Look at the different prayers used in the liturgy during this season:

- "Grant, almighty God, / through the yearly observances of holy Lent, / that we may grow in understanding / of the riches hidden in Christ."[241]

- "O God . . . / be pleased, we pray, / to nourish us inwardly by your word, / that, with spiritual sight made pure, / we may rejoice to behold your glory."[242]

- "For you have given your children a sacred time / for the renewing and purifying of their hearts."[243]

There is nothing sad or somber about any of the truths expressed in those prayers! The joy to which Lent calls us is a quiet joy that prepares us for Easter. This joy is more like that of a mother lovingly holding her sleeping baby. It's a joy that permeates our being; a constant, permanent joy that never goes away. It's the kind of joy that is nuanced by peace and security, a sense of constancy and assurance. This joy comes from the faith we have that Christ's Death has brought us life. It's a joy that is like the assurance of St. Paul: "God, who is rich in mercy, out of the great love with which he loved us even when we were dead through our trespasses, made us alive together with Christ."[244] In that, there is reason for rejoicing!

Recommitment to Our Baptism and Deepening Conversion

"What are you doing for Lent?" This is a question that we ask of ourselves and each other as Lent approaches. Especially in our American culture, we don't feel useful unless we are doing something! Lent is not so much a time for us to concentrate on what we are to do, as much as on what God wants to do with and through us, namely, make us disciples of Christ! At the same time, who we are is both shaped and expressed by what we do. With that in mind, let's take a look at how Lent can help us to be better disciples of Christ.

In order to understand what Lent is today, we need to look at its origins. In the early Christian community, when adults were preparing for initiation into the church, they (the catechumens) prepared for a lengthy and significant period of time, sometimes a few years. The whole community rejoiced and prepared along with them. The last forty days were an intense preparation for initiation into the community during which the elect (those about to be baptized), along with the community, would pray, fast, and give alms, leading up to the celebration of the sacraments at Easter. This period of preparation eventually came to be identified with what we call Lent.

As time went on and infant Baptism became more popular, the season of Lent continued but without focus on the initiation of new adult disciples. The Christian community continued to use the time to focus on penitence as a return to the baptismal state of grace. Self-denial, the endurance of suffering, mortification, sacrifices, and an emphasis on the suffering, Passion, and Death of Jesus became the foci of Lent. Penitents (public sinners seeking reconciliation) were marked with ashes and sent forth from the church on Ash Wednesday before being readmitted on Holy Thursday. As an expression of solidarity with those who were temporarily expelled, the entire community was marked with ashes on Ash Wednesday and joined in the reflection on the suffering, Passion, and Death of Jesus as well as the mortification.

Since the restoration of the adult catechumenate following the Second Vatican Council, the season of Lent has been reinvigorated as a time for the whole Christian community to prepare along with the elect (those preparing for Baptism), for entering into deeper relationship with Christ in Baptism. Today, the focus is on our Baptism: what does it mean to be a disciple of Christ, a member of his Body, the Church? We still pray, fast, and give alms, but not as an end in themselves. Rather we practice these traditional disciplines as a way of strengthening our discipleship through the conversion of our hearts. We don't endure Lent as though waiting for the suffering Jesus to expire on the cross. We know that Jesus died once and for all to save us from sin and now lives no more to die. Catholics believe in dying with Christ and being "born again"—and again, and again, and again, etc. That's why we return to Lent every year. Lent is a season that exists only because of Easter! Unless our focus is on preparing to celebrate the glorious triumph of Easter and the renewal of our Baptism in Christ, Lent has little meaning for us.

"By the solemn forty days of *Lent* the Church unites herself each year to the mystery of Jesus in the desert."

(Catechism of the Catholic Church, 540)

The Church uses the Scriptures of Lent to assist the elect and the entire assembly to reflect upon our baptismal commitment to discipleship. The Gospel on the First Sunday is always focused on Jesus's temptation in the desert while the Second Sunday is always focused on the glory of Jesus's Transfiguration. From the Third to the Fifth Sunday, the focus depends on the cycle of the Lectionary (meaning, that it is different in Year A, Year B, and Year C).

In Year A, we read three powerful passages from John: the Samaritan woman, the man born blind, and the raising of Lazarus. These three Gospel stories provide the elect and the assembly with an opportunity to reflect upon how Jesus satisfies our thirst, restores our sight, and raises us to new life. In Year B, Matthew's Gospel stories for these three Sundays calls us to focus on the meaning of the pending Passover of our Lord. In Year C, the Gospel stories of Luke and John focus on repentance and conversion. Finally, on the sixth Sunday, Palm Sunday, all three Lectionary cycles focus on the story of our Lord's Passion and Death. Throughout Lent, the First Readings come from the Old Testament and focus on themes of the covenant between God and Israel, and the Chosen People's journey of faith that was marked by sin and reconciliation. Through these powerful Scripture readings, we are challenged to reflect upon our own journey of faith and our need for reconciliation with God through Jesus Christ.

The Symbols of Lent

The Elect

During Lent, one of the primary symbols is a group of people who have been chosen to receive something of great value they have not earned. They are the elect. For many months, a group of people referred to as catechumens (literally "someone who is taught by mouth") have been learning about the disciple's way of life through the process of the Rite of Christian Initiation of Adults, or RCIA. Now, those who feel ready to embrace that life through the waters of Baptism are sent to the bishop for the Rite of Election where sponsors, godparents, and catechists give witness to their readiness. The bishop then declares them to be members of the elect, which means "chosen." They have been chosen in the same way that Jesus called his first Apostles to leave their nets and follow him. The Rite of Election celebrates this action on God's part and allows the elect to publicly embrace this unearned invitation.

As these chosen ones use Lent to make their final preparations for Baptism at Easter, the entire Christian community prays for them and prepares with them. Like newlyweds who remind long-married couples of a time when their commitment was all-consuming, the elect remind the entire Christian community of the all-consuming nature of discipleship. In a very real sense, the elect act as an example to the rest of us of what it means to truly desire the gentle yoke of discipleship. Their eagerness serves as a sign and a reminder for the already-baptized to approach the sacraments once again with renewed enthusiasm and commitment.

"These Elect, whom we bring with us to the Easter sacraments, will look to us for an example of Christian renewal. Let us pray to the Lord for them and for ourselves, that we may be renewed by one another's efforts and together come to share the joys of Easter"

(Intercessions for the Elect, Rite of Election, *Rite of Christian Initiation for Adults*)

Fasting, Praying, Almsgiving

If Lent is all about repentance (conversion) and deepening our discipleship, how do we do this? Traditionally, Catholics have focused on three disciplines: prayer, fasting, and giving alms. Notice that the words *disciple* and *discipline* come from the same root word, which means "follower." To be a disciple (follower) of Jesus means to practice discipline (following). Lent, then, is our practice season, an intense training camp for would-be disciples of Christ. In so many small ways during Lent, we practice allowing our old selves to die so that a new person may be born in Christ and celebrated with the Christian community at Easter. Ronald Rolheiser refers to these traditional Lenten disciplines as "non-negotiables" for Christian discipleship.[245] We practice these disciplines in an intense way during Lent, knowing that, as disciples of Christ, we will be called upon to exercise them year-round.

"Prayer with fasting is good, but better than both is almsgiving with righteousness."

(Tobit 12:8)

Here are a few suggestions for how to practice these Lenten disciplines:

Prayer (communication with God):

• Pray regularly. Consider setting aside time to read Scripture for about 10–15 minutes each day.

• Give yourself quiet time every day to just dwell in the presence of God.

• Pray with others. You might gather with a group each week for prayer, or talk to a friend about your prayer life. Consider attending a Lenten retreat or prayer day at your parish.

• Keep a Lenten journal.

• Try using different media to stimulate your prayer, such as prayer books, spiritual CDs or DVDs, or sacred music.

Fasting (self-denial, self-control, doing without):

• Avoid seeing fasting as a means for punishing yourself. Instead, think of it as a string around your finger—something that reminds you to make this period of time significant. Each time you experience physical hunger, let it remind you that Jesus alone satisfies the hungry heart.

• Fast from your usual menu of food and snacks not as a means of losing weight, but as a way of sensitizing yourself to those in need and reminding yourself that God alone can fulfill.

• Fast from the clutter in your life. Cut down on noise, TV, the Internet, emails, iPods, CDs, and car radios.

• Fast from sinful or addictive behaviors, and avoid using activity to mask emotional unrest. Fast from unnecessary shopping, gossip, having the last word, constant chatter, negativity, procrastination, finger-pointing, and emotional manipulation of others.

• Use the time, money, and emotional energy that you conserve from fasting to reinforce your prayer life and in service of others.

Almsgiving (giving to those in need)

• Consider ways in which you can give of your time and talent, not just your treasure.

• Make amends with society by doing service work or giving to charities that promote social justice.

• Make amends with friends by sending cards, letters, or emails, or by making phone calls or paying visits.

• Perform acts of kindness and charity not just for self-improvement, but to help heal others.

• Make amends with your body by consuming healthy foods, drinking enough water, and exercising regularly, not out of vanity, but out of reverence for the body that God gave you.

• Be generous with others in small ways. Take someone out to eat and pick up the bill. Loan someone your umbrella when it is raining.

• Clean out your drawers and closets and give clothes to the Society of St. Vincent de Paul or another local charity.

Someone once said that Lent was easier when it was harder, referring to the rigorous discipline of Lents gone by. Remember, the object of Lent is not to make life harder, but to make life more meaningful through a deeper relationship with Jesus. That takes discipline. Through the disciplines of Lent, we remind ourselves that it is not our jobs, our money, the food we eat, the status we have, the clothes we wear, the style of our hair, the popularity we have, or the car we drive that sustain us. God alone sustains us. Without that glorious power, we are dust.

The Cross: Journey to Jerusalem

When I was a kid, my dad used to drive the family to various fun places, one of which was old Comiskey Park, where the Chicago White Sox used to play. Not having any sense of direction, my siblings and I used to look for landmarks that would indicate how close we were to reaching our destination. As we inched along through traffic down 35th Street, we would eagerly look out the windshield window to see who could spot the light fixtures on the roof of the ballpark. Finally, one of us would spot them and shout, "I see the lights! I see the lights!" Once we could see the lights of Comiskey Park, we knew we were heading in the right direction and were close to arriving at our destination.   **~Joe**

During Lent, the cross stands before us as a "landmark" indicating where our journey is heading. Lent itself is a journey to Jerusalem. When we see the cross during Lent, we know that our baptismal journey leads us through death to life. Lent is not a time for us to continuously ponder the suffering and Death of Jesus, but rather, a time for us to ponder our destination. It is a time to remember that, if we are truly followers of Christ (disciples), then we must keep our eyes on the cross knowing that it is on Calvary that we arrive at our destination; that place where our lives will be transformed in glory.

In the Gospel for the Fifth Sunday of Lent, Year B, two Greeks (or Gentiles) make the following request: "We would like to see Jesus."[246] The response they get to their request is rather disturbing. They are answered with Jesus's prediction of the death he would endure. "If you want to see Jesus," the Gospel seems to say, "then look to the cross." The liturgies of Lent call us to journey with Christ, through his Passion and cross, into life. Through our own self-emptying and self-giving, we are called to follow in the Lord's footsteps "so that, being made by his grace partakers of the Cross, / we may have a share also in his Resurrection and in his life."[247]

"Very truly, I tell you, unless a grain of wheat falls into the earth and dies, it remains just a single grain; but if it dies, it bears much fruit"

(John 12:24, Gospel for the Fifth Sunday of Lent, Year B)

Forty Days: Our Exodus Experience of Conversion

Just how do we "count" the forty days of Lent? First, we need to recognize that the number forty is symbolic. How often we see this number in Scripture! It rained on Noah's ark for forty days and forty nights. Moses spent forty days on the mountaintop before descending with the Law. The Israelites spent forty years wandering the desert. Jesus spent forty days in the desert before beginning his ministry. The number forty is a symbolic number.[248]

In biblical tradition, the number forty represents a significant period of time during which a person or people are tested and strengthened for what lies ahead. Lent is to be a period of significance for us: a time to be tested and strengthened for our mission to serve as disciples of Christ. Like the people of Israel, who wandered the desert for forty years in search of the promised land, we experience our own journey of conversion during Lent as we grapple with our temptations and deepen our commitment to follow Jesus as he leads us from slavery to freedom.

With that in mind, it should be noted that the counting of the forty days of Lent is not scientific. One popular method is to count from Ash Wednesday to Easter Sunday, minus the Sundays of Lent, since Sundays are not days of penitence. Unfortunately, some Catholics use that formula as a convenient excuse to do all those things on Sunday that they were giving up the rest of Lent! Another method of counting the forty days is to begin counting the forty days beginning with the First Sunday of Lent, not from Ash Wednesday when Lent begins, and continue up to the evening on Holy Thursday when Lent ends and the Triduum begins with the Mass of the Lord's Supper. Neither of these methods actually counts each day of the season of Lent, though, so the number forty is symbolic.

Of these forty days, the first four weeks are primarily shaped by the readings, the penitential rites, and the rites related to Christian initiation. On the Fifth Sunday of Lent, the focus of the liturgy shifts to Christ's Passion and this continues through Holy Week, beginning on Palm Sunday of the Passion of the Lord and continuing through to the beginning of the Mass of the Lord's Supper on the night of Holy Thursday. With this celebration, Lent officially ends and the Sacred Paschal Triduum begins (see Chapter 22).

The Lenten Liturgy

The Absence of the Gloria/Alleluia and the Sparseness of Decoration

As we mentioned above, one of the disciplines of Lent is fasting. Catholics have a very rich understanding of fasting that goes way beyond the notion of simply giving up food. Our fasting is multi-dimensional: we fast not only from food, but also from certain habits, behaviors, and activities. In our Lenten liturgy, we ritually experience this fasting or "doing without." For forty days, we do without the proclamation of "Alleluia" before the Gospel. The absence of this Easter word reminds us that we are immersing ourselves into a season of fasting. In fact, Catholic tradition often involves literally "burying" the Alleluia. On the day before Ash Wednesday, many Christian communities will invite people to gather in a courtyard where a hole is dug and a sign with the word "Alleluia" painted on it is buried for the forty days.

In the same way that we fast from the singing of "Alleluia" during Lent, we also fast from the singing of the Gloria for forty days as well. The "emptiness" during this part of the Lenten Mass reminds us that our fasting is in full swing. Likewise, decoration of the altar is kept to a minimum, as another image of fasting—even our environment is participating in this fasting, or doing without. Our fasting is, indeed, audio-visual!

Some parishes follow the tradition of covering the cross in the final two weeks of Lent in anticipation of unveiling it for the Triduum, our glorious celebration of Jesus's triumph over death. Traditionally, these last two weeks were known as "Passiontide," acknowledging the more direct focus on the Passion of the Lord in the texts and the readings of the Mass during these weeks. Though that distinction is no longer made, the tradition may continue. Other images may also be covered, extending this visual fast. These would then be uncovered before the beginning of the Easter Vigil on Holy Saturday night.

Lent's Royal Violet

As we noted in our discussion of the color of Advent the use of color "has as its purpose to give more effective expression even outwardly whether to the specific character of the mysteries of faith to be celebrated or to a sense of Christian life's passage through the course of the liturgical year."[249] While the violet of Advent is a bluer tone suggestive of the darker late autumn skies, Lent's color maintains a royal violet that is more reddish, specifically suggesting the penitential spirit of Lent as well as the suffering of our Lord Jesus. Like the violet of Advent, Lent's violet suggests the kingship of Jesus, but now with a focus on how that was achieved through the suffering, Death, and Resurrection of the King of Glory. From vestments and banners to altar cloths and tastefully placed fabrics, Lenten violet surrounds us and calls us to enter the season with reverent joy.

"And the soldiers wove a crown of thorns and put it on his head, and they dressed him in a purple robe. They kept coming up to him, saying 'Hail, King of the Jews!'"

(John 19:2-3)

Penitential Rite

During Lent, the Penitential Rite of the Mass takes on a much more prominent character. In some communities, the priest invites the congregation to kneel for this part of the liturgy. In these cases, the pace of the liturgy is slowed and the invocations of the penitential litany are prayed with deliberateness and purpose. The theme of penance is given unique expression in this rite.

The communal nature of the Lenten call to conversion is particularly key to this part of the Eucharist. The Penitential Rite is not something that we do only as individuals. This is the time for the whole community to acknowledge the great and abundant mercy of God and its need to respond to that mercy by continued conversion of heart. Even if the Confiteor is used, which begins in the singular, "I confess to almighty God,"[250] the experience of hearing many voices joined together can be a powerful communal statement of our common human brokenness.

The Scrutinies of the Elect

Every so often, I get a request from someone to serve as a reference for them in their job search. Inevitably, a call will come in from the prospective employer inquiring about this person that I am recommending. During the conversation, the character, qualities, experience, and potential of the applicant are scrutinized. If the employer likes what he or she hears from me, then of course, further scrutiny takes place at the actual interview before this person is (hopefully!) hired.   **~Joe**

What does it mean for something or someone to come under scrutiny? The word *scrutiny* literally means "to search." When we scrutinize something or someone, we are searching, usually for flaws or areas that need attention or fixing. During the liturgies of Lent, we are called, along with the elect, to undergo scrutiny or, in other words, to search out that which is sinful or weak in our hearts as we prepare to enter (or renew) our baptismal relationship with Jesus. These Lenten rites of searching take place on the Third, Fourth, and Fifth Sundays of Lent. In the early church, those who submitted their names for Baptism were questioned after a significant period of preparation. Likewise, their sponsors and other acquaintances were questioned, usually about the moral character of the applicant. Though the practice of celebrating the scrutinies waned with the rise of infant Baptism and the decline of the catechumenate, the restoration of the Rite of Christian Initiation of Adults (1972) restored the celebration of the scrutinies to their rightful place in our Lenten liturgies.

"The scrutinies are meant to uncover, then heal all that is weak, defective, or sinful in the hearts of the elect; to bring out, then strengthen all that is upright, strong, and good. For the scrutinies are celebrated in order to deliver the elect from the power of sin and Satan, to protect them against temptation, and to give them strength in Christ, who is the way, the truth, and the life."

(Rite of Christian Initiation of Adults, 141)

During the scrutinies, the elect are called forward with their sponsors and the entire assembly prays for them that they may scrutinize their hearts and honestly recognize all that is weak and sinful and in need of healing, as well as to strengthen all that is strong and good. The Gospel readings of these Sundays, taken from John, are the heart of the celebrations of the scrutinies. Almost from the beginning of the Church, these Gospel readings have been used in these rites. From the middle of the first millennium, the Church has recognized the power of these three Gospel stories and has relied on them to help the elect in their self-searching. These stories focus on spiritual thirst (the woman at the well), blindness (the man born blind), and death and decay (the raising of Lazarus). In the scrutinies, these Gospel stories act as a light that shines on the lives of the elect and illumines those areas that need to be healed. The light from these Gospel stories is also cast upon the figure of Jesus, who is revealed to the elect as the One who is able to quench their thirst, restore their sight, and raise them to new life. In other words, Christ is shown to the Elect to be Savior and Redeemer. They, in turn, are shown their need for Christ's salvation and redemption.

At the same time, the entire assembly is called to scrutinize their own hearts, in the light of these Gospel stories, to determine what needs healing in order to renew their Baptism. The Church prays that the Elect will be free from Satan's grasp and the power of sin. These are called prayers of *exorcism*, not to be confused with the Hollywood notion that exaggerates (or perhaps, *simplifies* would be better!) exorcism into a ghastly encounter with monster-like demons. The truth is, evil exists within and all around us in some very subtle (and other not-so-subtle) ways. Through honest scrutiny, we come to identify these areas of sin that need healing (exorcism) so that, come Easter, we can truly say that only the power of Christ compels us!

The scrutiny rite ends with intercessions, in which the community prays specifically for the elect. What is so special at this point in the rite is that this is one of the few times when those preparing for Baptism are part of the community's intercessory prayer (the other time is during the rite of acceptance). Remember, they are not yet fully part of the community of the Church. It is the duty and the responsibility of the baptized to intercede for the Church, the world, the poor, and the local community. This is why those who have not yet become part of the Church are normally dismissed from the assembly before the intercessions are prayed. It is not yet their duty and responsibility. It is only after they have died in the waters of Baptism, when they become part of the Body of Christ, that they join their voices with those of the whole priestly community in its prayer to God on behalf of the world and the Church.

» During Lent, incorporate more silent time for prayer, identify something to fast from and a day or time to do so, and participate in an almsgiving project.

» Keep a "Scrutinies" journal. On each of the Sundays that these rites are celebrated, reflect and write about those areas of your life that are in need of healing.

» Write a letter to one or more of the elect of your parish telling them what it means to you to be a disciple of Christ and assuring them of your prayers and support during Lent.

» If Lent can be thought of as a "training ground" for would-be disciples of Christ, what "training regimen" would you recommend to your "trainees?"

» What is it that you thirst for in life? How can Jesus quench that thirst? In what ways are you experiencing blindness? How can Jesus restore your sight? In what ways are you bound head to toe and entombed like Lazarus? How can Jesus call you to new life?

» What bad or unnecessary habits can you fast from during Lent? If these habits could be compared to junk food, what would bring better health to your life this Lent?

CHAPTER 22

THE MYSTERY OF THE SACRED PASCHAL TRIDUUM

The Themes of Triduum

Our Defining Moment

How do we begin to address the most profound, the most holy, and the most solemn of our Catholic rites and rituals? How do we find words to describe the defining celebration that marks us as Christians and identifies us as followers of the crucified and risen One? How do we begin to reflect upon the depth and beauty, the symbols and gestures, the demands and the responsibilities that anyone who dares to enter these liturgies must accept?

What we are about to explore are the liturgies of the Sacred Paschal Triduum—the three-day celebration of Holy Thursday night, Good Friday, Holy Saturday, and Easter Sunday. These are not, as many people might think, three separate liturgical celebrations. It is all one liturgy, which takes three days to celebrate. It begins on Thursday evening and does not end until Easter Sunday evening. It is a defining moment, this three-day liturgy: defining because it tells us, once again, who we are as a community and as individual members of that community. Defining because it tells us, once again, who God is for us and what God has done and is doing for us: how God has been and continues to be active in our lives. Defining because it reminds us of who we are to each other and what our lives are to be about. Defining because it tells us from where we've come, who our ancestors are, and what they have passed on to us. Defining because this three-day liturgy has the power to shape us, to form us, and to make us anew.

"Beginning with the Easter Triduum as its source of light, the new age of the Resurrection fills the whole liturgical year with its brilliance."

(*Catechism of the Catholic Church*, 1168)

Most importantly, this three-day liturgy is defining because it is about our life and our death. It is about our life in Jesus Christ, who died, rose, and now lives in us and in the Church. Christ lives in us now, not two thousand years ago. Christ lives in us, as members of his Body, the Church. Christ lives in those whom we baptize in his name: Christ Jesus, risen, alive in those who will be new members of his Body, alive in the midst of our parish communities, alive in us. For us Catholics, the Paschal Triduum is the very heart of our liturgical year. Everything else that we do liturgically —every feast day, every holy day, and most especially, every Sunday—flows out of the

Paschal Triduum and its commemoration of the Lord's Death and Resurrection. It is the summit of our liturgical year. It is the very source of our liturgies, our prayers, our spirituality, and our whole faith.

"Christ accomplished his work of human redemption and of the perfect glorification of God principally through his Paschal Mystery in which by dying he has destroyed our death, and by rising restored our life, the Sacred Paschal Triduum of the Passion and Resurrection of the Lord shines forth as the high point of the entire liturgical year."

(Universal Norms for the Liturgical Year and the Calendar, 18)

The Three Days

As stated, although these are three separate days, the rites that mark them are considered only one liturgy. "But wait!" you might say, "Holy Thursday, Good Friday, Holy Saturday, and Easter Sunday—that's four days. So why do we refer to the Triduum as 'the three days'?" Perhaps this reference to time would be a good place to begin getting a better sense of how the Church asks us to look at these most sacred nights of our year.

The season of Lent officially ends during the day on Holy Thursday. As the sun sets that evening, we end Lent and begin the Triduum. During the next three days (*day* meaning 24 hours), the Church uses the ancient measure of time that counts a "day" from sunset to sunset, instead of the usual way of marking it sunrise to sunrise. So, "the three days" then become obvious: the first day of the Triduum is from Holy Thursday night to Good Friday night; the second day is from Good Friday night to Holy Saturday night, when the Triduum reaches its highest point at the Vigil; and the third day is from Holy Saturday night to Easter Sunday night, when the Triduum officially ends with the celebration of Easter Vespers (sung Evening Prayer).

In every way that we approach this three-day celebration, the Church calls us to acknowledge its uniqueness. The Church seems to be telling us, "these days are so special that we even count their passing differently than we normally do!" This gives us a clue as to how we should be approaching these holy days. They are special. They are unique. These days are set up in such a way to be, literally, a time of retreat for us. They are a time to cease our normal daily routines. These days are set aside for us to do things we don't normally do, things that we do only during these days. We are called to be different during these days. For, during these days, we accept the responsibility and the duty to "proclaim [his] Death . . . until [he comes] again."[251]

Focus of the Season

The Triduum is the shortest season of our liturgical year. It has a season of preparation —Lent. Likewise, it has a season of celebration—Easter Time. It is not really a part of either of those seasons. It is, rather, a season and a feast unto itself.

As the Triduum maintains the unity of the three days, so too does it maintain the unity of the events of the Paschal Mystery. Contrary to what many may think, the Triduum does not mark three separate events of Jesus's life (the Last Supper, the Crucifixion, and the Resurrection). Over the course of these three days, we are not celebrating a three-act passion play. Nor are we reenacting a different event from

Christ's last days on earth on each of these days. Rather, the Triduum, as a single three-day celebration, commemorates the single event of Jesus's Paschal Mystery, which is marked by those three moments, which Catholic theology has always understood as three elements of one single reality.

So, although the ritual of each day may mark a specific event (Holy Thursday marking the Last Supper, Good Friday marking the Crucifixion, Holy Saturday marking the Resurrection), each event is seen in the larger context of the one single Paschal Mystery. This is the framework for the Triduum celebration. It is the backdrop, so to speak, of each of the days and each of the specific rituals that make up the whole feast—the washing of feet, the procession with the Blessed Sacrament, the veneration of the Cross, the rites of initiation in the Easter Vigil.

"He humbled himself and became obedient to the point of death—even death on a cross. Therefore God also highly exalted him and gave him the name that is above every other name."

(Philippians 2:8–9)

Final Preparations

Earlier, we viewed the season of Lent through the experience of the elect, those who have participated in the RCIA and who are preparing for initiation. From that perspective, we saw what the season is to be for those of us already baptized. Similarly, to approach the Triduum in this way reveals what it can be for the whole parish community.

For the elect, these days are the final moments of their preparation for Baptism, Confirmation, and the reception of the Eucharist. For forty days they have been involved in spiritual reflection, prayer, and discernment. Their hearts have been scrutinized and their intentions have been verified. Now, like athletes in their final preparation for a significant competition, the elect spend these final days in silent reflection and intense prayer before their initiation.

So, too, should the Triduum be for those of us who are already baptized: these are the final days before the annual renewal of our Baptism, the final days before we once again commit ourselves to truly being the images of Christ that we were baptized to be. Like the elect, we have spent forty days in recollection and prayer, hoping to make ourselves ready for this significant, annual experience. Like the elect, we have fasted, given alms, and prayed with fervor. Like the elect, we have searched our hearts and our souls to see where in our lives we have wandered from the covenant that God made with us in the waters of the baptismal font. And like the elect, the three days of the Triduum should be ones of intense final preparation. For all of us, baptized or preparing for Baptism, these days are the culmination of a well-observed Lent.

The Paschal Fast

Have you ever been so excited, so full of anticipation and expectation, so consumed with an approaching event, that you just couldn't eat? It's not that the excitement and anticipation upset your stomach, or that you were so full of anxiety that the thought of food made you nauseated. It's that the approaching event was so significant, that you were just too excited to think of food. That's what the paschal fast of the Triduum is supposed to be.

"Let the paschal fast be kept sacred. Let it be observed everywhere on Good Friday and, where possible, prolonged throughout Holy Saturday, as a way of coming to the joys of the Sunday of the resurrection with uplifted and welcoming heart"

(Constitution on the Sacred Liturgy, 110)

This is not the same as the penitential fast of Lent. During the Triduum, we don't continue fasting in the spirit of self-denial and repentance. The fast of the three days is one of joy and expectation, single-mindedness and preparation. The early Church Fathers and Mothers used the analogy of an athlete to talk about the paschal fast. As a competitor fasts in order to maintain clarity and in order to remain focused on the approaching competition, so do we fast in order to remain focused on the commemoration of the Paschal Mystery.

The Church calls us to recognize the uniqueness of these three days. That may mean that keeping the paschal fast extends beyond food. Abstaining from unnecessary activity, or activity that we "usually" do on Thursday, Friday, and Saturday, is another way of observing the fast. It may mean not going to that Friday night movie, or running the normal Saturday morning errands. It may mean making a special request for a vacation day at work to ensure that you are able to fully take part in the rites of the three days. It may mean that you unplug the television or shut down the computer for these days. In a sense, we are called to do whatever it takes to mark these days as "different." Keeping the paschal fast may very well mean taking extraordinary measures to ensure that you are able to observe these extraordinary days.

The Liturgies of the Triduum

Holy Thursday

Remember, Holy Thursday is not a reenactment of Jesus's Last Supper and his agony in the garden. Although these things did happen on the night he was betrayed, they are not our primary focus. Our focus for the Mass of the Lord's Supper on Holy Thursday night is the same as it is every night of the Triduum—the Passion, Death, and Resurrection of Christ and the life that flows from that mystery. Holy Thursday's Mass of the Lord's Supper celebrates this through two main actions: the meal of the Eucharist, and the washing of feet. Both of these actions represent the ultimate reality of the cross: Jesus's total giving of himself to God.

Jesus told us to share the meal in memory of him, and so we do. In sharing the Eucharist, we are united to one another and to Christ in the giving of himself to others and to God. As Christ gave himself totally, so, too, are we called to give of ourselves to others and to God. This is made even more evident in the second main action of this liturgy, the washing of feet.

Many scholars believe that this ritual foot-washing was part of early baptismal liturgies. It demonstrates the Christian life to which we are called. This ritual is called the *mandatum*, which is the Latin word for "commandment." It refers to the "new commandment" that Jesus gave his disciples to love one another as he has loved them.

Washing feet puts that commandment into action. "For I have set you an example, that you should do as I have done to you" Jesus said.[252] And so we do. In kneeling and washing feet, we are united to one another and to Christ in the total giving of himself to others and to God. In this ancient and beautiful ritual, the Church sees an expression of the discipleship to which we are called through our Baptism. In preparation, then, to renew that Baptism, it seems fitting that we renew our understanding of the responsibilities that Baptism places upon us.

Good Friday

The celebration of the Lord's Passion on Good Friday is one of the few liturgies that has no beginning—no music, no procession, no "In the name of the Father, and of the Son, . . ." no greeting—just silent prayer. This is because the Mass of the Lord's Supper had no conclusion. The greeting and the beginning took place then, and since that point, we have been in the midst of the Paschal Triduum. On Good Friday, we simply take up publicly what we have been doing all along—reflecting, praying, and commemorating the Passion, Death, and Resurrection of Jesus Christ.

This day's celebration contains a multitude of contradictions. On the one hand, there is sorrow and grief surrounding the Lord's Death. On the other hand, we cannot pretend that we are unaware of the Resurrection and his triumph over death. For this reason, Good Friday must not be seen as a reenactment of the crucifixion and Death of Jesus. The Good Friday liturgy is not a wake where we grieve over the loss of a loved one. Rather, it is a celebration of the deep mystery of our faith that says that the cross and death lead to life. We celebrate that mystery in three ways this day. First, we read the Passion according to John. In the midst of our prayer and reflection, the community gathers and once again listens to the proclamation of Jesus's total giving of himself to God. In this proclamation, we hear of our own birth, the birth of the Church from the side of the dead Christ.

It is as Church, then, that we move to the second point of focus for this liturgy: the intercessions. These are different from the intercessions we pray at Mass on a typical Sunday. Here, they are more intense, embellished, and more urgent. The sense is that, on this day, we pray as if our lives depend upon it. We pray for the Church and her leaders. We pray for our world and for those who lead its nations. We pray for our Jewish brothers and sisters. We pray for all those who do not share our beliefs in the one true God or in Jesus Christ. We pray for those who are preparing for Baptism. We pray for the sick. With each of these intercessions, the pattern is the same: the intention is announced, there is a period of silent prayer while we kneel and actually pray for what was just announced, and then we stand while the priest concludes the intercession. It is here that we do, quite seriously and with deliberation, what we were baptized to do. We intercede to the Father, through Christ, on behalf of the world and the Church. This is our duty and our responsibility as members of the body of Christ. United in these prayers, we move forward to the third point of focus in this liturgy: the veneration of the crucifix. Together, we move to touch the crucifix, to kiss it, to embrace it, to bow in reverence before it.

"Behold the wood of the Cross, / on which hung the salvation of the world."

(The Showing of the Holy Cross, Friday of Holy Week, *The Roman Missal*)

Only after we have done all this (proclaimed the Passion, offered our prayers, and venerated the wood of the cross), do we quietly and simply share communion. With little more than what is absolutely necessary, we bring the reserved sacrament that was consecrated the night before. We pray the Lord's Prayer and we share the Bread of Life. Just as there was no formal beginning to the liturgy of the Lord's Passion, neither is there a formal conclusion: no blessing, no dismissal. We simply once again return to the silent reflection with which the liturgy began: no ending, for the Triduum continues into the following day, Holy Saturday, when, at the Vigil, we mark our own Passover from death into life.

Holy Saturday: The Easter Vigil

I once took part in an Easter Vigil that literally lasted all night. It was while I was on a Holy Week retreat and it began around 11:00 PM on Holy Saturday night. We started outside with the fire, then processed into the chapel of the retreat center, where we kept vigil for the rest of the night by proclaiming the readings, chanting the psalms, and sitting in prolonged periods of reflective silence. It was one of the most moving experiences of the Vigil that I have ever had. Yes, I caught myself dozing off periodically, but then so did most of the other people there. What was so comforting was that when I would wake up from these little naps, the rest of the people were still there, carrying on the prayer of the Vigil as I napped. Then I would once again join the prayers or the chants while others drifted off.

The culmination of that celebration of the Vigil, since there were no Baptisms, was the celebration of the Eucharist. Its timing was profound. From the darkness of the night, through which we kept watch, the eastern sky began to fill with light as the preparation of the gifts began. Soon, the lights of the candles were no longer needed as the light of the rising sun (pun intended) filled the room in which we were proclaiming Christ's Resurrection through the celebration of the Eucharist. We had kept vigil through Saturday night and, as Sunday dawned, we truly celebrated the Paschal Mystery. That experience of the Easter event was like no other since.   **~Todd**

The Roman Missal calls the Vigil of Holy Saturday night "the mother of all Vigils,"[253] and makes it explicit that the Vigil is to begin after nightfall. The Exsultet (the song sung immediately after the paschal candle enters the church) says that this night "dispels wickedness, washes faults away, / restores innocence to the fallen, and joy to mourners, / drives out hatred, fosters concord, and brings down the mighty."[254] The sense is given that this is a most important and sacred night. Indeed, it is.

> "This is the night
> that even now, throughout the world,
> sets Christian believers apart from worldly vices
> and from the gloom of sin,
> leading them to grace
> and joining them to his holy ones."

(The Exsultet, the Easter Vigil, *The Roman Missal*)

[The Easter Vigil begins in the darkness of night. In the midst of that darkness, which represents all that threatens to come between us and the love of our God, a great fire is lit. This fire is great enough, bright enough, and strong enough to chase the darkness away. It overcomes darkness. It reminds us of Christ, the Light of the World. This fire, as the prayer which blesses it says, is to "[bestow] on the faithful the power of [God's] glory."[255] It is to inflame us "with heavenly desires, / that with minds made pure / we may attain festivities of unending splendor."[256]

"The Easter Vigil, in the holy night when the Lord rose again, is considered the 'mother of all holy Vigils,'[257] in which the Church, keeping watch, awaits the Resurrection of Christ and celebrates it in the Sacraments. Therefore, the entire celebration of this sacred Vigil must take place at night, so that it both begins after nightfall and ends before the dawn on the Sunday."

(*Universal Norms on the Liturgical Year and the Calendar*, 21)

From this great fire, we light a great candle, a candle that is bigger than any other candle in our parish church, a candle that, once blessed on this night, will stand burning at every Baptism as well as at every funeral in the next year. For this is our Christ candle! As this candle is lit, we hold it high and the deacon or priest proclaims loudly, "The light of Christ!" to which the whole church answers, just as loudly, "Thanks be to God!"[258] Then a marvelous thing happens: like the pillar of fire that once led the Israelites through the night, this candle leads us through the night and into the church, where the fire of that candle is spread and shared by every one.

Then, in the light of this Christ-candle, we call upon all of creation, all of heaven and earth, to rejoice and exult, for "Christ broke the prison-bars of death / and rose victorious from the underworld."[259] This is the Easter song: the Exsultet. It is sung with only the light of the candles burning and it proclaims that "this is the night!" This is the first song of Easter, the first notes accompanying the words of our praise to God for Christ's Resurrection. It is the first hymn raised in joy of this night. It is Easter's proclamation of victory over sin and death.

"Exult, let them exult, the hosts of heaven,
exult, let Angel ministers of God exult,
let the trumpet of salvation
sound aloud our mighty King's triumph!
Be glad, let earth be glad, as glory floods her,
ablaze with light from her eternal King,
let all corners of the earth be glad,
knowing an end to gloom and darkness.
Rejoice, let Mother Church also rejoice,
arrayed with the lightning of his glory,
let this holy building shake with joy,
filled with the mighty voices of the peoples."

(The Exsultet, the Easter Vigil, *The Roman Missal*)

After we have sung the Easter song, still in the light of the paschal candle, we hear again the sacred stories of our faith, stories which are told only on this night: the story of creation, the story of the sea splitting in two, the poems of Isaiah and Ezekiel. And in these sacred stories, once again, we are reminded of who we are, and whose we are. St. Paul reminds us in the epistle from this night, "Do you not know that all of us who have been baptized into Christ Jesus were baptized into his death? Therefore we have been buried with him by baptism into death, so that, just as Christ was raised from the dead by the glory of the Father, so we too might walk in newness of life."[260]

The Roman Missal notes that "the reading of the Word of God is a fundamental part of this Easter Vigil."[261] These are the stories of our salvation history. Presently, the Liturgy of the Word during the Easter Vigil numbers up to nine readings. Throughout our history it has included as many as fourteen! These stories tell us of God's love and of God's action and presence throughout our history. This is the story of our relationship with God. It is *our* story. We tell it this night because this night we renew that identity in the renewal of our Baptism. Not only that, but we also tell the story this night so that those who are to join us in Baptism hear what it is they are becoming part of.

For the elect, the stories they hear during the readings tell them about the faith they are entering. The stories tell them about us—the community of Jesus, the Body of Christ. In a very real sense, we tell this story again because during the liturgy of this night, those who are to be baptized become the next chapter in the story. If this is the story that tells of God's presence and action from the start of the world, then the Baptisms that are celebrated during this night are the next instances of God's presence and action. The history of salvation continues in them! It seems most fitting, then, that after the story is proclaimed, we lead the elect to the waters of Baptism and to the fragrant oils that seal this new life just birthed into the Church and into the world: Christ Jesus, risen, alive in these new members, alive in each of us.

It is through the abundance of God's love and mercy that the elect are immersed into the Death and Resurrection of Jesus Christ. It is within the abundance of God's love and mercy that they are anointed with sacred chrism in Confirmation. And, as it is every Sunday for those of us already baptized, it is within the abundance of God's love and mercy that we gather around the table of the Lord this night and share the body and blood that brings each of us eternal life!

"You have put on Christ, in him you have been baptized. Alleluia, Alleluia!"

(Baptismal Acclamation, *Rite of Christian Initiation of Adults*)

Easter Sunday

The Triduum ends on the evening of Easter Sunday. After the fasts are broken and the Resurrection proclaimed, after the water is blessed and the elect are baptized, after they are welcomed around the table and Easter dawn breaks on a renewed body of Christ, we bask in the glory of the profound mystery of God's love for us.

For centuries, the Church has made the final proclamation of the Triduum through the celebration of Easter Vespers, a form of sung Evening Prayer. In a solemn celebration, we sing of Christ risen in the light of the Easter candle, which was blessed the night before. With this rite of Evening Prayer, we begin the fifty-day celebration of the Resurrection. Amid Alleluias and bells, amid the sprinkling of holy water and renewing our baptismal promises, amid the stories of the early Christians and the Resurrection appearance of Christ, the Church keeps Easter Time.

In reaching this point, the Church experiences again some of the richest and most symbolic rituals of our tradition. Through them, we are made anew, fashioned again into an image of the resurrected Christ, more closely bound to the Savior of the World. It is what we were created for; it is what we are called to. Renewed in the Spirit and in faith, we once again proclaim to the world that Christ Jesus is alive! Alleluia!

REFLECTION

» Determine ways in which you can ensure your own full and conscious participation in the rites of the Triduum: the foot washing of Holy Thursday, the centrality of the Passion, the intercessions and the veneration of the cross on Good Friday, and the Sacred Vigil of Holy Saturday night.

» How do you see these three days in relationship to the weekly parish celebration of the Eucharist? In what ways do you mark these special, most solemn days? Which of the rituals do you find the most profound? Why? Does one or another of the rites speak the most to you in your ministerial role?

» How is the fact that the Triduum is the central celebration of our Catholic tradition reflected in your own faith life? In your own prayer life? How do you see what we do every Sunday as flowing out of the three-day feast of the Triduum?

» The Church calls us to make the three days of the Triduum unique and different, because we are called to be different. In what ways do you make these days different? What are your own traditions or customs that surround these most solemn days? How do they help you to connect to the Church's wider celebration of these days?

CHAPTER 23

THE MYSTERY OF EASTER TIME

The Themes of Easter Time

Christ Is Risen: New Life, Eternal Life and the Destruction of Death

Imagine if shopping malls decorated for Easter the way they do for Christmas. You're probably thinking, "they do, don't they?" Sure, shopping malls put up huge Easter eggs, bunnies, baby chicks, and giant jellybeans just as they put out snowmen, Santas, elves, and reindeer for Christmas. There's one difference. At Christmas, it's not unusual to see a crèche mixed in with all of the secular decor: Jesus, Mary, and Joseph alongside jolly old St. Nick! Wouldn't it be interesting to walk through a shopping mall at Easter time and see an empty tomb in addition to the bunnies and jellybeans? This is not likely to happen! Society finds it much more palatable to celebrate the birthday of the historical Jesus than to celebrate the Resurrection of the Christ! To celebrate a birthday is simply acknowledgment of a past event. To celebrate the resurrection is a statement of faith about the present.

For Christians, the celebration of Easter is the very core of our faith. Unless we believe that Jesus is risen from the dead and lives among us, we have no reason to pay attention to anything else in this book. Without the Resurrection, this whole enterprise we call "Christianity" is a waste of time. St. Paul did not mince words when dealing with this same issue: "If . . . Christ has not been raised, then our proclamation has been in vain and your faith has been in vain. . . . If for this life only we have hoped in Christ, we are of all people most to be pitied."[262]

"The Resurrection of Jesus is the crowning truth of our faith in Christ, a faith believed and lived as the central truth by the first Christian community; handed on as fundamental by Tradition; established by the documents of the New Testament; and preached as an essential part of the Paschal Mystery along with the cross."

(*Catechism of the Catholic Church*, 638)

During Easter Time, we do not so much recall an event as much as we proclaim a belief about the present: namely, that Christ is risen! We cannot proclaim that Jesus is alive and present among us and still live our lives unchanged. Easter celebrates a lifestyle. It celebrates the change that happens in people when they live their lives knowing that Jesus is risen, alive, and present in their every action!

We call this new way of living "new life" and "eternal life" because it is a life unlike our earthly one. It is new life because it takes away our old way of living, which was bogged down in the false belief that we were alone and without hope. It is eternal life because it is a life that transcends the limits of this earthly life and gives us a share in the life of the risen Christ who transcends all things, including time and space. Knowing that the risen Christ is present among us, we can face any adversity with a new perspective just as St. Paul so eloquently preached to the Romans: "If God is for us, who is against us? . . . For I am convinced that neither death, nor life, nor angels, nor rulers, nor things present, nor things to come, nor powers, nor height, nor depth, nor anything else in all creation, will be able to separate us from the love of God in Christ Jesus our Lord."[263]

During these fifty days (longer than Lent's forty days: we feast more than we fast!), the Church invites us to ponder the significance of the Resurrection in our lives. Certainly, the Gospel readings call us to exult in the empty tomb. The same Gospel, however, also calls us to grapple with it. What does the empty tomb mean for me this day and every day? We are challenged to consider what it means to believe without seeing. We marvel at the appearances of the Risen Christ. We embrace the image of the Good Shepherd. We consider the Spirit's gift of ministries within the Resurrection community and the role of the Spirit of the risen Christ in the Church today. We hear Jesus's prayer for us and contemplate the mission of the Spirit in the Church as encountered in the mystery of Pentecost. And, in the end, we emerge as a people who do not walk alone, but instead carry within us the new and eternal life of the Spirit of the risen Lord who is truly present and conquers all things, even death!

"Therefore, *Easter* is not simply one feast among others, but the 'Feast of feasts,' the 'Solemnity of solemnities.'"

(*Catechism of the Catholic Church,* 1169)

The Symbols of Easter Time

The Neophytes

Every sports team likes to have a good mix of veteran players and outstanding young rookies. The veterans bring their experience, skill, and poise to any situation. They serve as mentors for the young players. The rookies bring a high level of intensity, enthusiasm, and raw desire. They serve as catalysts for the veteran players, reigniting battle-weary warriors to play with the level of intensity they had when they were rookies.

During Easter Time, the Christian community delights in this blend of "veterans" and "rookies" as well. Those who have been disciples of Christ for some time have been serving as mentors for those "apprentices" who celebrated their initiation at the Easter Vigil. Now, the newly baptized, or neophytes, are, in a sense, thrust into the spotlight. They themselves become a symbol or sacrament for the entire Christian community that is celebrating new life in the Risen Christ. The neophytes embody the fervor and excitement of one who is newly called by Jesus to follow as a disciple. Their conscious and intentional decision to change their way of life and accept Jesus as their Lord reminds the entire Christian community of the depth and seriousness of our commitment.

"Veteran" Christians find themselves challenged to avoid simply going through the motions, so to speak, when all around them, they see "rookie" Christians consumed with the notion of how to live the Gospel of Jesus. Their names and pictures are placed in the parish bulletin and newsletters. Their photos and biographies are posted in the church vestibule. They are the guests of honor at receptions following various Masses. They are invited to meetings of various parish organizations and ministries. They may be invited to share a reflection after communion on one of the Sundays of Easter. The important thing is, the neophytes themselves are not being honored or "worshiped," but rather, the power of Jesus manifested in their change of life is being proclaimed and praised as each of us prays that the Lord will renew and fill our hearts with the same fervor!

"The neophytes . . . should experience a full and joyful welcome into the community and enter into closer ties with the other faithful. The faithful, in turn, should derive . . . a renewal of inspiration and of outlook"

(Rite of Christian Initiation of Adults, 246)

Water

When we think of the symbolic meaning of water, we tend to get a little bit romantic. In other words, we think of all of the positive images of water: it refreshes, washes clean, quenches, cools, nourishes, gives life, and so on. All of these attributes of water are quite correct. Unfortunately, we sell the full symbolic meaning of water short if we only focus on those positive images. The fact is that water also kills! Water can destroy and cause chaos. Water can be terrifying.

Each of us can most likely recall a time in our own lives when water's less romantic qualities unleashed its forces against us. Perhaps your basement once flooded, or maybe you were caught in a torrential rainstorm that forced you off the road. As a child, you may have fallen into water before you could swim, or had your head held underwater by an older sibling or a bully. Perhaps you've seen or experienced firsthand the damage caused by the wind and rain of a hurricane. Sadly, some of us have lost loved ones to drowning. Water, indeed, has its "dark" side.

Why bring all of this up? What could all of this "negativity" have to do with the glory and joy of Easter? Remember, Easter is our celebration of Jesus' triumph over death; a horrible death that truly happened. Easter is death transformed, not death vanished. Resurrection is inseparable from death. Easter Sunday is inseparable from Good Friday. Water's ability to give life, refresh, renew, and wash clean is inseparable from water's ability to destroy, cause chaos, frighten, and, yes, kill. Water, like the mystery of God, can be described using the traditional Latin phrase of *tremendum et fascinans*, meaning "fearful and fascinating" (see Chapter 7, "The Mystery of Reverence").

In Scripture, this double-edged understanding of water is quite evident (there are over 600 biblical references to water). Throughout the Bible, water's twofold nature is revealed: it is essential for life, and yet it destroys life. It is no surprise, then, that after the Israelites in the desert were saved by water from the rock, the only thing that stood in the way of their escape from slavery in Egypt was a body of water.[264] In order to pass over from slavery to freedom, they would need to pass through death! This crossing of the Red Sea in the Exodus story serves as the main imagery for the blessing of the water in our baptismal font each Easter Vigil. This is the water that we once entered and continue to enter in order that our old selves may die and we may be reborn in the Risen Christ who alone walks on water (and thus, has control over the forces of chaos, destruction, and death). Without a proper understanding of the Passover/Exodus story and the central role of water in that experience, our understanding of our own Baptism as a crossing over and the Eucharist as our new Passover meal is severely diminished.

Our Easter celebration of fifty days is a time to reflect upon our own baptismal experience of entering the waters that signify the death of our old self and emerging again, signifying our birth as a new creation. Throughout Easter Time (and not only at the Easter Vigil), we are reminded time and again of the waters of Baptism. On each of the Sundays of Easter, the priest may sprinkle us with holy water so that we can feel once again the waters that remind us of our death and call us to new life. Our baptismal fonts are flowing with living waters, reminding us of the mystery of our Baptism.

"Graciously bless this water. / For you created water to make the fields fruitful / and to refresh and cleanse our bodies. / . . . / Through water, which Christ made holy in the Jordan, / you have renewed our corrupted nature / in the bath of regeneration. / Therefore, may this water be for us / a memorial of the Baptism we have received, / and grant that we may share / in the gladness of our brothers and sisters / who at Easter have received their Baptism."

(Rite for the Blessing and Sprinkling of Water, During Easter Time, *The Roman Missal*)

Full Celebration of the Eucharist

There are all kinds of reasons why we go to a restaurant: the service, the ambiance, the entertainment, the location, the prices, and so on. Ultimately, however, there is really only one reason we go to (and return to) a restaurant: the food! We may enjoy the uniforms worn by the waiters and waitresses, or the decorations on the walls and tables, or the entertainment and lively music, but ultimately, the reason we go is to eat! If the food is not what we were looking for, we have no reason to come back.

In the same way, there are many reasons why people choose to become Catholic. Perhaps we are attracted by the tradition, or by a warm and hospitable community, or by a pastor who is a particularly charismatic preacher. We are drawn to the waters of Baptism and enter into a community of faith. Ultimately, however, we come into this community of faith for one reason: the food! Yes, Easter is all about our Baptism and the confirmation of that Baptism. The reason we are baptized and confirmed, however, is so that we may be led to the table of the Lord where a very special meal awaits us. If Easter is all about Baptism and Baptism leads us to Eucharist, then, ultimately, Easter is all about Eucharist!

During Easter, our attention to the Eucharist is not to be distracted by water, fire, oil, and flowers. Rather, all of these are meant to heighten our awareness of the centrality of this meal that is the climax of every action that we participated in during the Triduum. In a sense, the Triduum (specifically the Easter Vigil's celebration of Baptism and Confirmation) entices us to enter more deeply into the mystery that we encounter so intimately in the Eucharistic meal. If the experiences of the Triduum do not lead us to a deeper awareness of the Eucharist, then they have failed, for the Eucharist is the way that we encounter the Risen Christ whom we celebrate at Easter and on every Sunday of the year. In a very real sense, we can say that Baptism leads to the Eucharist. The Bread of Life and the cup of salvation are what we were baptized for! After all, the Eucharist is the only repeatable sacrament of initiation. Each time we come to the table, then, we encounter our Baptism and we renew the life first received there.

Like the two disciples on the road to Emmaus in Luke's wonderful Easter story, we, too, may have difficulty recognizing the Risen Lord in our presence unless we see him in the breaking of the bread! Easter Time is a season for us to revel in the Eucharistic meal, allowing the Risen Christ to open our eyes and set our hearts on fire through the breaking of the bread that is his real presence. The waters of Baptism indeed quench our thirst for new life in Jesus, but only the Bread of Life can satisfy the hunger we have for intimate union with the Risen Christ.

"Almighty and ever-living God, / who restore us to eternal life / in the Resurrection of Christ, / increase in us, we pray, the fruits of this paschal Sacrament / and pour into our hearts the strength of this saving food."

(Prayer after Communion, Sixth Sunday of Easter, *The Roman Missal*)

The Spirit of the First Disciples

One of the most distinctive features of the Easter liturgies is hearing the stories of the early Christian communities in the Acts of the Apostles. In all three cycles of the Lectionary readings (Year A, B, and C), the First Readings of Mass during Easter Time come from the Acts of the Apostles. We hear of how the power of the Risen Christ was made known through the first followers of Jesus, and how "they praised the word of the Lord; and as many as had been destined for eternal life became believers."[265]

One can only imagine the joy and the excitement of the first members of those early communities. Talk about being filled with the Spirit and having your life and your world turned upside down by God! The people we hear about in these First Readings during Easter Time are the models the Church gives us each year for guidance and for direction in terms of how we should be celebrating Christ's Resurrection.

"May the wondrous flame that appeared above the disciples, / powerfully cleanse your hearts from every evil / and pervade them with its purifying light"

(Solemn Blessing, the Holy Spirit, *The Roman Missal*)

The spirit in which the early Christian communities lived out their faith should be the same spirit with which we celebrate Easter in our faith community. The joy and conviction, the enthusiasm and the life, the overpowering awareness of Christ's presence among us that those first Christians lived with are the same things that we should be striving for in our own lives. To be on fire with the Spirit of God through the power of Christ's Resurrection is what we celebrate during Easter Time. We need to be open to that Spirit as the early church was. Then, as the Lord adds to our community day by day, through his gifts to us, through his presence among us, through his life in each of us, then indeed will we be the Easter people that God calls us to be!

Return of the Gloria and the Alleluia

Every holiday and especially at Easter, I bake a loaf of bread following a recipe that I got from my wife's grandmother many years ago. We call the old family recipe "Busia's" bread (pronounced BOO-sha which is Polish for "granny" or "grandma"). As it is baking, the aroma fills the entire house, building our desire for our first bite. Finally, when we do sit down to eat it, the only sound to be heard is each of us respectively uttering "Mmmmmmmm!" As our taste buds jump for joy, we all realize just how much we have missed this bread since the last holiday!   ~**Joe**

As we celebrate Easter Time, the Christian community enjoys a feast that involves all of the senses! After fasting on many levels (see Chapter 21, "The Mystery of Lent"), we now dive with ravenous appetites into a fifty-day banquet that we call Easter. After fasting, we realize just how much we have missed that from which we abstained. In our Lenten liturgies, we have been fasting from the singing of the Gloria and the Alleluia. Now that Easter is here, we realize how much our souls long to sing these words! After six weeks of fasting from the singing of these hymns, we find our spiritual "taste buds" exploding with the taste of praise!

On Easter, in the midst of flowers (also noticeably gone for six weeks!), with a font overflowing with living water, we sing the Gloria and Alleluia. We spent some time looking at the Gloria during our treatment of Advent (see Chapter 18). Let's take a closer look at this unique word: Alleluia! It has a nice ring to it, doesn't it? Alleluia! It's a Hebrew word that is actually untranslatable, but for the most part means "Praise God!" and it has come to symbolize a whole host of meanings, different for each person who says it or hears it.

"These are the days above all others in which the Alleluia is sung."

(Universal Norms on the Liturgical Year and Calendar, 22)

"Alleluia"—it means life and light. More precisely, it means life after death and light out of darkness. It means an Easter candle: tall, majestic, and standing high so that everyone can see it, proclaiming as it does that, "He is not here, among the dead. He is risen!"

"Alleluia"—it means washing and cleansing. It means being reborn or re-created in living water, leaving the old self behind in the tomb of the font and rising, as Christ did, to the new life that God has promised.

"Alleluia"—it means death is no more. The last thing that could ever possibly separate us from God or from Christ or from each other is itself dead!

"Alleluia"—it means the wonderful smell of lilies and other flowers, proclaiming that the long reign of winter and darkness is over and that the new season of spring is among us, like the kingdom that Jesus preached.

"Alleluia!"—it means "Peace to you," the kind of peace that comes after reconciling to another, to yourself, to your family, to your Church, and to God. It means the kind of peace that comes when the wounds have at least begun to heal.

"Alleluia"—it means the Bread of Life and the Cup of Salvation to which we are all called in the life of Baptism, and to which we all say, "Amen" (another untranslatable Hebrew word).

"Alleluia!" Before the tremendous and awesome mystery that we celebrate during Easter, no word, no phrase, no explanation, and no theology is more appropriate than simply to babble, like a child, this simple, wonderful word.

Celebration of Baptism and Other Sacraments

In addition to fasting from the Gloria and Alleluia during Lent, some parishes may also have been fasting from celebrations of Baptism, first Communions, and Confirmations. Now, with the arrival of the fifty days of Easter Time, the Christian community erupts in a spiritual festival of sacramental celebrations! As a way of reconnecting these three sacraments of initiation that were celebrated in unified fashion at the Easter Vigil, the Church often celebrates a flurry of infant Baptisms, first Communions, and Confirmations during Easter's fifty days. In this way, the Christian community sees clearly that the new life of the Risen Christ that we celebrate during Easter is deeply and profoundly manifested in the celebration of the sacraments.

Likewise, those who were baptized as infants and are now coming forward for Confirmation and Eucharist are reminded that the purpose of their Baptism, celebrated some years before, was to bring them to this day. Thus, the past is made present and the Baptism celebrated some years before is celebrated and renewed once again! In addition to these sacraments of initiation, the Church also uses these fifty days of spring to rejoice in celebrations of Marriage and Holy Orders, two sacraments that echo the dying and rising of Baptism, as people die to their old selves and emerge as a new creation in the Risen Christ to be at the service of the communion of the Church. Finally, celebrations of anointing are also common during this "sacramental festival" of fifty days, as the Church celebrates the healing power of the risen Christ who overcomes all sickness, and even death.

"Baptism, the Eucharist, and the sacrament of Confirmation together constitute the 'sacraments of initiation,' whose unity must be safeguarded."

(*Catechism of the Catholic Church*, 1285)

The Fifty Days: "Unpacking"

One summer I went on, what is still to this day, the best vacation I have ever had. For two full weeks I went camping along the banks of the St. Lawrence River in Quebec City and Montreal, Canada. I remember being faced with the tedious task of unpacking when I returned. Most of us know people—maybe ourselves!—who do not like unpacking. Unpacking takes time. Strangely enough, however, something began to happen as I went about it. Each time I took something from a suitcase or bag, I would hold it and examine it. I would recall at what point in the vacation I acquired each memento. In a real sense, what I was doing was reliving the vacation as I unpacked.   **~Todd**

The season of Easter is very much like that post-vacation experience. It is meant to be, very literally, the "unpacking" period for us who have just celebrated the Death and Resurrection of Jesus Christ. The events that surround our celebration of Easter are too much to take in all at once, and they need to be unpacked, slowly and deliberately, with care and attention given to each element of the experience. How long does it take for the Christian community to "unpack" the mysteries of Easter? Fifty days! Fifty whole days to rejoice and exult! Fifty wonderful days to revel in the celebration of Christ's victory over death and the grave! Fifty days to reflect on and digest all that we have just been a part of in the liturgies of Holy Week, all that we have just heard in the readings proclaimed, the prayers voiced, and the rites celebrated during the Triduum. Fifty days to unpack what we have just gone through. For, truly, as a people of faith, we have just gone through our own experience of death and resurrection.

The Church views the fifty days of Easter as one continuous feast. Yes, that's right: one, single feast which takes fifty days to celebrate. It is like a prolonged celebration of Sunday, a seven-week festival of Easter, a "week of weeks" as the early Christians called it. This season of Easter is the longest liturgical season in our Church's calendar, outside of Ordinary Time. From Easter Sunday evening until the day of Pentecost, we celebrate one continuous feast during which we revel in the joy and the glory that comes from Christ's Resurrection. We do this by singing hymns and songs of Easter throughout the season, by keeping the worship space full of Easter flowers for the full fifty days, and by leaving the decorations that marked the feast of the Vigil and Easter Sunday morning.

> "The fifty days from the Sunday of the Resurrection to Pentecost Sunday are celebrated in joy and exultation as one feast day, indeed or better as one 'great Sunday.'[266]"
>
> (*Universal Norms on the Liturgical Year and the General Roman Calendar*, 22)

Why fifty days? Why keep the festival alive for seven weeks? Because, quite simply, it takes at least that long to do everything that we have to do in order to truly celebrate Easter. First, we take fifty days to show that being Christian is more about feasting than fasting (compare the fifty days of celebration with the forty days of Lent). It takes at least fifty days to let the "Alleluia" sink in after six weeks of not hearing it. It takes at least fifty days to let the sweet smell of the sacred chrism and the smell of fresh, new flowers chase away the dryness and barrenness of a well-observed Lent. It takes at least fifty days for the wet oil to dry on the heads, hands, and spirits of those who were anointed on Holy Saturday night. It takes at least fifty days for those who were baptized to look back on the Triduum and discover what it all means in their lives now that they are members of the Body of Christ. Easter, unlike Lent and Advent, is not a period of preparation for anything, but is, rather, a prolongation. We do not celebrate the Sundays *after* Easter, we celebrate the Sundays *of* Easter, recognizing that this feast is not limited to one day, but goes on and on and on.

Finally, it takes at least fifty days for any faith community to understand everything that took place during the Triduum. What does it mean to wash feet within the community? What does it mean to approach the wood of the cross and to kiss it, embrace it, and touch it? What does it mean to gather in the darkness of night, light a fire, bless it, and proclaim Jesus's Resurrection? What does the empty tomb mean? What do we make of these rumors and mysterious reports of one who was dead but now lives? What do we make of these stories of doubt, misunderstanding, and lack of recognition among Jesus's most loyal followers? The liturgies of Easter Time, in the prayers, readings, and rites, invite us to unpack all that we have done and heard and to explore these events, celebrations, and rituals. We need these fifty days to be a time of rich and joyful "unpacking," head-scratching, and reflection! Take your time—you've got fifty days!

Renewal of Baptism

There are two ways to try to make a point. One is by understatement. Perhaps through subtlety, people will take notice of our message. The other is by hyperbole or over-statement. In a sense, we make a point by pounding people over the head with it so that they won't be able to miss it! One of the "messages" of Easter that is very difficult to miss is the relation between Christ's Death and Resurrection and our Baptism. There is no subtlety going on here! Easter Time calls every one of us to reflect on and to be renewed in the Baptism that has given us a share in the Resurrection we celebrate. The importance of Baptism as the very thing that connects us to Christ's Resurrection cannot be overlooked during this season or underestimated in how often we are reminded of it. Take notice of how often Baptism is referred to in the liturgies on the Sundays of Easter. Just look around your church during Easter Time and you can't miss the connection: baptismal water flowing, the presence of the paschal candle burning brightly at every liturgy, the renewal of our faith and our baptismal promises every Sunday, and the presence in the assembly of the neophytes. How could we miss Easter's connection to Baptism when week after week for seven weeks, we celebrate the rite of being washed again as the whole assembly is sprinkled with holy water?

"And so, now that our Lenten observance is concluded, / let us renew the promises of Holy Baptism."

(The Renewal of Baptism Promises, Sunday of the Resurrection, *The Roman Missal*)

The greatest of all mysteries—the love of God shown to us through Christ's Passion, Death, and Resurrection—is the mystery that gives us life and destroys our death. As a people who are "washed clean in the blood of the Lamb," we must recognize and recover the intimate relationship between our Baptism and Christ's Resurrection; between his dying and rising and our share in that newness of life that has been promised to us. You can't miss it!

REFLECTION

» Brainstorm ways in which you might more closely see the connection between Easter's focus on Baptism and our celebration of the Eucharist. Focus on how Baptism's water, fire, oil, and so on serve, not as distractions, but as invitations to deeper participation and understanding of the Eucharist.

» Take notice of and reflect upon the dual nature of water in your everyday living. Observe how water is essential for life and yet destroys it. Reflect upon the significance of this for the celebration of Baptism.

» Read over selected passages of the Acts of the Apostles used as the First Reading during Easter Time and draw comparisons between the spirit of the first disciples and the spirit of your parish community.

» How can you effectively use the fifty days of Easter to "unpack" the celebrations of the Triduum? What specifically needs unpacking?

» What does it mean when we say celebrating the Resurrection is a statement of faith about the present, as opposed to simply acknowledging a past event?

CHAPTER 24

THE MYSTERY OF ORDINARY TIME DURING SUMMER AND FALL

The Structure of the Season

The Cycle of Nature

I'm the kind of person who could never live in a climate that doesn't experience the change of the seasons. Growing up in the Midwest, I have learned to appreciate and to love the various seasons and all that they bring: the messiness of spring, the heat and humidity of summer, the colors of autumn, and the snow and cold of winter. I love the changes that come from the four seasons.

I especially enjoy the seasons of summer and autumn. The Midwest experience of June through November can involve a myriad of different weather conditions—anything from mild temperatures to dangerous extremes of oppressive heat or bone-chilling cold; from lethal dryness to deluges and thunderstorms; from slow and lazy breezes off Lake Michigan to the whipping winds of a tornado. Of course, the standard joke in Chicago's part of the Midwest is that, if you don't like the weather, "stick around for fifteen minutes . . . it'll change!" **~Todd**

Throughout the summer and autumn months, row upon row of crops and vegetables spread out along the interstate highway system. Orchards flourish in this area of the country and roadside fruit stands are a standard element of the season's landscape. All of it melds together to create a series of scenes by which you can measure the passing of the two seasons. From planting, to harvest, to sale, the cycle marks the turn of summer into autumn.

"Today we seek God's blessing on these seeds and the crops they will produce. Christ reminds us that, unless the seed is planted in the earth and dies, it will not yield fruit. As these seeds grow and are cared for, may they be signs of new life that comes from God."

(Order for Blessing Seeds at Planting Time, *Book of Blessings*)

Some of the most enjoyable civic holidays occur during the seasons of summer and fall. From the heralding call of Memorial Day and the picnics and fireworks of the Fourth of July, through Labor Day's signal of summer's end and the harvest-laden atmosphere of Thanksgiving, the seasons' holidays give ample opportunities for rest, reflection, celebration, and renewal. In many ways, these days embody the spirit that winds in and throughout this segment of the calendar. They provide another kind of clock by which we mark the passing of the year. They are like signposts along the journey from the season's early months, through its maturity, and into its later stages.

The Liturgical Cycle and the Lectionary

The season of Ordinary Time in summer and fall is the longest season of the liturgical year. Though technically it is the continuation of Ordinary Time that began after Christmas (see Chapter 20), this is the season that governs our liturgies for almost six months, stretching from early or mid-June to late November or early December. It is the season that takes us through family vacation and the "dog days" of summer to the start of another school year and the start of shorter days and cooler nights. It is the season that will lead us to harvest, the feasts of All Saints and All Souls, and the close of yet another liturgical year with the great Solemnity of Our Lord Jesus Christ, King of the Universe.

As the longest season, it is most easily viewed in two major parts. Though they are not official titles, we will refer to these two parts simply as Ordinary Time during summer and Ordinary Time during fall. Despite the titles, it's not the seasons of nature that distinguish the two parts. Remember that the length of Ordinary Time depends upon the date of Easter. Thus, it is the Church's liturgy and the readings that are proclaimed within it that help to distinguish the different aspects of this long season. As we saw in Chapter 20, the Lectionary gives Ordinary Time its theme and its focus, its shape and its nuance. Through the readings and the prayer texts of the Sunday Mass, the themes of Ordinary Time take shape.

During the Second Vatican Council, it was decided that the faithful should be exposed to a more complete proclamation of the Scriptures during the celebration of the Eucharist. To ensure that this happened, the Lectionary was revised so that throughout Ordinary Time the semi-continuous reading of the books of the Bible would be heard during Mass. It was this principle that gave rise to the three-year cycle in which the readings of each year are dominated by a specific Gospel text. As we have seen, in Year A it is the Gospel according to Matthew, in Year B it is the Gospel according to Mark, and in Year C it is the Gospel according to Luke. For all three years, the First Reading was chosen to connect in some way to the Gospel. The Second Reading, however, was set up to be a semi-continuous reading of one of the New Testament epistles, the Acts of the Apostles, or Revelation. Taken all together, the three readings help to give a sense of flow to the liturgies of Ordinary Time.

"The treasures of the Bible are to be opened up more lavishly, so that a richer share in God's word may be provided for the faithful. In this way a more representative portion of Scripture will be read to the people in the course of a prescribed number of years."

(*Constitution on the Sacred Liturgy*, 51)

During Ordinary Time, the readings proclaimed at Mass work to flesh out the person of Jesus of Nazareth. As we saw in Chapter 20, the readings during Ordinary Time in winter concentrate on the beginning of Jesus's earthly ministry. By the time we get into Ordinary Time in summer and fall, the readings are focused on the mission of Christ and the life of discipleship. In the summer part of the season, the readings of all three cycles paint a picture of what a life in Christ entails. Based upon Jesus's preaching, the miracles during his public ministry, and his teaching on the kingdom, we are given a sense of what we are called to as disciples.

Through the Scriptures that are proclaimed in the liturgy, the demands of discipleship are presented in contrast to the way of the world. Being a disciple, we hear, means looking beyond the conventions and ideologies of the world to see the life offered through Christ, which is dramatically different. "What I say," Jesus says through the Gospel, "is love your enemies and pray for those who persecute you."[267] This is a very different way of living from what our culture or society advocates. It is the way of life that sees beyond the present world and its structures to the world that Jesus came to establish: a world of peace, justice, equality, and compassion. It is the life that we are called to live as baptized members of Christ's Body.

During the late summer and early fall, the readings and the texts proclaimed in the liturgy change focus. They move from describing the life of discipleship to describing the complete transformation of the world in light of the kingdom that Christ came to establish. This complete transformation is what theologians call the "eschaton" or the "end times." This refers to the world and our way of life in it once the kingdom is completely established. It is a vision of existence in the reign of God, which will be in its totality when the Son of Man returns in glory. The second coming of Christ will bring a world in which all the promises of God, from the time of Eden on, are fulfilled. It is the "new heaven and a new earth" that John the Evangelist writes of.[268] It is the kingdom of peace and justice of which the prophets wrote. It is the life that Christ came to bring through his life, Death, and Resurrection. It is God's initial plan and hope for his creation, before it was altered by sin. It is what we might call "heaven."

During this latter part of the season, the readings of the liturgy present images and descriptions of these "end times." The prayers and texts of the Mass point us toward that time and call us to stand in hope and confidence. The world of which we hear is the world that our Baptism has destined us to live in. It is the fulfillment of the covenant that God made between himself and all of humanity. This vision of the world and our life in it culminates in the belief that Christ will return in glory to rule over all creation as king and Savior. It is what we celebrate in the solemnity of Our Lord Jesus Christ, King of the Universe the last Sunday of the liturgical year. For us Catholics, this is our New Year's Eve. After this solemnity, our liturgical year ends and another Advent comes, beginning a new year of grace, a new year of conversion, a new year in which we move ever deeper into the mystery of Christ Jesus.

"It is from Scripture that the readings are given and explained in the homily and that psalms are sung; the prayers, collects, and liturgical songs are scriptural in their inspiration; it is from the Scriptures that actions and signs derive their meaning."

(Constitution on the Sacred Liturgy, 24)

The Liturgies of the Season

Ordinary Time during Summer

For many of us, the summer months can be the best months of the whole year (just ask any student). The simple slowness and relaxed air of summer present us with the chance to revel in the most ordinary of experiences. When else but on a summer evening can you take such enjoyment from watching fireflies or lazily walking in the warm breeze? When else can you experience the simple beauty of a full and bountiful garden? When else can you feel the drain of tension and the ebb of stress that comes from the heat of the sun, high in the afternoon sky? Summer is the time to experience the extraordinary graces of relaxation, slowed pace, and getting away in the ordinary experiences of family, friends, and nature.

This very same dynamic is also at work in the Sunday liturgies as we enter into this second stretch of the season of Ordinary Time, beginning in the summer. The readings of the Mass during the summer do much to present the extraordinary grace of God's presence in the most ordinary of life situations. The Scriptures are full of summer images. Believers are compared to seeds buried in the ground in order to live in Christ, flourishing like the green grass. Stories are told involving summer storms on the lake and special trips in order to come away for a while and rest.[269] Promises are made of goodness flowing like a cool, lazy river for those who have faith and there are special stories of visitors and weddings, banquets and celebrations. All this is the context that the liturgies present during this season, and in this context Jesus reveals God among us.

"You visit the earth and water it, you greatly enrich it; / . . . / You water its furrows abundantly, settling its ridges."

(Psalm 65:9a, 10)

It is interesting that in Years B and C, the story of the feeding of the multitudes is proclaimed in the readings of the Sunday Mass during the summer. In Year A, during which we hear from Matthew's account of the Gospel, it is proclaimed at a weekday Mass. In John's account of the story, which we hear in Year B, the multiplication of the loaves and fish is the Gospel that introduces the five-week period in which we hear the "Bread of Life discourse." As if on any one of the many summer picnics we ourselves may take, the story recounts Jesus, who instructs the people to sit on the grass in the heat of the day so that he may nourish, renew, and strengthen them. These are the everyday, ordinary events of our summer lives. The liturgy presents them to us as doors for God's extraordinary presence and action among us. Our lives and the liturgies we celebrate are intimately connected. Our liturgies proclaim that God goes with us through the "dog days" of fun and relaxation, vacation and warmth. Blessed are we who have the eyes to see this and the ears to hear it!

Ordinary Time during Fall

Often, toward the end of summer, some people find themselves beginning to itch for fall. We begin to desire cooler nights, changing colors, the crisp quality of the air, and the leaves that swirl and dance and crunch under feet. The harvest that just seems to explode during fall conjures up cravings for pumpkin pie and apple cider. The produce section of the grocery store just seems to overflow with fruits and vegetables, and roadside farmers' markets pop up all over. Fall is a time of fulfillment, a time of culmination, and a time of abundance.

W hen I was in high school, I worked for an orchard that was near my home. Though it was open all year round, the busiest and most rushed time of the year was from late summer through the fall and into the first part of winter. During this time, while all the apples and other fruit were coming in from being harvested, there was never even one second of "down time." Mr. Porter (the orchard's owner) hired a tremendous number of "extra hands" to help accommodate the harvest, to help in the storage-barns, and to assist in the store.

People came to the orchard from all over the area, and even beyond, for the autumn fruits, cider, hay rides, and donuts. Every weekend the parking lot was overflowing and the cash register lines wound through the store, out the door, and onto the land outside. Everyone seemed to be electrified with excitement, and there was just such an urgency in the air: workers rushing around to accommodate all the customers, field hands rushing through the store with bins of ripe fruit, teams of pickers winding in and out of the rows of trees. It was harvest time and there wasn't a second to lose! There was an abundance to be had!   **~Todd**

"Let us now bless the Lord, who has once again bestowed on us the fruits of the earth. Abel offered his first fruits to God; let us also learn to share our blessings for the good of those in need, so that we may be true children of the Father, who bestows his gifts for the benefits of all the peoples of the earth."

(Order of Blessing in Thanksgiving for the Harvest, *Book of Blessings*)

From the end of October until the Solemnity of Our Lord Jesus Christ, King of the Universe in late November, the readings, the prayers, and the feast days all call us to the same urgency, the same excitement, the same sense of "fulfillment" that is present in the natural cycle of this season. As the ebb of the season begins to draw us into falling leaves and temperatures, overcast skies and browning landscape, so too do our liturgies point us to the "end times" and the fulfillment of God's eternal promises, which will come to pass with the return of Christ in glory.

In the liturgies of this part of the season, the abundance of God's gifts is presented as available for all who follow! Vineyards and harvest scenes more and more command our attention as we hear God's Word. Reminders and exhortations of what it means to be a disciple and all that is demanded in following Jesus sound as the year winds down. We hear parables calling for the need to be prepared. The feasts of All Saints and All Souls explicitly call us to look at our own fleeting state of "temporary-ness," and the time left before the "coming of the Lord's great and glorious day."[270] The liturgies of fall help us to place things in order as the year closes—to prepare ourselves, even as nature prepares herself for the darkness of winter, for the coldness of the earth, and for the promise of another spring.

"See, the day is coming, burning like an oven, when all the arrogant and all evildoers will be stubble; the day that comes shall burn them up. . . . But for you who revere my name the sun of righteousness shall rise, with healing in its wings. You shall go out leaping like calves from the stall."

(Malachi 4:1–2, First Reading, Thirty-third Sunday in Ordinary Time, Year C)

Solemnities and Feast Days of Ordinary Time during Summer and Fall

As with Ordinary Time in winter, during the months of Ordinary Time in summer and fall, our Church's calendar is filled with opportunities to celebrate the Paschal Mystery of Christ in ways that have shaped our public worship since the earliest days of our tradition. Numerous solemnities, feasts, and memorials of the saints give us wonderful opportunities to celebrate the Gospel as it is lived out in a significant way in the lives of our brothers and sisters who have gone before us.

We celebrate eight solemnities during this season. These four celebrate aspects of the mystery of our Lord:

- Solemnity of the Most Holy Trinity (first Sunday after Pentecost)

- Solemnity of the Most Holy Body and Blood of Christ, also called *Corpus Christi* (Sunday after the Most Holy Trinity)

- Solemnity of the Most Sacred Heart of Jesus (Friday after the second Sunday after Pentecost)

- Solemnity of Our Lord Jesus Christ, King of the Universe (the end of the liturgical year)

The following four solemnities celebrate events in the lives of Mary and the saints:

- Solemnity of the Nativity of St. John the Baptist (June 24)

- Solemnity of Sts. Peter and Paul, Apostles (June 29)

- Solemnity of the Assumption of the Blessed Virgin Mary (August 15)

- Solemnity of All Saints (November 1)

The special nature of solemnities will be addressed in more detail in Chapter 25.

During Ordinary Time in summer and fall, our Church celebrates many of our brothers and sisters whose lives have mirrored Christ's in unique and wondrous ways. They include:

- St. Boniface (June 5)

- the Immaculate Heart of Mary (June 8)

- St. Barnabas (June 11)

- St. Thomas the Apostle (July 3)

- St. Benedict (July 11)

- St. Mary Magdalene (July 22)

- St. James the Apostle (July 25)

- Sts. Joachim and Ann (July 26)

- the Transfiguration of the Lord (August 6)

- St. Dominic (August 8)
- the Exultation of the Holy Cross (September 14)
- the Archangels (September 29)
- St. Francis of Assisi (October 4)
- Sts Simon and Jude, Apostles (October 28)

These, and many others, are the days that proclaim the Paschal Mystery of Christ. They help us to live our own faith, and are a wonderful way to mark our tradition of worship and prayer. Like the cycle of nature or the calendar of summer and fall holidays, they help us to mark the passing of the season. For people of faith, who mark time with an "alternative" calendar, these days lead us ever deeper into the mystery that we proclaim each Sunday: the mystery of our salvation in Christ.

REFLECTION

» As you enter the liturgies of Ordinary Time in summer and fall, be mindful of the various "parts" of the season.

» Consider the many ways in which you can mark the passing Ordinary Time in your own life. Be mindful of the many extraordinary graces that God offers you through ordinary experiences. Strive to be aware of the ways that the liturgies of the season connect to your own personal experience of summer and of autumn.

» Which aspect of this period of Ordinary Time speaks loudest to you? How do the readings and the prayer texts help you to experience this portion of our liturgical year? How do you mark any of the many saints and feast days in your own prayer?

» How do the readings of the liturgies during this season help you to understand the life of discipleship? How do the summer liturgies help you to understand the demands of following Jesus? How do the autumn liturgies help you to hope in the return of Christ in glory?

» "Ordinary Time" simply refers to the time that is counted, or ordered, around the celebration of Easter. What connections do you make between the celebration of the Resurrection and the liturgies of Ordinary Time? How is your life as a disciple influenced or directed by Ordinary Time in summer and fall? How do the liturgies of this season help you to understand the person of Jesus Christ?

CHAPTER 25

THE MYSTERY OF SOLEMNITIES, FEASTS, AND HOLY DAYS

Marking Days in Our Faith

As we've already noted, Sunday was the original feast day in the historical development of the Church's liturgical calendar. This was the day for the weekly gathering of the community to hear the Scriptures proclaimed and to share in the breaking of the bread. For a while, this sustained the early Christians in the way they marked their life in Christ. Week by week, they would proclaim their faith that Christ had died, was risen, and would come again. Before too long, however, as the Church grew and took root in other regions and lands, celebrations of various aspects of the Paschal Mystery other than the marking of Sunday began to surface. The life of the Church took on slightly different characteristics in different cultures among different peoples. Local communities, influenced by the societies and the distinct situations in which they lived, celebrated their faith in ways that were particular to them.

This was, perhaps, most obvious in the development of special days which were observed in the lives of individual communities. These days were dedicated to the memory of members of the community whose lives exemplified the Paschal Mystery of Christ in unique ways. These people were primarily martyrs of the early church. By the middle of the second century, such memorials were part of just about every Christian community. Marking the day of their death—or rather their "birth" into eternal life—the cults of the martyrs spread throughout Christianity. Initially, this was a practice that gave witness to the honor, respect, and devotion that communities had for certain of its members who displayed virtue, hope, and faith in the face of persecution.

Beyond individual communities, such memorials were held all over for the Apostles who had lived with Christ and who gave witness to his teaching, preaching, and miracles, and whose own preaching and witnessing gave rise to many of these very communities of the early church. After the era of persecution, this practice of remembering applied to the memorials that communities would hold for other local heroes of the faith: bishops, holy men and women, and venerated teachers or preachers.

In a way, this is a practice with which we are familiar in our own times. In Chicago, for example, during the early spring month of March, we observe and celebrate Casimir Pulaski day. A Polish Nationalist who fought in the Revolutionary War, Pulaski is revered by the Polish community, a very sizable group in the greater fabric of Chicago. And so, on the first Monday of March, there is a parade in the city, and we mark the life of one of our heroes. A similar dynamic is at work in the early development of our Church's liturgical calendar of solemnities, feasts, and memorials of Christ, Mary, and the saints. As a way of "fleshing out" the Paschal Mystery of Christ, these feasts and memorials celebrate an aspect of our faith that helps us to see what it means to live a Christ-like life. This cycle of feasts and memorials, called the sanctoral cycle, is an ordering of days, outside of Sunday and the liturgical seasons, by which we mark our faith and its celebration.

"The Saints who have universal importance are celebrated in an obligatory way throughout the whole Church; other saints are either inscribed in the calendar, but for optional celebration, or are left to be honored by a particular Church, or nation, or religious family."

(*Universal Norms on the Liturgical Year and the Calendar*, 9)

The Great Solemnities

Among the days that we as Catholics observe and celebrate, solemnities take precedence. These are days that rank above any other day in terms of the celebration being kept. In a way, we treat them as a Sunday in the order of the importance we give it, and in fact, during Ordinary Time, a solemnity can take precedence over Sunday (when, for example, the solemnity of All Saints falls on a Sunday). These days are so important to us that we observe them and celebrate them to the fullest extent no matter what day they may fall upon during the year. On these days, the Church calls us to gather for the celebration of the Eucharist, and perhaps to even mark the day with special rituals or customs, such as a Eucharistic procession on the Solemnity of the Most Holy Body and Blood of Christ, or a blessing of the harvest on the Solemnity of the Assumption of the Blessed Virgin Mary.

Those of us who grew up attending Catholic schools, in fact, can recall that solemnities were school holidays. Though they had the feel of a holiday, the idea behind the practice was to allow us to observe the day to its fullest. By being relieved of our normal duties during that day, we could give more of ourselves to a full celebration of the solemnity. Though our culture and society no longer support that kind of observance of these special days, we are nonetheless called to mark them in the most faithful way that we can. Even though we are obliged to attend school or to go to work, our faith calls us to do what we can to make these days special and unique. They are real opportunities to celebrate what God has done, in Christ, through the lives of these holy ones, or through the special aspect of Christ that the day celebrates.

The solemnities that we observe in our present liturgical calendar are made up of three "kinds." There are those that are solemnities of the Lord. These are days that celebrate a specific aspect of the life, Death, and Resurrection of Jesus Christ. They are either an observance of a specific event of the life of Christ as recorded in the Gospel (for example, the Solemnity of the Ascension of the Lord), or they are an observance of a particular aspect of our faith in the crucified and risen One (for example, the Solemnity of the Most Holy Body and Blood of Christ, which does not celebrate a specific event as much as it celebrates an idea or theological concept that stems from our faith in Christ).

Of these particular solemnities, there are seven:

• Christmas, which is the Solemnity of the Nativity of the Lord

• the Solemnity of the Epiphany of the Lord (the Sunday that falls between January 2 and 8)

• Easter, the Solemnity of the Resurrection of the Lord

• the Solemnity of the Ascension of the Lord (either Thursday of the Sixth Week of Easter, or the Seventh Sunday of Easter)

• the Solemnity of the Most Holy Trinity (Sunday after Pentecost)

• the Solemnity of the Most Holy Body and Blood of the Lord (the second Sunday after Pentecost)

• the Solemnity of the Most Sacred Heart of Jesus (the third Friday after Pentecost)

• the Solemnity of Our Lord Jesus Christ, King of the Universe (the last Sunday of the liturgical year)

Beside the solemnities of the Lord, there are also the solemnities of Mary, the Mother of God. There are three of these:

• the Solemnity of Mary, the Holy Mother of God (January 1)

• the Solemnity of the Assumption of the Blessed Virgin Mary (August 15)

• the Solemnity of the Immaculate Conception of the Blessed Virgin Mary (December 8)

These days, in particular, celebrate the Church's ancient devotion and honor to Mary of Nazareth, whom God chose, from the beginning of time, to be the Mother of Christ. Her faith, trust, and total reliance on God are held before us as a model. In her, we see what it means to be a disciple.

Finally, there are the solemnities of the saints. These are days that are so important to us in our yearly observance of God's holy ones that we give them heightened attention. We celebrate four of these:

• the Solemnity of St. Joseph, Spouse of the Blessed Virgin Mary (March 19)

• the Solemnity of the Nativity of St. John the Baptist (June 24)

• the Solemnity of Sts. Peter and Paul, Apostles (June 29)

• the Solemnity of All Saints (November 1)

Let's take a closer look at some of these great days in our sanctoral cycle.

The Solemnity of the Most Holy Body and Blood of Christ (Second Sunday after Pentecost)

"Nourishing your faithful by this sacred mystery, / you make them holy, so that the human race, / bounded by one world, / may be enlightened by one faith / and united by one bond of charity."[271]

This richly worded preface brings us to the fullness and the richness of what this solemnity commemorates. In this prayer, the Church gives direction for our prayer and a guide for our minds and hearts as we come together to remember God's saving action in our world, in our community, and in our own lives. On this feast, we worship God who lives among us—in Christ, in the Spirit, and, most obviously, when the Christian community comes together to share the meal that is the Body and Blood of the Lord. It is in the breaking of the bread and the sharing of the cup that the Christian community is sustained and nourished and becomes the Body of Christ for the rest of the world. The prayer expresses what it means to be fed and nourished by God's presence and what our response should be: "May [we] be enlightened by one faith / and united by one bond of charity." We cannot experience Christ in sharing his Body and Blood and then keep it to ourselves. The Concluding Rites of the Mass make this obvious: "Go and announce the Gospel of the Lord."[272] We announce the Gospel of the Lord by loving and serving one another.

This day's celebration reminds us that the Eucharist is never an individual event. Sharing the Body and Blood of Christ with one another is always done within the worshiping community. It is only when the Christian assembly gathers, gives thanks, and remembers the love of God and God's saving action in our lives that the union promised in the Eucharist can take place. Only then are we truly God's people. Only then are we the true body of Christ.

"Grant, O Lord, we pray, / that we may delight for all eternity / in that share in your divine life, / which is foreshadowed in the present age / by our reception of your precious Body and Blood."

(Prayer after Communion, Solemnity of the Most Holy Body and Blood of Christ, *The Roman Missal*)

The Solemnity of the Most Holy Trinity (Sunday after Pentecost)

Images and references to the Trinity run consistently throughout our Catholic liturgies. We hear them from the very beginning of our liturgy: "In the name of the Father, and of the Son, and of the Holy Spirit." We hear them in the Profession of Faith that unites each and every one of us, living and dead: "I believe in one God, / . . . / maker of heaven and earth, / . . . / [and] in one Lord Jesus Christ, / the Only Begotten Son of God, / . . . / [and] in the Holy Spirit, the Lord, the giver of life."[273] We hear them in the great prayer over the bread and wine: "For with your Only Begotten Son and the Holy Spirit / you are one God, one Lord."[274] "You are indeed Holy, O Lord / . . . / for through your Son our Lord Jesus Christ, / by the power and working of the Holy Spirit. . . . "[275] Whenever we gather as a community of faith, we acknowledge and celebrate the life-giving relationship of the Father, Son, and Holy Spirit.

Being in relationship is a very intricate and intimate part of being human. Human beings cannot survive without some level of relationship with something outside of themselves. Whether it is with our family members, our friends, our spouses, our partners, or our coworkers, we need to be in relationships. They give us strength and hope. They fuel us with love and support. They bless us with grace and life. Sociologists say that it is through relating to others that human beings learn to define themselves as people, as individuals, as unique persons with unique qualities and gifts. The great German philosopher Martin Buber said it best: "One learns to be 'I' by first being 'we.'"[276]

The solemnity of the Trinity has that same effect—it tells us something about ourselves. We were created in the image and likeness of a God who is in relationship— three Persons so intimate, that God is one. This Trinitarian God is also in relationship with the world, with the people whom God has called to be his own, and with all of creation. The mystery of the Trinity is the mirror in which we should see all of our relationships—intense and passionate union, supportive grace, self-giving sacrifice, undying life, and great love. This is the grace, sacrifice, union, life, and love that are given to us from God. Because of that, it is to permeate our own lives, our own relationships, our own selves. It is what we are called to when we gather as brothers and sisters, when we worship, when we give thanks, when we remember, when we eat and drink, when we celebrate.

"Grant us, we pray, that in professing the true faith, / we may acknowledge the Trinity of eternal glory / and adore your Unity, powerful in majesty."

(Collect, Solemnity of The Most Holy Trinity, *The Roman Missal*)

The Solemnity of All Saints (November 1)

When I was growing up, my mom's side of the family had the custom, every four or five years, of holding huge family reunions. People would come, literally, from all over the country. I remember these reunions very, very fondly. They were great experiences for a young kid who often understood "family" as being only that small circle of people whom I saw on a regular basis. At every one of these family reunions, someone whom I had never met before would be introduced to me as my aunt, great uncle, or cousin. Even though it might have been my first time meeting these people, if they were identified to me as family, well, that was good enough for me! They would always get a family greeting: a hug and a kiss. Somehow, being introduced to me as family put this person into a context for my young mind. It was a context that felt safe and comfortable. This context gave me a sense of the kind of relationship I had with the other person.   **~Todd**

The Solemnity of All Saints provides a context for us and all those who have gone before us, marked with the sign of faith. It puts us in relationship with one another. It makes a connection between us. Very simply put, it makes us "family." What unites us to these others is that we share, as St. Paul says, "one Lord, one faith, one baptism."[277] We are united by a bond that is born in the font, and that is strengthened at the table of the Lord. So powerful is this bond of water and sacramental food that nothing can break it or sever it. Not even death can separate us once we are joined together in Christ Jesus. What this means is that as we are united to our brothers and sisters still living, so too are we united in our bond of faith with the all those who now stand with joy in the presence of our loving God. We do nothing alone when we do it as Church. Being Christian means never being alone. We come to this recognition as we celebrate this solemnity, recognizing that we stand with countless others who are our "family."

The Solemnity of Sts. Peter and Paul, Apostles (June 29)

"For by your providence / the blessed Apostles Peter and Paul bring us joy: / Peter, foremost in confessing the faith, / Paul, its outstanding preacher, / Peter, who established the early Church from the remnant of Israel, / Paul, master and teacher of the Gentiles that you call."

(Preface to the Eucharistic Prayer for the Solemnity of Sts. Peter and Paul, The Roman Missal)

There is so much to feed our prayer, our worship, and our faith in the liturgy of this solemnity. As the Entrance Antiphon for the Vigil Mass reminds us, "Peter the Apostle, and Paul the teacher . . . / . . . have taught us your law, O Lord."[278] Since the very beginning of our tradition, the Apostles and prophets have held a special place in our prayer and worship, in our history and our self-understanding. The Apostles were eyewitnesses to the Christ-event (his life, his Passion, and his Resurrection), and it is on their experience that our Church's faith is based. We are the offspring of their faith. It is in the spirit of their convictions and their refusal to let go of them during the tumultuous beginnings of the Church that we are able to pray for encouragement in our own faith.

Both Peter and Paul are reported to have been martyred under the Emperor Nero (AD 54–68)—Peter by crucifixion (upside down as the legend says, because he didn't feel worthy to die in the exact manner as his Master) and Paul by beheading. They "planted the Church with their blood; / they drank the chalice of the Lord / and became the friends of God."[279] Their faith becomes a model for our own faith— sometimes it seems that it isn't any easier to be a Christian in today's world than it was in their time.

We bring all of this to our celebration today, and our faith is wed to experience: "Grant us, O Lord, / . . . / so to live in the Church, / that, persevering in the breaking of the Bread / and in the teaching of the Apostles, / we may be one heart and one soul, / made steadfast in your love."[280] On Peter's faith (as shaky and threatened as our own is sometimes) and on Paul's preaching, we long for what today's solemn blessing prays: "So that by the keys of St. Peter and the words of St. Paul, / and by the support of their intercession, / God may bring us happily to that homeland / that Peter attained on a cross / and Paul by the blade of a sword."[281]

The Solemnity of Our Lord Jesus Christ, King of the Universe (Last Sunday of the Liturgical Year)

On this day, we celebrate the last great day of our liturgical year. Even though it's the last feast of the year, we first get glimpses of it months earlier. It is no accident that this solemnity is connected to the service of light celebrated at the Easter Vigil on Holy Saturday night. On that night, we proclaim the faith that we express in this solemnity: "All time belongs to him."[282] In fact, we celebrate Christ the King only because we first celebrated Easter months earlier. The solemnity of Christ the King is a celebration of a king who gives his own life so that we might live, and whose reign is eternal.

The Second Reading proclaimed in this day's liturgy helps us to focus on this crucified king: "To him who loves us and freed us from our sins by his own blood, and made us to be a kingdom, priests serving his God and Father, to him be glory and dominion forever and ever. Amen."[283] This reading goes on to echo the prayer from Holy Saturday night: "'I am the Alpha and the Omega,' says the Lord God, who is and who was and who is to come, the Almighty."[284] This crucified servant, this Risen Lord, this king is one and the same. He is the Alpha—the very beginning of our life in faith, and he is the Omega—the very end of our life in faith. Everything that we have—our days, our time, our accomplishments; our failures, our joys, our belongings, our sorrows, our very selves—belongs to him. We belong to him! This is what we celebrate this day.

Feasts, Memorials, and Occasional Masses

In our Church's liturgical year, we make similar distinctions (i.e., some celebrations are seen as taking on more significance than others). Thus, in addition to the *solemnities* discussed above, the Church also celebrates feasts and memorials as part of the sanctoral cycle. It is clear from our discussion above that solemnities are seen as the most significant of the three. As such, their celebration actually begins with First Vespers (Evening Prayer from the Liturgy of the Hours) on the preceding day. Some may even have their own Vigil Mass, which is celebrated the evening of the preceding day. Finally, as mentioned earlier in this chapter, solemnities supersede the Sunday liturgy (during Ordinary Time) when their date (which is always the same) falls on a Sunday.

Closely related to solemnities are feasts, such as the feast of the Holy Family of Jesus, Mary, and Joseph (Sunday after Christmas), the feast of the Presentation of the Lord (February 2), or the feast of the Exaltation of the Holy Cross (September 14), which celebrate a specific event or aspect of the Paschal Mystery. "Feasts are celebrated within the limits of the natural day,"[285] meaning that their celebration does not begin at Vespers of the preceding day as with solemnities. Finally, memorials are those days on which we recall certain saints, such as St. Polycarp, February 23; St. Catherine of Siena, April 29; and St. Pius X, August 21. Their celebration may be either "obligatory or optional,"[286] and typically commemorates the date of the death of the saint being honored. By marking certain days of the year with such memorials, the Church helps us to connect our daily living with the lives of the saints, who exemplify what it means to be disciples of Christ.

In our secular calendar, certain celebrations are fixed. For example, Thanksgiving will always be the fourth Thursday of November. At other times, however, civic leaders may feel the need to proclaim certain days in honor of a particular person, group, or cause, such as "National Take Your Child To Work Day." Such days allow us to celebrate or commemorate specific needs or occasions without being tied to a particular day in the calendar year.

Likewise, in addition to all of the solemnities, feasts, and memorials tied to specific dates, the Church also provides us with "occasional Masses" to mark occasions that arise in the lives of the faithful but are not necessarily related to a particular time of the liturgical season. Some of these Masses provide prayers for various needs and occasions: for the pope, for the unity of Christians, for Congress, for prisoners, for rain, for a happy death, and so on. Other Masses provided for in the Roman Missal, although not a part of the liturgical year, may be used for certain events or occasions such as the dedication of a church, a wedding Mass, or for specific people who have died such as a pope, a priest, or a married couple. These liturgies are provided as a way of reminding us that, while we follow a liturgical year, our life experiences do not always follow a calendar. Various needs and events arise at any time during our liturgical year, calling us to celebrate life's mysteries through the Eucharist on any given day.

REFLECTION

» Reflect on how you mark and celebrate the great days of our faith throughout the liturgical year. Identify those solemnities that go "unnoticed" or that can be developed in your own observance. Begin to develop patterns of celebration or customs around these great days of faith.

» Pay attention to the sanctoral cycle and begin to develop a sense of the rhythm and the flow of the saints' days, solemnities, and feasts. Become familiar with this way of marking the passing of the year.

» Given that our society and culture do not necessarily support our Church's observance of Holydays of Obligation, feasts, and solemnities, consider how you might "keep" these days special. Develop ways that you can mark these special days and feasts.

» Which of the many feasts and holy and days are your favorites? Why?

» The days that we mark as festive are those that are given over to specific people and events in our faith's history. How do they influence or shape you as you continue your faith journey? What value can you find in observing these days and feasts?

» What feasts or solemnities have shaped your own faith the most? How has your observance of these days helped you to be a better disciple of Christ? How have they formed you as a member of Christ's Body, and of the Church?

EPILOGUE

If you haven't figured it out, both authors of this book love the whole prospect of gathering with friends or family around a table and sharing with them a great meal. Much of this book, in fact, was hammered out in a Greek restaurant in the near west side of downtown Chicago! Who among us doesn't like to gather with others, those who mean the most to us, and share with them great food, great libation, and great sharing?

For any of us with culinary aspirations, the situation can only be enhanced if the meal around which our loved ones gather is one that *we* have created. In truth, there can be no greater joy, for one who likes to cook, than, after greeting and gathering the guests, to have them sit down and share a meal that you yourself have prepared.

One of the outcomes we hope for most is that those who share our culinary creation will do so with enjoyment and great satisfaction. We hope that they will taste the subtleties of the ingredients or the contrasts of flavors. We hope that they will "mull over" the food and that the food itself will contribute to the whole experience of sharing the meal; that it will contribute to the conversation, to the fellowship and to the actual relationship we have with those sharing it. In a word, we hope that our guests will savor the meal that we have prepared.

To savor something is a very specific, very deliberate action. It cannot be done quickly. It's the opposite of gulping! It takes time and some concentration—even some reflection. To *savor* is to slowly take in what is being presented and to let it "settle." To savor is to actually ruminate. It's to let whatever is savored lead us, in our minds and in our hearts, to a deeper awareness, a fuller and a more meaningful experience.

And when we actually savor, what happens? Memories are often stirred; other experiences or people are called to mind; we are touched on a certain level; something is revealed. In other words, connections are made. Suddenly, the food (and the experience) we are savoring take us to another place, another experience in our lives. As a result, the meal takes on a deeper meaning, another aspect of the relationship is revealed or another aspect of the memory is revealed—the whole experience is intensified.

Liturgy and catechesis, when combined for the great prayer of praise and thanksgiving that is the Eucharist, both call us to savor: to savor the readings proclaimed at Mass; to savor the hymn we sing or the music we hear; to savor the homily; to savor the whole experience. And when we do, connections are made for us! Something is revealed to us! We are taken to a deeper, more profound level.

But what happens when the meal flops? What happens when that great lasagna recipe fails? What happens when the roast is burned to a crisp? What happens when the meal at the restaurant just doesn't match up to past experiences? Does that mean that the connections between those gathered are lost? Does that cause the relationships that are made manifest in the gathering to suddenly fracture? Does it rob the evening or the celebration of all meaning? Of course not. We know that even then, the laughs and the intimacy and the fellowship that are part of the gathering are not lost. We know that even then, connections are made and the levels of friendship are intensified and the epiphanies that we experience are just as true!

So too with liturgy. Sometimes, the liturgy isn't celebrated as we had hoped. Sometimes, the music, or the preaching, or the presiding, or the Scripture proclamation isn't what we had hoped for. Does any of that mean that Jesus Christ, crucified, dead, buried, and risen in glory hasn't been proclaimed? Does that mean that God the Father hasn't acted in this place, at this moment in our community's life? Does that mean that the Spirit hasn't been present to manifest the great love and mercy of God? Does that mean that the Eucharist hasn't been celebrated? Of course not.

In the end, liturgy and catechesis do not depend on us. They are, after all, the means and the vehicles for the great I AM. They are the means which the All-Powerful Creator of the universe uses to shape us and mold us and continually form us into images of his beloved Son. These are the means that God uses to reveal himself more and more to us, his beloved creation. They are the means through which Jesus Christ continues to be present and active to his holy people—his Body, the Church.

This, of course, is no excuse to take lightly our approach to celebrating liturgy, as if we can relax knowing that God will come through even when we don't. On the contrary, while the liturgy does not depend on us, its profundity deserves nothing less than our best efforts. Whatever our role may be in the assembly, we are called to recognize what God is doing in the liturgy and to respond with our very best, savoring each and every moment and element of the Mass.

To become a disciple of Jesus is to savor the mystery that is celebrated. This can only be done when catechesis and liturgy work hand in hand. Jesus models this intimate connection between catechesis and liturgy in the powerful Gospel account of the road to Emmaus:

"Then beginning with Moses and all the prophets, he interpreted to them the things about himself in all the scriptures. As they came near the village to which they were going, he walked ahead as if he were going on. But they urged him strongly, saying, 'Stay with us, because it is almost evening and the day is now nearly over.' So he went in to stay with them. When he was at the table with them, he took bread, blessed and broke it, and gave it to them. Then their eyes were opened."

(Luke 24:27–31)

Sharing a great meal with those who mean the most to us is in many ways a mystery. We trust that when we give ourselves over to the experience, somehow, a new level of awareness will emerge. Ultimately, however, that is beyond our control. It requires a power beyond ourselves to transform a simple gathering of people around a meal into a transforming experience of life, love, family and friendship. When we bring catechesis and liturgy together and we allow the mystery to lead us, disciples of Christ emerge. And then we are able to acknowledge: "Without a doubt, the mystery of our religion is great: He was revealed in flesh, vindicated in spirit, seen by angels, proclaimed among Gentiles, believed in throughout the world, taken up in glory."[287]

1. Acts 2:42.

2. *Catechism of the Catholic Church*, 1075.

3. Blake, Michael, *Dances With Wolves*.

4. John 13:5.

5. John 13:12.

6. John 13:5.

7. *General Directory for Catechesis*, 90.

8. Acts 2:42.

9. *Catechism of the Catholic Church*, 1074.

10. *Sacramentum Caritatis*, 64.

11. Smith, Cyprian, *The Way of Paradox: Spiritual Life as Taught by Meister Eckhart*.

12. Shatner, William, Gene Roddenberry, Harve Bennett, and David Loughery, *Star Trek V: The Final Frontier*.

13. *De Potentia*, q. 7, a. 5, ad 14, as quoted in McBrien, Richard P., *Catholicism*.

14. *Liturgy of St. John Chrysostom*, Anaphora.

15. Buber, Martin, *I and Thou*.

16. *Summa Contra Gentiles*, lib. 1, cap. 30, n. 4, as quoted in the *Catechism of the Catholic Church*, 43.

17. Collins, Patrick, *More Than Meets the Eye: Ritual and Parish Liturgy*.

18. *Constitution on the Sacred Liturgy*, 2.

19. Penitential Act, *The Roman Missal*.

20. Ryken, Leland, James C. Wilhoit, and Tremper Longman III, ed., *Dictionary of Biblical Imagery*, 335.

21. Cf. Isaiah 45:15; Judges 13:18.

22. 1 Kings 19:12.

23. Westley, Dick, *Redemptive Intimacy: A New Perspective for the Journey to Adult Faith*.

24. John 14:9.

25. John 11:42.

26. Cf. Philippians 2.

27. John 17:25.

28. Genesis 3:8.

29. Exodus 33:12–17.

30. Song of Solomon 5:10.

31. Cf. 1 Kings 19:13.

32. Psalm 139:15.

33. 1 Corinthians 13:12.

34. Westley, Dick, *Redemptive Intimacy: A New Perspective for the Journey to Adult Faith*.

35. Mark 1:11.

36. Proverbs 3:4.

37. Acts 7:46

38. Luke 1:29.

39. Concluding Doxology, *The Roman Missal*.

40. Cf. Philippians 2:6–11.

41. See Cyril of Alexandria, *Commentary on the Gospel of John*, book 11, chapters 11–12.

42. Cf. Ephesians 2:12–22.

43. *Catechesi Tradendae*, 5; cf. *Catechesis of the Catholic Church*, 426; *Ad Gentes*, 14a. In relation to this christological end of catechesis see Part 1, chapter 1 and Part II, chapter 1. "Jesus Christ mediator and fullness of Revelation" and that which is said in Part II, chapter 1 "Christianity of the evangelical mission."

44. *Catechesi Tradendae*, 20c.

45. Cavalletti, Sofia, *The History of the Kingdom of God, Part 1: From Creation to Parousia*.

46. *The Roman Missal*.

47. Rolheiser, Ronald, *The Holy Longing: The Search for a Christian Spirituality*.

48. Exodus 20:2–3.

49. Synod of Bishops, *Message to the People of God, Cum iam ad exitum* on catechesis in our times, 9.

50. CT 23.

51. *General Directory for Catechesis*, 30.

52. *Catechism of the Catholic Church*, 1074.

53. Stuhmueller, Carol, ed., "Faith," *The Collegeville Pastoral Dictionary of Biblical Theology*.

54. *Evangelii Nuntiandi*, 24.

55. Cf. *Catechism of the Catholic Church*, 1146. Cf. GIRM, 288.

56. Boynton, Sandra, *Blue Hat, Green Hat*.

57. Cf. *Catechism of the Catholic Church*, 1148, 1152.

58. Rowling, J.K., *Harry Potter and the Goblet of Fire*.

59. Dr. Seuss, *How the Grinch Stole Christmas!*

60. Baum, L. Frank, *The Wonderful Wizard of Oz*.

61. Genesis 9:12–15.

62. Cf. Ezekiel 20:12.

63. Cf. *Constitution on the Sacred Liturgy*, 59; *Catechism of the Catholic Church*, 1075.

64. *Constitution on the Sacred Liturgy*, 49, 52.

65. *Lumen Gentium*, 10; cf. 1 Peter 2:4–5.

66. Cf. *Lumen Gentium*, 10, 34; *Presbyterorum Ordinis*, 2.

67. *Constitution on the Sacred Liturgy*, 14.

68. 1 Peter 2:9; see 2:4–5.

69. Cf. *Constitution on the Sacred Liturgy*, 11.

70. Lewis, C.S., *The Lion, the Witch, and the Wardrobe*.

71. Cf. Genesis 23:7, 33:3; Ruth 2:10; 1 Samuel 24:8; 2 Samuel 14:4; 1 Kings 1:16.

72. Cf. *Constitution on the Sacred Liturgy*, 30; *Musicam Sacram*, March 5, 1967, No. 17; *Acta Apostolicae Sedis* 59 (1967), p. 305.

73. See 1 Kings 19:12–13.

74. Mt 5:21.

75. Cf. Mt 5:22–39; 5:44.

76. *Catechism of the Catholic Church*, 1180.

77. *Rite of Dedication of a Church and an Altar*, 2. Cf. CIC, 1214.

78. See St. Augustine, Epis. 161, *De origine animae hominis*, 1, 2; PL XXXIII, 725, as quoted in Pope Pius XII, Encyclical *On Sacred Music (Musicae Sacrae Disciplina)* (MSD), no. 5.

79. St. Augustine, *Sermo* 336, 1 (PL 1844–1855, 38, 1472).

80. See Luke 10:27.

81. Day, Thomas, *Why Catholics Can't Sing: The Culture of Catholicism and the Triumph of Bad Taste*.

82. Foley, Edward, and Carol Stuhmueller, ed., "Music and Bible," *The Collegeville Pastoral Dictionary of Biblical Theology*.

83. Genesis 4:21.

84. Ryken, Leland, ed., "Music," *Dictionary of Biblical Imagery*.

85. Psalm 137:4.

86. Exodus 15:21.

87. 1 Corinthians 14:13–19.

88. Ephesians 5:18–19.

89. Revelation 14:3.

90. *Musicae Sacrae Disciplina*, 31, see 33.

91. See *Constitution on the Sacred Liturgy*, 30.

92. See 1 Corinthians 10:17.

93. See *Gaudium et Spes*, 1.

94. *Constitution on the Sacred Liturgy*, 24.

95. See Luke 2:14.

96. Isaiah 61–63.

97. Preface of the Solemnity of Our Lord Jesus Christ, King of the Universe, *The Roman Missal*.

98. Cf. Lk 9:31; 22:7–20.

99. See Daniel 3.

100. Exodus 19:16–25.

101. Exodus 33:7.

102. See 2 Samuel 7 and 1 Kings 5.

103. Psalm 132:7, 13–14.

104. Ryken, Leland, James C. Wilhoit, and Tremper Longman III, ed., *Dictionary of Biblical Imagery*.

105. John 2:19.

106. 2 Corinthians 6:16.

107. 1 Peter 2:4–5.

108. *Built of Living Stones*, 51.

109. *Built of Living Stones*, 58.

110. 1 Corinthians 11:26.

111. *Rite of Dedication of a Church and an Altar*, 3.

112. 1 Corinthians 11:26, cf. Revelation 19:9.

113. *General Instruction of the Roman Missal*, 296.

114. *Mediator Dei: On the Sacred Liturgy*, 21.

115. *Built of Living Stones*, 70.

116. *Code Iuris Canonici: Code of Canon Law*, 938 § 1.

117. *Built of Living Stones*, 71.

118. *Built of Living Stones*, 130.

119. 1 Kings 7:48–50.

120. Romans 13:14.

121. Fink, Peter E., ed., *The New Dictionary of Sacramental Worship*, p. 1306.

122. See Isaiah 6:1–4.

123. *General Instruction of the Roman Missal*, 332.

124. Rohr, Richard, *Hope Against Darkness: The Transforming Vision of St. Francis in an Age of Anxiety*.

125. Rolheiser, Ronald, *The Shattered Lantern: Rediscovering a Felt Presence of God*.

126. See 1 Corinthians 1:17–31.

127. Matthew 16:24, Mark 8:34, Luke 9:23.

128. *Catechism of the Catholic Church*, 1098.

129. See Galatians 6:18; 2 Timothy 4:22.

130. 2 Peter 3:9.

131. Genesis 1:2.

132. *General Instruction of the Roman Missal*, 29.

133. See Genesis 1:3.

134. John 1:1.

135. John 1:14.

136. Cf. *Constitution on the Sacred Liturgy*, 33.

137. *General Instruction of the Roman Missal*, 55.

138. Introduction, *Lectionary for Mass*, 13.

139. *Fulfilled In Your Hearing: The Homily in the Sunday Assembly*, p. 20.

140. *General Instruction of the Roman Missal*, 66.

141. Harris, Daniel E., *We Speak the Word of the Lord: A Practical Plan for More Effective Preaching*.

142. Cf. *Lectionary for Mass*, English translation of the Second *Editio-Typica* (1981) no. 24.

143. *General Instruction of the Roman Missal*, 67.

144. See Luke 4:21.

145. *Gathered Faithfully Together: A Guide for Sunday Mass*, 62.

146. Cf. Luke 22:18.

147. Liturgy of the Eucharist, *The Roman Missal*.

148. *General Instruction of the Roman Missal*, 30.

149. The Blessing of Baptismal Water, Easter Vigil, *The Roman Missal*.

150. Eucharistic Prayer III, *The Roman Missal*.

151. Prayer over the Offerings, *The Roman Missal*.

152. See Isaiah 11:1–10.

153. Matthew 5:23–24.

154. See Acts 2:42; *General Instruction of the Roman Missal*, 83.

155. See John 1:36.

156. See Exodus 12.

157. See Revelation 5, 19:9.

158. See Matthew 8:8.

159. Acts 2:42.

160. See Mark 10:38.

161. Prayer after Communion, Ritual Mass for Vocations to Religious Life, *The Roman Missal*.

162. Matthew 26:39.

163. Concluding Rites, *The Roman Missal*.

164. 1 Corinthians 11:26.

165. Aykroyd, Dan, and John Landis, *The Blues Brothers*.

166. *General Instruction of the Roman Missal*, 90c.

167. Geller, Bruce, David Koepp, Steven Zaillian, and Robert Towne, *Mission: Impossible*.

168. See 2 Corinthians 5:20.

169. *General Instruction of the Roman Missal*, 90c.

170. Aleichem, Sholom, and Joseph Stein, *Fiddler on the Roof*.

171. See Genesis 27.

172. Solemn Blessing, Sunday of the Resurrection, *The Roman Missal*.

173. Concluding Rites, *The Roman Missal*.

174. *Sacramentum Caritatis*, 51.

175. *Evangelii Nuntiandi*, 14.

176. *General Directory for Catechesis*, 47.

177. *Evangelii Nuntiandi*, 18.

178. *Go and Make Disciples: A National Plan and Strategy for Catholic Evangelization in the United States*, 46.

179. Ibid., 53.

180. Ibid., 56.

181. Genesis 1:14.

182. Psalm 46:11.

183. The Blessing of the Fire and Preparation of the Candle, the Easter Vigil, *The Roman Missal*.

184. Preface V of the Sundays in Ordinary Time, *The Roman Missal*.

185. Sample Invocations for the Penitential Act, *The Roman Missal*.

186. Nicene Creed, *The Roman Missal*.

187. Memorial Acclamation, *The Roman Missal*.

188. Eucharistic Prayer III, *The Roman Missal*.

189. Eucharistic Prayer IV, *The Roman Missal*.

190. Luke 1:46–55.

191. Luke 1:54–55.

192. Luke 1:67–79.

193. Luke 1:72–73.

194. Genesis 12:2.

195. Collect, Friday of the Second Week of Advent, *The Roman Missal*.

196. Luke 2:10.

197. Memorial Acclamation, *The Roman Missal*.

198. Cf. Revelation 22:17.

199. Communion Rite, *The Roman Missal*.

200. *General Instruction of the Roman Missal*, 346.

201. Luke 1:78–79.

202. See Luke 1:52–53.

203. Isaiah 62:5, First Reading for the Mass During the Night on the Solemnity of the Nativity of the Lord.

204. Prayer after Communion, Mass During the Day on the Solemnity of the Nativity of the Lord, *The Roman Missal*.

205. Isaiah 2:2.

206. Isaiah 64:1.

207. Jeremiah 33:14.

208. Collect, Vigil Mass for the Solemnity of the Nativity of the Lord, *The Roman Missal.*

209. Luke 2:10–11.

210. Isaiah 9:6.

211. Preface I of the Nativity of the Lord, *The Roman Missal.*

212. Antiphon before the *Magnificat*, Evening Prayer on the Solemnity of the Epiphany of the Lord, *Liturgy of the Hours.*

213. Matthew 3:17.

214. Collect for the Feast of the Baptism of the Lord, *The Roman Missal.*

215. Alternative Collect for the Feast of the Baptism of the Lord, *The Roman Missal.*

216. Solemn Blessing for the Solemnity of the Epiphany of the Lord, *The Roman Missal.*

217. Collect for the Vigil Mass of the Solemnity of the Epiphany of the Lord, *The Roman Missal.*

218. Isaiah 49:18.

219. Matthew 2:9.

220. Shea, John, *Starlight: Beholding the Christmas Miracle All Year Long.*

221. *Universal Norms on the Liturgical Year and the Calendar*, 32.

222. Gloria, *The Roman Missal.*

223. Titus 2:14.

224. Hebrews 1:3b–4.

225. John 1:11.

226. Luke 2:34–35.

227. The Memorial Acclamation, *The Roman Missal.*

228. Blessing of the Paschal Candle, the Easter Vigil, *The Roman Missal.*

229. Memorial Acclamation, *The Roman Missal.*

230. Mark 1:15, Gospel for the Third Sunday in Ordinary Time, Year B.

231. Dickens, Charles, *A Christmas Carol.*

232. Luke 2:14.

233. Introductory address, the Feast of the Presentation of the Lord, *The Roman Missal.*

234. Blessing of the candles, the Feast of the Presentation of the Lord, *The Roman Missal.*

235. Luke 2:32.

236. Jonah 4:2.

237. 2 Corinthians 6:2.

238. See 2 Corinthians 6:2.

239. Entrance Antiphon, Fourth Sunday of Lent, *The Roman Missal.*

240. Preface I of Lent, *The Roman Missal.*

241. Collect, First Sunday of Lent, *The Roman Missal.*

242. Collect, Second Sunday of Lent, *The Roman Missal.*

243. Preface II of Lent, *The Roman Missal.*

244. Ephesians 2:5–6.

245. Rolheiser, Ronald, *The Holy Longing: Guidelines for a Christian Spirituality.*

246. See John 12:21.

247. The Commemoration of the Lord's Entrance into Jerusalem, First Form: The Procession, Palm Sunday of the Passion of the Lord, *The Roman Missal.*

248. For more detailed treatment of this issue, see Chapter 7 of *The Bible Blueprint: A Catholic's Guide to Understanding and Embracing God's Word* by Joe Paprocki.

249. *General Instruction of the Roman Missal*, 345.

250. Penitential Act, *The Roman Missal.*

251. Memorial Acclamation, *The Roman Missal.*

252. John 13:15.

253. The Easter Vigil in the Holy Night, *The Roman Missal*, 20.

254. The Exsultet, the Easter Vigil, *The Roman Missal.*

255. The Blessing of the Fire and Preparation of the Candle, the Easter Vigil, *The Roman Missal.*

256. The Blessing of the Fire and Preparation of the Candle, the Easter Vigil, *The Roman Missal.*

257. St. Augustine, *Sermo*: 219: PL 38, 1088.

258. Procession, the Easter Vigil, *The Roman Missal.*

259. The Exsultet, the Easter Vigil, *The Roman Missal.*

260. Romans 6:3–4.

261. The Easter Vigil, *The Roman Missal*, 21.

262. 1 Corinthians 15:14, 19.

263. Romans 8:31, 38–39.

264. See Exodus 14.

265. Acts 13:49, First Reading for the Fourth Sunday of Easter, Year C.

266. St. Athanasius, *Epistula festalis*: PG 26, 1366.

267. Matthew 5:44.

268. Revelation 21:1.

269. See Mark 6:31.

270. Acts 2:22.

271. Preface II of the Most Holy Eucharist, said on the Solemnity of the Most Holy Body and Blood of Christ, *The Roman Missal.*

272. Concluding Rites, *The Roman Missal.*

273. Nicene Creed, *The Roman Missal.*

274. Preface to the Eucharistic Prayer, Solemnity of the Most Holy Trinity, *The Roman Missal.*

275. Eucharistic Prayer III, *The Roman Missal.*

276. Buber, Martin, *I and Thou.*

277. Ephesians 4:5.

278. Entrance Antiphon, Solemnity of Sts. Peter and Paul, Apostles, Vigil Mass, *The Roman Missal.*

279. Entrance Antiphon, Solemnity of Sts. Peter and Paul, *The Roman Missal.*

280. Prayer after Communion, Solemnity of Sts. Peter and Paul, *The Roman Missal.*

281. Solemn Blessing for the Solemnity of Sts. Peter and Paul, *The Roman Missal.*

282. Blessing of the Fire and Preparation of the Candle, the Easter Vigil, *The Roman Missal.*

283. Revelation 1:5–6.

284. Revelation 1:8.

285. *Universal Norms on the Liturgical Year and the Calendar*, 13.

286. *Universal Norms on the Liturgical Year and Calendar*, 14.

287. 1 Timothy 2:16.

BIBLIOGRAPHY

Roman Documents

Book of Blessings. Washington, DC: International Commission on English in the Liturgy (ICEL), 1984.

Catechesi tradendae, Apostolic Exhortation, Pope John Paul II, 1979.

Catechism of the Catholic Church (2nd ed.). Washington, DC: Libreria Editrice Vaticana—United States Conference of Catholic Bishops, 2000.

Constitution on the Sacred Liturgy, Second Vatican Council, 1963.

Dedication of a Church and Altar, Congregation for the Sacraments and Divine Worship, 1977.

Evangelii nuntiandi, Apostolic Exhortation, Pope Paul VI, 1975.

General Directory for Catechesis, Congregation for the Clergy, 1997.

General Instruction of the Roman Missal, ICEL, 2012.

Lectionary for Mass, Confraternity of Christian Doctrine, 1998.

Lectionary for Mass: Introduction, ICEL, 1998.

Liturgy of the Hours, ICEL, 1975.

Rite of Baptism for Children, ICEL, 1970.

Rite of Christian Initiation of Adults, Congregation for Divine Worship, 1988.

Roman Missal, ICEL, 2012.

Sacramentum Caritatis, Apostolic Exhortation, Benedict XVI, 2007.

Universal Norms on the Liturgical Year and the General Roman Calendar, ICEL, 2012.

Documents of the United States Conference of Catholic Bishops

The following documents are all published by and available from the United States Conference of Catholic Bishops (USCCB), Washington DC.

Built of Living Stones: Art, Architecture and Worship, 2000.

Fulfilled in Your Hearing: The Homily in the Sunday Assembly, 1982.

Go and Make Disciples: A National Plan and Strategy for Catholic Evangelization in the United States, 1993.

Sing to the Lord: Music in Divine Worship, 2007.

Other Works Cited

Aleichem, Sholom, and Joseph Stein. *Fiddler on the Roof.* Directed by Norman Jewison. Performed by Topol, Norma Crane, Leonard Frey, et al. Twentieth Century Fox Home Entertainment, 1971.

Augustine. *The Confessions of St. Augustine,* translated by John K. Ryan. New York: Doubleday Image Books, 1960.

Baum, L. Frank. *The Wonderful World of Oz.* Chicago, IL: George M. Hill Company, 1900.

Aykroyd, Dan, and John Landis. *The Blues Brothers.* Directed by John Landis. Produced by Universal Pictures. Performed by John Belushi, Dan Aykroyd, Cab Calloway, et al. 1980.

Blake, Michael. *Dances With Wolves.* Directed by Kevin Costner. Performed by Kevin Costner, et al. MGM/UA Home Entertainment, 2003.

Boynton, Sandra. *Blue Hat, Green Hat.* New York, NY: Little Simon, 1984.

Brown, Raymond. *An Adult Christ at Christmas Time.* Collegeville, MN: The Liturgical Press, 1978.

Buber, Martin. *I and Thou.* New York, NY: Collier Books/Scribner, 1958.

Cavalletti, Sofia. *The History of the Kingdom of God, Part I: From Creation to Parousia.* Translated by Rebekah Rojcewicz. Chicago, IL: Catechesis of the Good Shepherd Publications, 2012.

Collins, Patrick. *More Than Meets the Eye: Ritual and Parish Liturgy.* New York, NY: Paulist Press, 1983.

Day, Thomas. *Why Catholics Can't Sing: The Culture of Catholicism and the Triumph of Bad Taste.* New York: Crossroad, 1990.

Dickens, Charles. *A Christmas Carol.*

Dr. Seuss. *How the Grinch Stole Christmas!* New York, NY: Random House, 1957.

Fink, Peter E., ed. *The New Dictionary of Sacramental Worship.* Collegeville, MN: The Liturgical Press, 1990.

Geller, Bruce (TV series), David Koepp, Steven Zaillian, and Robert Towne. *Mission: Impossible.* 1966 (TV series), 1996 (film).

Harris, Daniel E. *We Speak the Word of the Lord: A Practical Plan for More Effective Preaching.* Chicago, IL: ACTA, 2001.

Lewis, C.S. *The Lion, the Witch, and the Wardrobe.* New York, NY: Macmillan, 1950.

McBrien, Richard P. *Catholicism.* New York: HarperCollins, 1981.

Newman, John Henry Cardinal. *Parochial and Plain Sermons.* San Francisco, CA: Ignatius Press, 1997.

Paprocki, Joe. *God's Library: Introducing Catholics to the Bible.* Mystic, CT: Twenty-Third Publications, 2000.

Pope St. Leo the Great, *De Passione Domini.*

Roddenberry, Gene, Harve Bennett, David Loughery, and William Shatner. *Star Trek V: The Final Frontier.* Directed by William Shatner. Produced by Paramount Pictures. Performed by William Shatner, Leonard Nimoy, DeForest Kelley, et al. 1989.

Rohr, Richard. *Hope Against Darkness: The Transforming Vision of St. Francis in an Age of Anxiety.* Cincinnati, OH: St. Anthony Messenger Press, 2001.

Rolheiser, Ronald. *The Holy Longing: The Search for a Christian Spirituality.* New York, NY: Doubleday, 1999.

—. *The Shattered Lantern: Rediscovering a Felt Presence of God.* Danvers, MA: Crossroad Publishing Company, 2005.

Rowling, J.K. *Harry Potter and the Goblet of Fire.* New York, NY: Scholastic, 2000.

Ryken, Leland, James C. Wilhoit, and Tremper Longman. *Dictionary of Biblical Imagery.* Downers Grove, IL: InterVarsity Press, 1998.

Shea, John. *Starlight: Beholding the Christmas Miracle All Year Long.* Chicago, IL: ACTA Publications, 2006.

Smith, Cyprian. *The Way of Paradox: Spiritual Life as Taught by Meister Eckhart.* London: Darton, Longman & Todd Ltd., 2004.

Stuhlmueller, Carroll, and Dianne Bergant, et al. *The Collegeville Dictionary of Biblical Theology.* Collegeville, MN: The Liturgical Press, 1996.

Westley, Dick. *Redemptive Intimacy: A New Perspective for the Journey to Adult Faith.* New London, CT: Twenty-Third Publications, 1981.